D0370907

HALF BAKED

Half Baked

The Story of My Nerves, My Newborn,
and How We Both Learned to Breathe

ALEXA STEVENSON

RUNNING PRESS
PHILADELPHIA · LONDON

Library of Congress Control Number: 2010926543

ISBN 978-0-7624-3946-1

Designed by Joshua McDonnell
Edited by Jennifer Kasius
Typography: Archer and Bembo

Cover Photograph by iStock: Pgiam

Running Press Book Publishers
2300 Chestnut Street
Philadelphia, PA 19103-4371

Visit us on the web!
www.runningpress.com

The names of some characters in this book have been changed.

To my mother,

for believing I could

What the American public wants in the theater is a tragedy with a happy ending.

—WILLIAM D. HOWELLS

Prologue

When you give birth to a baby who weighs less than two pounds, no one knows what kind of flowers to send. A big, congratulatory bouquet of daisies, or an arrangement that strikes a more somber note? Perhaps something pretty but blue, like a hydrangea, or something tiny, like a bonsai tree. No baby's breath, since the baby in question is likely to be breathing with the aid of a ventilator. How do you say it with flowers, when what you want to say is *"Congratulations on creating a whole new person! I hope she makes it through the week"*?

The day after my daughter was born, I tried to modulate my expression while the doctors discussed her condition. A wall of IV pumps chirped mournfully in the background, and Simone lay sprawled in her isolette, her limbs glistening and bruised. There was grave talk of blood pressure and electrocardiograms, yet my brain played only a delirious loop of *"I have a baby! A beautiful baby!"* Maybe it was the hormones, or the morphine, or maybe my sputtering neurons simply couldn't comprehend the place they found themselves: somewhere between joyous, endorphin-soaked new motherhood, and the bleak landscape of tiny burial plots.

Gray areas were never my strong suit. Which is unfortunate, because gray areas account for about 96% of human experience. But in my mind, there were only ever two options: everything goes well, or the world is swallowed in a lake of fire. Personally, my money was on "lake of fire," and I figured it didn't hurt to be prepared. Why sit around waiting for fate to spring from what appears to be a perfectly ordinary birthday cake, when you could be researching signs your headache may be an aneurysm or cataloging suspicious moles? I diagnosed my own infertility by reading too much and expecting the worst—the same way I'd diagnosed my first kidney stone ten years before. The doctor back then said "bladder infection," but I knew better, and two weeks and a trip to the ER later, I was proven right. Two weeks after *that*, in an airplane bathroom, I peed a tiny, tangible pebble of my victorious pessimism into a plastic strainer. Analysis showed the stone was mostly calcium, but it might as easily have been a crystallization of anxiety, turned to rock the way diamonds are formed—under extreme pressure, over time.

The list of things I found insupportably risky as a child included handsprings, swimming underwater, amusement park rides other than the carousel, base—or any other—ball, tire swings, and bicycling on unpaved roads. And fireworks, of course, partly because of an episode of *Lassie* in which Timmy befriended a boy blinded by a firecracker, and partly because of my oft-stated maxim that while suicide bombers or errant landmines may be beyond our control, surely choosing not to detonate explosives for *sport* is a small, sensible measure we can all take to prolong our time on earth. Like whitewater rafting, or living in California or New Orleans, fireworks were against the code I lived by: *Don't Borrow Trouble.*

The mistake I made—and would keep making, over and over—was in believing that my apprehension had a protective quality; that preparing for the worst would arm me against misfortune. Regrettably, the disaster you expect is seldom the one visited upon you. Maybe that headache isn't an aneurysm, but the first in a string of debilitating migraines that will plague you for years. Between the best and worst case scenarios are the "moderately tolerable scenario," the "better than expected scenario," and "really bad, but at least it's not cancer."

The night before I started my IVF cycle, a bridge ten minutes from my home buckled and collapsed, sending a freeway full of cars sliding into the Mississippi. I'm sure some of those people were brooding as they sat in traffic, wondering whether their spouse was cheating, worrying about a cough they'd had for weeks (*Lung cancer? Emphysema?*), nervously massaging the steering wheel while playing an improbably terrible scene in their heads.

But I am willing to bet that none of them—not one—was expecting the concrete under their tires to give way.

And in an admittedly less dramatic fashion, I can relate. Your standard, run-of-the-mill human gestation lasts 40 weeks, and I had completed 19 of those when a woman walked up to me and chuckled knowingly. Strange women are always chuckling at you once you're pregnant, women who were pregnant themselves once, years ago. They see you trundling toward the bathroom, or being hoisted from your chair via a series of pulleys, and they laugh, thinking: *You poor motherfucker.*

"You look exhausted!" said the chuckler. I gave her a wan smile. She eyed my belly, which dwarfed the rest of me, hovering over my torso like an eclipse. "Well," she said, "At least it can't be much longer! You must be due any day now!"

I was due on May 17th. It was December. Being pregnant with twins meant that even in the second trimester, I was the size of an orca.

"Actually," I said, "I still have a long way to go."

And I was right, in a way—just not in the way that I thought.

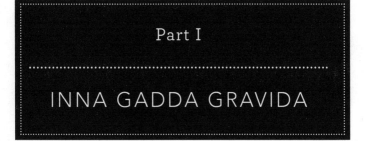

Part I

INNA GADDA GRAVIDA

CHAPTER
······························
One

Infertility has much in common with those reality shows in which the contestants eat live, writhing scorpions washed down with a warm tumbler of pus. In both cases one endures and even seeks out a series of indignities, all in the tenuous hope of receiving a prize that will make the process ultimately worthwhile. I once collected all of my urine for 24 hours in an orange vat shaped like a gas can, and then transported the sloshing receptacle back to the clinic on the seat of my car. I stage-whispered the phrase "SEMEN ANALYSIS" over the phone to a half-deaf receptionist, while my colleagues pretended not to listen. I welcomed specula, nozzles, small scalpels, catheters, thermometers, ultrasound wands, swabs, a syringe of radioactive dye, and—by my count—nine highly trained medical specialists into my vagina.

Nine. That's a baseball team.

But secretly, I continued to harbor a suspicion that—like the ulcer and the lactose intolerance—my barrenness would turn out to be a small thing I had blown out of proportion, requiring nothing more complicated than a prescription. As a little girl, whenever I feigned sickness to avoid an odious task, or lingered too long over a list of symptoms in my beloved *Mayo Clinic Family Health Book*, a mysterious mind-body alchemy would conspire to make me truly ill. Surely something similar, a combination of paranoia and magical thinking, was at work here?

The nurse poked my rear with a meaty finger.

"Right here. One quick motion, like you're throwing a dart."

I braced myself against the seat of the chair—the chair I was bending over, my pants around my ankles. I could feel Scott behind me, panic emanating from him in waves.

"You want me to..." he stammered. "I'm really going to *inject* her?"

I knew how he felt. I had assumed we would be practicing on a prosthetic ass of some kind. WHERE WAS THE PROSTHETIC ASS?

In the instructional video we'd just finished watching, the vaguely Swedish-looking actors approached each injection with barely contained glee, the wife straightening afterward to beam insanely at the camera. Scott and I had giggled through most of the film, but now, feeling the breeze on my naked legs, it seemed more sinister than amusing. Who were those people, and what the hell had they been smiling about?

Then: a tiny stab.

"Just *do* it," I hissed, annoyed at my husband for stopping with only the tip of the needle engaged.

But he hadn't stopped. It was all done, and now *I* was the one grinning like a maniac. I turned to see Scott looking smug and exhilarated. Maybe the Swedes were on to something.

Scott left for work, and I put my pants back on, moved to an exam room, and took them off again. It occurred to me that this was more or less how I had spent my free time for the past 24 months—moving from exam room to exam room, removing my pants. Thankfully, I did not have time to pursue this singularly depressing line of thought, because a nurse entered and snapped on a pair of gloves.

I had taken five days of a breast cancer medication used off-label to strong-arm my ovaries into growing an egg or two, and it was time for an ultrasound to see whether this pharmacological trickery had been successful. If it had, Scott would put his newly minted injection skills to use: a shot of hormone would release the eggs, which I imagined floating down a fallopian tube, glowing roundly in the murky uterine half-light. My husband's genetic contribution would be delivered via catheter, and if we were lucky, an egg would fertilize and then implant, growing from clump of cells to creepy amphibiate embryo to fat, healthy human baby. After two years of diagnostics, we were dipping our first toe into the chemically polluted water of fertility treatment.

The ultrasound machine hummed as I positioned myself in the stirrups and craned my head to see the screen. My ovaries swam into view, lumpen swirls of gray studded with black. The nurse began to count and measure, clicking the edges of each large black oval that might house an egg. Eggs! I felt smug and fertile, like a chicken.

"Hmmm," said the nurse, "Huh." She frowned. I craned. She continued her clicking, and I began to feel a creeping sense of dread.

On its own, my body couldn't be bothered to mature an ovum more than once in six months, but a medical nudge had matured so many that my insemination was canceled, and when she entered, my reproductive endocrinologist warned that a lapse in chastity could land me with septuplets. For a desperate moment I thought septuplets might not be so bad—I could name them after the days of the week, or the moons of Saturn!—but that soon passed, and I sat dumbly on the edge of the table, holding my paper sheet.

My reproductive endocrinologist was a former veterinarian, but I hadn't doubted her credentials until that day, when she looked at me with her kind, dog-loving eyes, and agreed that the best way to avoid a litter would be to skip directly from the kiddie pool of insemination to the bends-inducing sea of IVF. This was more than a few days of pills and a catheter snaked through what I'd once called my private parts. A cycle of in vitro fertilization would mean surgically removing my eggs, fertilizing them outside my body, and replacing an embryo or two. Left alone to pull on my pants one final time, in defeat, the worry began. I had pushed my doctor through diagnosis, requesting specific tests and deluging her with photocopied journal abstracts. Had I been too convincing? Had this erstwhile vet misread the evidence? Had I *thought* my ovaries into mutiny? Maybe it was a mistake, and I wasn't infertile at all. Oh, how we'd laugh, someday!

Leaving the clinic, a packet of IVF consent forms and informational material poked out of my handbag, including a thick sheaf about the egg retrieval procedure. It featured an illustration of the large ultrasound-guided needle used to access the eggs, a contraption that resembled a penis with a spear extending from its head, or maybe a narwhal. Looking at it made me deeply uncomfortable, though not as deeply uncomfortable as I imagined I'd be after its use. I was so accustomed to overreacting that it was a shock to realize that for once—maybe for the very first time—I was even worse off than I'd expected.

Like tax law, IVF is generally only interesting to and understood by a small, obsessive coterie of practitioners. To the rest of the world, the world that doesn't spend its lunch hours reading back issues of *Fertility and Sterility*, in vitro fertilization is a nebulous medical procedure, more science fiction than science. I was born only a year or so before the original Test Tube Baby, and when I was young the term was bandied about frequently in the news. Back then I imagined Louise Brown's conception as something between cloning and the creation of Frankenstein: a whole, miniaturized infant growing in a glass vial. She'd be yawning pinkly and bobbing in her fluid, while bespectacled, white-coated men wrote things on clipboards.

But by the time I was officially diagnosed as an evolutionary cul de sac, I knew more about fertility treatment than most physicians, thanks to the Internet and my subscription to a variety of medical databases. When I wasn't reading about egg quality or the lifespan of human sperm, I was entering increasingly frantic keywords into search engines late at night, a glass of wine at my elbow. *"Ovulation induction treatment"* I typed, *"polycystic ovaries protocol success rate."* As the hours wore on and my glass emptied, I used my computer less for data collection than as a very expensive Magic 8 Ball: *"When will I have a baby?"* I queried uselessly, *"Pregnant teenagers: WHY?"*

Six weeks after the ultrasound that sealed my fate, I received the medications for my first IVF cycle. If ever there is a test of one's desire to hear the pitter patter of little feet, it is opening a box the size of a schnauzer to find it entirely filled with needles.

"This seems...wrong," I said, hoisting a fat plastic bag of syringes. "I can't possibly need this many." Scott came up behind me to look, and began to laugh. I threw an aggrieved glare over my shoulder.

A second schnauzer-sized box was almost empty, the bottom lined with ice packs protecting a few slender packages of medication. The free needles would displace my food processor and hand mixer in a deep kitchen drawer, but all $1400 of fertility medication fit neatly into my refrigerator's butter compartment, each $60 vial an inch tall and the width of my pinkie. They were suspiciously nondescript for agents of reproduction, and I would have liked a little drama, say in the form of trumpets that sounded when you popped the plastic cap: *Dun duh-da* DAAAH!

I once had a secondhand microscope and a case of vials not unlike these, each (with the exception of the one holding a whole dead bee) containing something unrecognizable to the naked eye. There were brine shrimp in one, tiny protozoa in another. When I peered through the eyepiece at a drop from the vial labeled "pond water," a formerly uniform liquid leapt to life: whip-like organisms squiggled across the surface, tiny fronds clustered in a corner. I tried to think of the expensive thimbles in my butter compartment as similarly filled with unseen potential, but it was hard, without the trumpets. Maybe if they'd been bigger, or carved from bone. Maybe if their labels had read "CAUTION: CONTAINS HUMAN BABY PRE-CURSOR!" instead of "*urofollitropin for injection.*" Maybe if I hadn't been so uncomfortably aware of the provenance of the contents—which was, technically, the distilled and powdered urine of post-menopausal nuns.

Oh ho ho! you are saying, *this is what they call artistic license!* But it's true: having no more practical use for them, post-menopausal women pee out vast quantities of the hormones used to grow eggs, and around 1950 an enterprising Italian gentleman discovered a way to extract these hormones for use in fertility treatments. He needed a reliable urine source, and nuns were the obvious choice, as they are clean living and dwell in packs.

I wondered how they did it, these nuns. Did they take turns lifting their gowns to squat over a collection vat, rosary beads swaying forward?

How did they reconcile their donation with the Pope's "MORTAL SIN!" stance on IVF? Would it help if they knew the Vatican once *owned* the largest manufacturer of fertility medication? Were they regular nuns, chatting from behind a bathroom stall, or the sort that have taken a vow of silence, the only sound the splashing of urine into a sterile container? Should I have used synthetic hormones instead, or was this a welcome human touch to a subtly dehumanizing process?

As a child, I played dolls with a fervor and commitment to my role that was unparalleled among my contemporaries. The fastest way for a playmate to invite my scorn was to say "Let's pretend it's the next day!" or "Now it's time to put the baby to bed!" One needed only to glance out the window at the glaring noonday sun to see that the latter was untrue, and while my disbelief could be suspended enough to allow for the pretense that a plastic toddler was my own, living flesh and blood, I took even sham motherhood very seriously.

I attended a daycare program—the glumly and unimaginatively named "Extended Day"—and often exasperated the staff by refusing to retire my pseudo spawn to a cubby. Not only did I resent being shuffled from mandatory activity to mandatory activity by adults with a wildly inaccurate estimation of just how enjoyable "capture the flag" really was, but I also felt they were perpetuating a dangerous misconception. One couldn't leave a REAL baby in a cubby, at least not without inviting the interest of local law enforcement. Having children was a responsibility, and when you tired of warming bottles or rocking fractious infants, you could not simply imagine the hours away.

Responsibility or not, having children was what I wanted most of all. I spent hours deciding upon their future names and debating the question of how many, exactly, I would bear. The summer before second grade, I convinced a friend that I was pregnant—the mechanism was unclear, though I recall something about a toilet seat—and before some older girls overheard us and spoiled it all with ridicule, I spent an idyllic week patting my belly and discussing whether I ought to find a nanny or take the baby to school with me in the fall. But eventually it was time to put aside childish things, and move on to writing execrable poetry, and then to experimenting with drugs and mooning over unsuitable boys. While I still planned to have children one day, I figured I would wait until I was too old and unhip to do anything else—probably sometime in my thirties. It would be a nice distraction, then, from the fact that I was no longer any fun.

This plan persisted until I was twenty-four, when the pathway to my rational, highly evolved neocortex—the part of one's brain that lounges atop the rest reading magazines about Danish design—was hijacked by a squelchier, more primitive portion, capable of emitting only one, deafening command.

"BAAAAABY!" it cried while I was doing laundry, or driving to work.

"BAAAAABY!" it moaned at the throngs of pregnant women that had appeared, overnight.

"BAAAAABY!" it would bleat as I shopped for produce, drawing me inexorably to the smallest, most adorable fruits—clementines, apricots, and tiny Saturn peaches.

It was unsettling to find myself in the grip of a passion beyond my control, my formerly many-branched personality pruned to a single, fertility-message-board-reading stalk. I studied the work of psychologists and anthropologists looking for an explanation, books with titles like *Maternal Desire, Mother Nature,* and *On Fertile Ground.* I perused academic papers on behavioral endocrinology and the interaction between mother apes and their infants. I learned that injecting prolactin into castrated male birds will cause them to grow broody and hover over nests of young, just like their female counterparts, and that the big eyes and large, bald heads of human babies were engineered to appeal to adult humans, just as the golden natal coat of certain monkeys endears them to their parents.

Shockingly, none of this information did a thing to quiet the insistent yodeling of my biological clock, which I pictured not as sleek and digital, but rather the sort of thing The Professor might have cooked up on *Gilligan's Island,* out of a coconut. How sophisticated could it be, if it insisted upon sounding a call I had no means to answer? It was a cruel evolutionary misstep, to divorce the desire to reproduce from the ability to do so. Thank God for nuns.

CHAPTER

·····························

Two

The morning of my first injection I rose early, poured a bit of rubbing alcohol onto my kitchen counter, and wiped it down with a paper towel. I opened a sterile syringe and drew up my dosage, just as the Swedes had shown me. I applied ice to my abdomen for a few minutes before using an alcohol wipe to clean the patch of skin. Then I grasped a pinch of belly fat and swiftly jabbed the needle into my flesh, a wee hara-kiri. As I depressed the plunger, I felt an unexpected steely thrill. Had I been a cartoon, my chest might have visibly ballooned as I pressed a cotton ball to the injection site, and it was all I could do to keep from pumping my pale fist in the air.

I'd always liked a rousing game of rummy, but anything more physical was out of the question. My mother, an avid baseball fan, was once hit in the neck by a line drive, and knocked flat and breathless. Medics carried her into the under-area (dugout?) and in time something horrifyingly livid developed atop her windpipe, the sort of bruise that has three dimensions. My mother and I had markedly different reactions to this event: she returned home ebulliently clutching an autographed ball, and I added "spectator" to the list of sports positions I had no desire to play.

In elementary school, I watched my classmates fling themselves around on the monkey bars and envied their obvious ignorance of the danger all around them. My first serious boyfriend owned a motorcycle, and in retrospect, this alone should have told me it wasn't meant to be—sooner or later he would tire of my excuses (Groin pull! Improper shoes!) and find someone who enjoyed the feeling of the wind in her hair. I was not that person. I avoided things that made me anxious until they imploded into disasters that made me more anxious still: I lost a car to parking tickets and ruined my credit by fearfully stuffing overdue bills into a drawer, or consigning them to the recesses of my handbag with the redundancies of pens and lip gloss, the untethered dollar bills, and the wallet and calendar I was too forgetful to use. I was nervous and obsessive, but lacked the redeeming compulsion for organization that often accompanied these traits, instead bumbling through life like a precociously informed child: all the curmudgeonly dread of a 70-year-old, without the basic life skills. My ancestors were hardy pioneer stock, but my fear of driving and suspicion of bees, the wave of dread I experienced before making a simple phone call—all of this evidence made me suspect I was not only weak and ineffectual, but fundamentally unfit for the life of an adult human.

A week into my IVF cycle I hardly recognized myself. There I was, stabbing myself with needles—me! a girl afraid of Frisbees!—and it didn't faze me in the slightest. There are women who play rugby and balance their checkbooks yet blanch at the sight of needles, and many patients delegate the shot-giving to a partner. They take deep breaths and wait for it to be over; they close their eyes and visit their Happy Places. I, however, performed every injection myself, and performed it with relish. I did not require visualizations of white sand beaches, and after years of finding difficult activities that others dispatched with ease, it was exhilarating to be on the other side of the Frisbee, so to speak. I'd never felt so sure and capable, despite years of therapy. It appeared I could have saved considerable expense by cultivating a confidence-boosting habit of IV drug use or self-mutilation. I dropped my used needles into a sharps container with DANGER! printed on the outside, and while I may not have laughed at it, I often glanced smugly in danger's direction as I left for work.

For all my newfound bravado, the barrage of hormones began to take a toll. The precision and ritual of injecting saline into a vial of powder or tapping the bubbles from a syringe had reminded me pleasantly of chemistry, my favorite of the sciences in school. But IVF wasn't chemistry, not really: it was biology, a class I'd hated for its surfeit of variables and mobius-like feedback loops. Glancing from a textbook illustration of clearly labeled organs to the inscrutable mishmash of yellow and gray in my belated frog, I'd felt weary and overwhelmed—apt descriptors of my mental state after twelve days of injectable mother superior. My uterus twinged and cramped, and one ovary rested directly atop my bladder, creating the sense that I was perpetually near incontinence. Near-daily monitoring made me late for work, and no one likes to begin her mornings with a cold ultrasound probe to the vagina. Blood draws left my arms bruised and track-marked, but the suspicions of my coworkers were easily allayed by the bloating that left me far too zaftig for heroin addiction.

My ovaries responded slowly at first, and when my dosage was doubled I began waking with night sweats, a sheet clinging clammily to my skin. After spreading a dry towel on the bed I'd lay on my back, feeling my ovaries floating heavily in my pelvis like overripe fruit, my mind scampering ahead through all the ways that things could go wrong. I might get pregnant, but even then there were miscarriage, stillbirth, and SIDS to worry about—not to mention the inevitable misery when my baby left for college and stopped returning my calls. My anxiety was so practiced and efficient that I could begin with a small thing in the present, and be fretting within moments about hypothetical events 20 years in the future.

Beside me slept my husband, untroubled. His understanding of the process we were undergoing was vague, and he'd only recently stopped referring to it as "IBF," possibly standing for something like INTRICATE BABY FACTORY. Bafflingly, Scott showed no interest in monographs about the benefits of luteal human chorionic gonadotropin over progesterone supplementation. He seemed certain of our success, brashly disregarding my warnings about chickens and the inadvisability of counting them during the gestational period. He'd already begun referring to our potential offspring as "Science Baby," returning from the bookstore where he worked bearing a volume of children's poetry. "I hope Science Baby likes cats," he mused, stroking one of our three while I frowned worriedly in the background.

At one time I'd have given anything for this paternal zeal. I was ready for children long before he was, and we'd had countless identical arguments on the subject: I'd mount an impressive case (once with the aid of a PowerPoint presentation), Scott would overrule me, then I'd sob while scrubbing the bathroom tile. Now he was the one with baby-shaped stars in his eyes, and I was bowed with pressure. His sperm were spry and numerous—in the wild, he'd have long since ditched me for a more productive female, and I would be left to build small inexpert fires by myself, scrabbling for grubs under tree bark and dying alone, my carcass picked clean by birds.

Thursday evening, Scott and I stood in the kitchen, pondering my backside. Our kitchen window faced another apartment building, and though the shades were drawn, I was certain our silhouettes were visible— me pinching my ample rump as my husband bent to get a closer look.

We were preparing to administer a shot to the "upper outer quadrant" of my buttock, an area that seems suddenly vague when you're about to plunge into it an inch-and-a-half-long needle the width of an uncooked spaghetti noodle. For once I was not the one doing the plunging, due to my limited view of the target. The shot had to be delivered at precisely 8:30 PM, 36 hours before my egg retrieval. The clock said 8:28. Scott rose to squint at a diagram while I twisted further to prod a spongy spot that was not quite hip, not quite ass.

"Here, right? I think it's here."

"That's too high. What if I paralyze you?"

"You're not going to paralyze me," I said, feeling confident that this was so. I was less confident that he would avoid an artery, or worse, bone. I could easily imagine the sickening sound it would make. *Kkrrrrugh.* Maybe the needle would break, and I'd have to remove it with pliers, or ride to the ER while balancing awkwardly on one cheek.

"Let's just do this," I said, leaning into the counter for support.

35 ½ hours later I was free of pants once more, wearing a hospital gown as I reclined with my feet in stirrups. The stirrups were in a procedure room at my fertility clinic, itself located in a drab medical office tower called the Riverside Professional Building. The building was attached to the University hospital by a series of skyways and subterranean tunnels, a proximity I found comforting, given the narwhal. An anesthesiologist fiddled with the IV in my hand as the lights were dimmed, and I worried about Scott, masturbating in a room down the hall. He'd been so averse to visiting that sterile-yet-pornography-replete chamber that all of his diagnostic samples had been collected in our apartment and raced to the clinic in a specimen cup. This wasn't allowed for IVF. The cycle had been rigidly orchestrated up to this point, and it was unnerving to know the whole production could be rendered null by my husband's inability to orgasm outside his comfort zone.

Something warm sluiced into my vein as I joked nervously with the nurses. Then, in a brief but luxurious lapse, I drifted out of and back into consciousness.

I was propped in bed in the recovery room, covered by a thin blanket, with a pulse oximeter gripping my finger. Less than half an hour had passed, but I felt refreshed and buoyant. I'd been anxious about the side effects of the anesthesia, but the only one I noted was a sudden desire to procure a supply of my own for recreational use. Anything that could cause euphoria in one whose vaginal wall has just been repeatedly punctured was all right by me, and I made a mental note of the drug. *Versed*, ladies. Ask for it by name.

Scott entered, looking reassuringly jaunty, and a nurse appeared with juice and a packet of saltines. I asked how many eggs they'd retrieved.

"Twenty-two," she said, smiling. The three of us grinned around at each other. I'd been told to expect fifteen, but obviously someone had underestimated me. The news was almost as intoxicating as the Versed. The nurse left to check on another patient, and I tucked into my snack. Worry had its downsides, but when things went well I enjoyed a degree of glee I might otherwise have missed. *My God*, I thought, *these saltines are delicious!*

After a bit more rest and two additional packets of saltines, Scott helped me into my clothes and the elevator, and we walked back along the skyway to the parking garage. Halfway across I stopped and looked through the glass at the building we'd just left. Soon, in a linoleum-tiled room on the fifth floor, an embryologist would be conceiving our potential children. Sperm would whip their way to my eggs while I was somewhere across town, watching television or napping. The triumphant entry, that first cleaving and merging of chromosomes: it would all happen not just outside of my body, but outside of my zip code. It felt strange to leave. But I turned away from the window and we resumed walking, climbing into the car, paying the parking attendant, and driving silently over the river toward home.

CHAPTER

Three

My second year of college was notable for the fact that I spent most of it in a haze of depression, over the end of my romance with a shaggy-haired boy with a morphine addiction and skittish, don't-fence-me-in approach to relationships. We also happened to live 1000 miles apart, and I know what you're thinking: HOW COULD THAT GO WRONG?

But it did, and misery followed, as did a raging ulcer. I couldn't eat, which was probably for the best as I lacked the energy to wash so much as a plate, and our apartment was beginning, my roommate remarked, to look as if we had a time-share arrangement with The Black Crowes. Another roommate was a sweet, Tarot-card-reading holistic medicine enthusiast, and it was on her recommendation that I finally turned to acupuncture.

The acupuncturist's office was in Nyack, a complicated train and bus ride from Sarah Lawrence, and though I do not recall the details, I remember that my first attempt to make the trip involved desperate retching over a railing, a near assault in a bathroom at the White Plains train station, and an eventual trudge back to my apartment, defeated and sobbing. The next time, my roommate drove, and finally I lay on a table by a window as a man lifted my shirt to pin needles on my stomach. The needles were curiously painless, jutting up around my umbilicus like a series of slender telephone poles. When he was finished, the acupuncturist adjusted the arm of a heating lamp so that it hovered over my belly, and then he left me to relax.

I did relax, a little; I tried. But mostly I eyed that lamp. It looked old. The hinge suspending it above me was a simple screw, and it was hard to be serene when the ancient threads could give at any moment, sending the lamp's heavy head plunging toward my midsection. And so I waited, either to be calmed, or to feel a ring of tiny spears driven through my delicate internal organs. Surprisingly, neither occurred.

I left acupuncture alone after that until ten years later, when clinical trials were showing that it improved IVF success rates. When science said jump, I asked how high subjects in the study had jumped, and then attempted to replicate that exactly. This time my acupuncturist was a svelte half-Asian twenty-something named Jennifer, working out of a yoga studio in Minneapolis. She placed the needles mostly in my feet and wrists, and improbably enough, her expensive poking acted upon me like a powerful sedative. After my first session I felt loopy, with an unfamiliar looseness of my joints that I supposed must be what it felt like to be free of tension. Sitting in the booth of a nearby restaurant, I began to panic. My mind interpreted any change as an excuse to become hypervigilant and nervy: *What am I feeling* NOW? it asked, running a quick survey of my mental and physical systems. *Is this normal, this languid sensation? How long will it last?*

But I got used to it, and soon I was going every week, sinking pleasantly into a candle-lit daze each Saturday morning while a flute moaned breathily in the background. Acupuncture was supposed to be especially helpful immediately before the embryos were placed in the uterus, and so on the morning of my embryo transfer, I was supine on a table in my acupuncturist's condo, where she'd agreed to treat me on her day off.

I tried to think tranquil, hospitable-to-embryo thoughts, but the unfamiliar environment distracted me. The heat was stifling, and I could hear Jennifer moving about in her kitchen beyond the door. It is difficult to ascend to another plane when this one is full of the sounds of a dishwasher being unloaded. Scott, who had accompanied me to the appointment, turned a page of his book, audibly. I slanted one eye open to look at him.

"You're supposed to be relaxing," he said.

"I am!"

"Your eyes are open."

"Eye," I corrected, closing it.

Seventeen of my eggs had fertilized, and for the past three days these seventeen embryos had been growing in their petri dishes across the river. Also experiencing growth was my abdomen, which was so swollen it now precluded my wearing anything more tailored than a caftan. This was sure to present a problem when I returned to work after my two days of post-transfer bedrest, but I wasn't supposed to be thinking about that. I was, after all, relaxing. I tried to focus on my breath.

…It felt forced, this breathing. Was this how I always did it? In, then out? I was having trouble with the rhythm and the pacing, and seemed to be a breath or two behind. Now lightheaded, I tried to go back to not noticing my breathing at all, but that was impossible. Shouldn't this come naturally?

"It's not working," I whispered, opening both my eyes this time and lifting my head to look at my husband.

"What's not working?" he sighed, closing his book.

"Relaxing. Usually I find this relaxing."

Scott looked suspiciously at the needle protruding from between my eyebrows.

"Really?"

There were footsteps outside the door. I reassumed the position.

Like the acupuncture before it, the Valium I took en route to the clinic failed to produce the expected effect. More specifically, it failed to produce any effect at all, prompting me to double check the instructions in case I'd misunderstood the timing of the prescribed dose. Timing wasn't the problem. It was the day the fruit of my loins would be returned to them, a day two months in the making. As with a rocket launch, there was no way to know whether the mission would be a success or, you know, the *Challenger*, but this was the day we pressed the button. Under these circumstances neither Eastern nor Western medicine could vanquish my anxiety—its power was too great.

Our embryologist was a handsome lacrosse-type named Christopher, with wire-rimmed glasses. Once I'd shed my panties, he led us into a darkened laboratory attached to a procedure room.

"Take a look," he said, gesturing to the microscope that cast a small patch of light on the counter. Our two best embryos, one with seven cells and one with nine, had been separated from the rest of the bunch, floating companionably together in a petri dish of culture medium.

"Oh *wow,*" I breathed, eye to the eyepiece. Scott and I took turns peering through the lens, exchanging looks of astonished awe.

I'd seen pictures of embryos before, but these struck me as exceptionally beautiful, each like a delicate collection of soap bubbles. I felt a surge of pride and protectiveness. We were transferring two at the doctor's recommendation, to increase our odds of ending up with any baby at all, but after seeing them—petite, well-behaved, symmetrical— I found it impossible not to root for them both. It occurred to me that if I gave birth nine months later, I would be in the unique position of having seen my offspring outside my body once before, pregnancy merely a brief hiatus in our external relationship. *You again!* I imagined myself saying in the delivery room. *My, look how you've grown!*

The doctor performing my transfer was the senior member of the practice, responsible for Minnesota's first IVF baby some twenty years before. He was diminutive and pink cheeked, with white hair and an impish smile. Today—along with his customary bowtie—he was wearing what looked like a mining headlamp as he sat on a stool between my raised and open legs. He'd inserted a speculum, and was probing me intently with a catheter, murmuring. Now I understood why they prescribed the Valium.

"You have very unusual anatomy," he said, raising his head.

I was unsure of how to respond. Thank you? I'm sorry?

"There's a C-shaped *bend* where your uterus meets the cervix," he continued, making the letter C with one of his small hands. "Would you mind if I invite our medical student to observe?"

"The more the merrier!" I burbled nervously, unable to help myself.

Up by my head, Scott rolled his eyes. Something about being in stirrups makes me relentlessly jokey, as if puns and jazz hands will distract us all from the awkwardness of the situation.

The medical student entered, clad in a hijab and a scrub top over long black skirting. Minneapolis has a large population of Somali Muslims, so this was not unusual in and of itself, but it added to the surreality of the scene: an extravagantly swathed Muslim woman and an elfin man wearing a bowtie and headlamp were deep in conference between my knees, my pubic area bathed with light in the otherwise darkened room. There was a joke in there somewhere, but I was blessedly unable to find it.

Let me tell you about the day I got pregnant, I imagined saying to my future children, or maybe: *an old man and a Muslim walk into a vagina...*

The doctor was bending the catheter, jerry-rigging it to snake around my unusual anatomy. The embryologist tenderly, carefully handed him the syringe holding our embryos.

"Here we go!" said the doctor, depressing the plunger.

And just like that, I was sixteen cells bigger.

I don't know if ignorance is bliss, but cognizance most definitely is not. My knowledge of the specifics of conception made the ensuing week tortuous, for if research had taught me anything, it was that it's a miracle anyone is born at all. For all the precisely calibrated machinations of an IVF cycle, in the end success comes down to implantation, an event you can only encourage. This is why many infertile women feel the urge to firebomb newspaper offices when yet another article about IVF uses the word "implant" to describe the process of placing embryos in the uterus. While a doctor can chuck your embryos into the appropriate internal chamber (and by "chuck" I mean "*transfer*"), no one can control whether those embryos implant and result in pregnancy. An embryo must synchronize its every developmental move with the uterus, and there is a harrowingly slight window sevenish-days after fertilization during which it must thrust its trophoblastic fingers into the blood supply to tap out a frantic chemical signal. *I'm here!* the signal says, *Please don't kill me!* If it fails to make contact, the embryo will be unceremoniously sloughed away.

It's all terribly dramatic, like a tiny pelvic James Bond movie.

The crucial window fell the weekend after my transfer, during a visit from Scott's parents. All day Saturday I could think of nothing but the cellular mission taking place inside me. *If only I were a rat*, I thought, riding spacily up and down an escalator while my in-laws shopped nearby. The implantation process for rat embryos is pathetically easy—the embryo simply sidles up to the uterine wall and waits to be embraced. Stupid, lazy rats.

The night before, the embryologist had called. None of our remaining fifteen embryos had developed well enough to freeze. This didn't inspire confidence in the two we'd transferred, their exceptional beauty notwithstanding, and Scott returned from work to find me sitting in the dark, my face swollen and slick with tears.

"I don't understand," I'd said again and again, and I didn't. I wasn't even thirty. My eggs should have been fresh and dewy and full of zeal, but instead they were as prematurely aged as the rest of me. We'd counted on having frozen embryos for backup, but now failure would mean at least a year of saving for another cycle, while my eggs grew more decrepit and I wandered Miss Havisham-like through our apartment, keening and clutching a onesie.

According to my studies, Monday was the earliest a home test might show a positive result, so when my eyelids sprang open at 4:00 that morning I darted quietly to the bathroom, debating whether it would be better to collect my sample in a cup to ensure an even moistening of the test stick or to use the classic midstream method, which might be expected to propel urine into the absorbent wicking with greater force.

When I'd completed the experiment, I labeled the stick with the date and sat on the toilet to interpret the data. I'd retrieved a previous day's negative test from the cupboard to use as a control, and I held the two side by side, watching the result window.

I watched and waited, and then I went back to bed.

When I woke again an hour later, I returned to my bathroom laboratory. I held that morning's test under the bright bulb above the mirror. I tilted it to, then fro. I pried the plastic case apart and removed the strip inside; I pressed it against a piece of plain white paper and squinted at the area where a line might be expected to appear.

Negative.

I dressed and drove to work, where I sat dully at my desk, eyes burning. Our two charming embryos had gone the way of their dozen brothers and sisters—I could feel it. Twelve more months stretched barrenly before me, and even waiting for the blood test to confirm my failure seemed an excruciating waste of time, time that could otherwise be spent drinking heavily and sobbing over unpasteurized cheese.

I would have comforted anyone else in my position with statistics, reminding her that in the majority of women, one week after a transfer of three-day embryos is too early for a positive result to register on any home test. I would have assured her that the probability of success only begins to drop significantly if tests are still negative, say, two days later. I would have told her that the early hCG these tests measure does not rise in a linear fashion, and levels can jump from zero one day to fifteen the next. *It's too soon to draw any reliable conclusions,* I would have said, adjusting my spectacles, secure in the scientific dispassion that is so much easier to maintain when counseling *other* people.

And you know what? I would have been right. I was pregnant.

One evening when I was five weeks along, Scott arrived home to see me sobbing on the couch, my work pants unbuttoned, mascara smeared across my cheekbones.

"What is it? What's the matter?" he asked, dropping his bag by the door and rushing to my side. I shook my head miserably and tried to get my breathing under control.

"L-L-LOLA!" I sobbed, finally. "She was bi-bi-bitten by a snake? And then she *draaagged* herself home, which took *days*, and when she *got* there, her OWN SISTER—"

"Wait," Scott interrupted, looking past me at the television, "Wait a minute. Is Lola a *meerkat*? Are we crying for meerkats now?"

Yes. Yes I was. I was crying for meerkats.

I'd gotten sucked into a meerkat reality show on Animal Planet, a channel I'd never watched before I was pregnant, not even once. I liked animals as much as the next girl, but had always assumed the people watching Animal Planet were the same individuals who bought commemorative plates featuring Cat Breeds of the World. I owned no such plates, and yet there I was, racked with sorrow over a glorified rodent.

In my defense, have you *seen* a meerkat? The way they stand on their hindquarters, front legs dangling atop their bellies? What chance did I have against that, given the quantities of progesterone gamboling through my bloodstream? I took a shot of the stuff every night, to mimic and supplement the hormones of early pregnancy. It was suspended in oil, and injecting it deep into my—now familiar—upper outer quadrant required a large needle and a high pain tolerance. These shots started the day after my eggs were retrieved, and three weeks later my hips were bruised and lumpy, my puncture-ridden skin becoming harder to pierce.

"It's like the hide of a rhinoceros!" observed my husband, who always knew how to make a girl feel pretty. I'd given up on administering the injections myself, and instead lay on the couch while Scott slowly depressed the plunger, the density of my flesh resisting mightily against the thickness of the oil. I bought numbing cream and applied it twenty minutes pre-shot to give it time to work, covering the glob with a taped-on bottle cap to prevent it from smearing.

Weeping in front of Animal Planet with my pants unbuttoned, a bottle cap taped to my leathery ass, I must have made a lovely tableau—the sort of thing you could show to teens as part of an abstinence program.

Internally I was no less a disaster, in a state of constant, terrified suspense. For all I knew, whatever had been growing inside me might have chosen *that very moment* to shuffle off its tiny mortal coil.

You probably know the gist of Schrödinger's famous cat-in-the-box paradox: should you seal a cat out of sight with something that might-or-might-not kill it—not that I'm suggesting you do such a thing, understand—said cat remains, for theoretical purposes, equally dead and alive until you unseal the box again and look inside. This certainly-unsanctioned-by-PETA thought experiment was a familiar topic in our family, and not just because we were such hopeless nerds that my childhood living room wall hosted a colorful rug-hooking of squares based upon the Fibonacci sequence. (Though, you know. We were.) Mostly, "Schrödinger" had a place in my youthful lexicon because his puzzle was the set-up for an oft repeated piece of legendary parental wit, when in response to an assertion of the doctor's death, my mother once deadpanned: "Are they sure?"

I thought of Dr. Schrödinger and his beleaguered cat frequently, in the early weeks of pregnancy. How could I not? I was essentially hosting the same experiment in my own abdomen, and I didn't like it one bit.

Scott and I had conceived twice before, when a fluke of chemistry freed one of my recalcitrant eggs. Alas, the same hormonal imbalance that made it hard for me to get pregnant made it equally difficult to stay that way, and I'd miscarried both times before the end of my second month. Our first pregnancy had been three years before, and back then at five weeks I'd basked obliviously in the private sense of importance I had as I went about my day. While I walked to the store for groceries I was secretly creating a spine, toes, and eyelids beneath my coat. I was multitasking; I was full of purpose. It may have looked like I was only slurping a milkshake, but my innards were up to miraculous things.

Even naïveté couldn't quite quash my customary nervousness, and though my midwife rolled her eyes at my desire for empirical evidence, she agreed to an ultrasound when I was seven weeks along. Scott had to work, and so my mother was with me that morning as I lay in the dark and gazed at the screen mounted high in the corner. There was nothing visible but a grey expanse punctuated by a small, empty circle of black.

"That's the gestational sac," said the technician, "But it's very small, and I don't see anything inside. How far along did you say you were?"

I miscarried that weekend on New Year's Day—at home, sick with grief and shame. There is nothing more foolish and pitiable than a character ignorant of the misfortune about to befall her, secure in a grotesquely unfounded happiness. We wince at these people when we see them in tragedies: Jackie Kennedy humming as she applies lipstick the morning of November 22nd; the Lindbergh parents cuddling their smiling baby. The comedic equivalent is the naked emperor strutting through the town square, and I was haunted by an image of myself as I must have looked driving to a party late on Christmas Eve, singing "Lullaby of Birdland" to a belly that contained nothing alive at all.

I'd resolved never to be so carelessly joyful again. This time, my OB had agreed to be aggressive in treating the tendency to kill my own young, and prescribed a steroid to slightly depress my immune system. He'd also decreed I could have as many ultrasounds as needed for reassurance, and my first was just before six weeks. My legs rattled in the stirrups, my eyes swimming with apprehensive tears. It was time to open the box, Dr. Schrödinger.

"Just tell me right away, whatever it is," I said to the nurse, who was petite and perky, like a sorority sister. She patted my knee as she began the ultrasound.

And then I saw them: two smudges inside two perfectly round circles, nestled companionably next to one another, just as they had been in their petri dish.

"OhmiGod!" squealed the nurse, "Two little sacs!"

I watched in tearful awe as she took measurements and pronounced everything as it should be, and at the end we gazed together at the picture she had printed for me, of my uterus and its newest inhabitants.

"They are just so *cute*," she said. And who was I to argue with a professional?

"TWO?" said Scott on the phone.

"For *now*," I said repressively.

"Twins!"

"*Maybe*," I reminded him. But I was smiling, God help me.

"Do you think both will...*stay*?" asked my mother, when I called her from my office.

"I don't know. It's too early to tell." I could hear laughter in the background, and the clinking of glasses. "What are you doing? What time is it there?"

My mother had moved to Switzerland six weeks before, for a three-year work assignment, and it would be another year before I mastered the time difference.

"Oh, it's seven. Jill and I are playing cards." Jill was my mother's boss, and a fellow transplant. I heard a deck being shuffled. "I'll put the money

I win in a fund for you," my mother said. "Can you imagine the cost of daycare if you end up with twins?"

I missed my mother. I'd asked her once why she'd moved away just as I began fertility treatment, and she'd said "Well I didn't think it would *work* right away. I figured it could take *years.*" My mother was a realist—whether the glass was half full or half empty, eventually the water would evaporate altogether. You might think this would be deflating, but I was relieved not to have to manage her expectations. Rather than assuming I'd deliver two babies in May, she saw things much as I did: two fetii now gave me a better chance of at least one living baby in the end. Or, as she put it delicately, after a later ultrasound: "It's unlikely that they'd *both* die, now."

My in-laws, on the other hand, were as unrestrainedly optimistic as my husband. Their enthusiasm was a clear, sunlit pool in which I occasionally allowed my feet a refreshing dangle, chattering on the phone to my mother-in-law in a fine impersonation of someone who didn't know better, a girl who took it for granted that elevator cables would hold. I'd join Scott in his speculations about the Science Babies—would they be boys, or girls, or one of each? What would be their favorite flavors of ice cream?

"I'm having kittens," I blurted to the cats one evening, alone with them in the apartment. I swung pendulum-like between my suspicious default and wild glee—a middle ground would have been ideal, but I was damned if I could find one.

At our discharge appointment, the bow-tied gentleman who had transferred our embryos handed me a pair of envelopes addressed to the clinic and two blank birth announcements to be mailed after the babies were born. The cards were cream, with pink and blue blocks. When Scott and I arrived the nurses had greeted us with excited smiles, and as we were shown to an exam room, the theme from *Rocky* swelled subliminally in the background. I half expected to be draped with a wreath of flowers, like the winning horse after a race.

I'd already had two scans courtesy of my obstetrician, but until the fertility clinic confirmed it with one of their own, my pregnancy wasn't official for their statistics. The ultrasound picture was far clearer than that at my OB's office, and the babies had grown. This machine had sound, and for the first time Scott and I heard the *BA-rumpBA-rumpBA-rumpBA* of the heartbeats. Doctor Bowtie performed the ultrasound himself, pointing out the contracting of tiny oyster-like ventricles and the red and blue pulsing of blood through the umbilical cords. I'd asked (as was my custom) about miscarriage risk, and the doctor said he'd be surprised if we didn't have two healthy babies come spring. He shook our hands, and in the car, Scott squeezed mine, and I squeezed back. We rode home like that, quiet and hopeful.

PLEEEASE, PLE-ASE, PLEASE, PLEASE! James Brown begged through the speakers, and oh, I knew exactly how he felt.

Five

"No ultrasounds? But how will we know if they're dead?"

It was my eight-week appointment, and my OB had suggested we curtail my weekly glimpses, now that the worst of the danger had passed. My response prompted him to begin a pretty speech about Worrying About That Which We Cannot Control, but he broke it off mid-sentence to laugh at my stony face.

"I can see this is a concept you're wrestling with."

"Only since birth," I said, drily.

I'd told myself I'd stop worrying once I heard a heartbeat, but this had been revised to "after the first trimester," and I suspected that as I moved forward, the worry finish line would be pushed along with me, to "after the 20-week anatomy scan," and then "once the babies are viable outside the womb."

I did have evidence that *something* was happening, even without sonographic proof. Ten days before, I'd been at work—walking the well-traveled path between my office and the bathroom—when the floor seemed to waver. I blinked. The walls wobbled inward, and I steadied myself against a cubicle. When I turned my head, the world staggered to catch up.

Has my office been moved aboard a ship, I wondered, *or is this the start of an honest-to-God pregnancy symptom?*

The next morning, doubled over the toilet, I had my answer. Only the infertile or paranoid—I had the distinction of being both—will understand the reassurance I felt with every heave. This was short-lived, however. As I would soon discover, there is nothing reassuring about vomiting undigested peas out of one's nose.

I was six and a half weeks when the nausea started, and it never entirely stopped. I tried ginger tea, ginger candy, ginger ale, and candied ginger. I used ginger-scented shower gel, and bought packets of a mysterious hot ginger drink from an Asian grocery. I sucked on lemon drops and ate spoonfuls of frozen lemonade; I nibbled sleeve upon sleeve of saltines. I took extra vitamin B and a variety of approved over-the-counter remedies, and walked around wearing acupressure wristbands, like a greenish, unwholesome-looking Olivia Newton-John. When I was unable to keep down even liquids, my doctor prescribed Zofran, a drug given to cancer patients undergoing chemotherapy. The flavor of the dissolvable tablets was like a robot's idea of cherry, but they were remarkably effective at keeping my stomach contents concealed from the public. For this alone I'd have considered naming the Science Babies Zofranny and Zooey, combining my love of Salinger with my gratitude for modern medicine, but Zofran was not without its problems.

I am Swiss, and because my bowels are normally as regular as the trains of my countrymen, I'd never given them much thought. This may explain why it took me six long days to notice that...service had been suspended. *Huh,* I thought to myself, as I became increasingly uncomfortable, *pregnancy is certainly full of surprises!*

Surprises were not, however, what I was full of. I added stool softeners to my prescribed regimen of vitamins, progesterone, and baby aspirin. Zofran may have vanquished the vomiting, but it left my queasiness intact, and had to be taken on a strict schedule. I woke myself at four each morning to eat two saltines, drink a glass of milk, and race to dissolve a tablet on my tongue before the amalgam of cherry and tin overwhelmed my gag reflex. If I overslept by an hour, it was too late, and I'd spend the morning retching into the nearest receptacle. When it happened, I consoled myself with comparisons to the summer I was fourteen, when a misfiring of hormones and blood sugar left me cheek to tile all season, whittling my already spindly frame to a scant 85 pounds. My mother took me to doctors, where I vomited in waiting rooms and had the same conversation, over and over:

DOCTOR: Could you be pregnant?

ME: No.

(DOCTOR *asks* MOTHER *to leave room.* MOTHER *exits.*)

DOCTOR: Could you be pregnant?

ME: No.

It was humiliating to assert this again and again, working to impress upon skeptical medical professionals just how sexually inexperienced I was, moving as necessary from my virginity to the fact that I had never been kissed, at last resorting to the shameful admission that no member of the opposite sex had yet so much as leered in my direction. Point finally taken, the doctors threw up their hands and pronounced me an enigma wrapped in a conundrum wrapped in a T-shirt covered in bile. I remained mentally unsteady long after my stomach settled, wondering with every bug or bout of indigestion whether it was the start of another gastrointestinal siege. Pregnancy, at least, gave my misery purpose.

My next appointment was at 11 weeks, and as Scott and I waited in the exam room, a carelessly placed fan blew up the paper sheet covering my lower half. I coquettishly pushed it down again, doing my best and breathiest Marilyn, but when the ultrasound began, all humor left me. The Science Babies were *moving.*

I gaped at the screen as they waved their arms and legs. Absent were the flippers of three weeks before; these creatures were distinctly human in appearance. I think I can pinpoint this as the instant I began to be, as they so aptly say, expecting—that it was possible things might not go wrong, after all.

"Put '*Science,*'" Scott urged me, pointing to the space on our intake paperwork for "*Father's Name*." We were in the office of a specialist, waiting for our genetic screening appointment. I'd just reached the magical mystical 12-week mark, and if everything went well that day I planned to stop scuttling to meetings while hiding behind a legal pad, and tell my coworkers about my pregnancy. The reveal was mostly a formality, as I'd been in maternity clothes for weeks. Only days before an older colleague had patted her stomach conspiratorially and asked whether I was "packing heat." She may have mangled the metaphor, but I had known what she meant and I'd panicked and hurried away, leaving her mortified.

The screening included a 3D ultrasound, and by now the babies were miniature people, small claymation figures kicking and rolling inside of me with distinct personalities of their own. Baby A was a good-natured ham, stretching out obligingly to be measured, waving, and turning upside down to waggle its long legs at us. In my favorite among the sheaf of ultrasound photos we collected, Baby A's legs are frozen upside down in the frame, extending up, lithe and frog-like, from a little round belly.

Baby B, on the other hand, had been difficult from the beginning—first measuring behind, then pronounced "excitable" for its high heart rate, then hiding as if it believed that ultrasonography might steal its fetal soul. During one appointment it curled like a cocktail shrimp high in a corner, refusing to move and frustrating the nurse. When I told my mother, she said "That's the lazy one, maybe."

"Well, but its heart was faster. It always is."

"Lazy and nervous then," she amended. "Aww! It's just like its mother!"

These glimmers of my tenants' humanity became vital as the second trimester began and my constant, feverish gratitude became harder to sustain. By late afternoon, my stomach was pressed so far toward my throat that I could scarcely eat, and sleep required a complicated arrangement of body pillows. Even with them my aching hips woke me frequently to turn from uncomfortable position to slightly-less-uncomfortable position, and once I was awake, I'd notice Scott's breathing, the way you might notice the sound of a train hurtling past you through a tunnel. I'd try pushing his mouth closed and shoving him indelicately onto his side before dragging my pillows to the living room couch, where I'd fantasize about how I might serve the divorce papers: stuffed in his open mouth while he snored, maybe, or rolled up and used to beat him out of a peaceful slumber. In my fourth month I woke to find a cat speculatively sniffing my nipple, and from then on I'd have to wear a bra stuffed with nursing pads to keep from being molested by pets or waking in a pool of my own leaking milk. Simple tasks exhausted me, things like typing or boiling water, and sharp ligament pains made me lurch from place to place like the wincing undead.

Late at night, though, I'd slip out of my clothes and stand in front of our full-length mirror to run my hands over my body—the only way to convince myself that the marvelous, round creature reflected was really me. My belly was smooth and firmer than it had been since college, shining either with promise or because its skin was stretched so tautly. I have a short torso, and the lack of available real estate left my expanding midsection nowhere to go but out. By eighteen weeks it would project from beneath my bosom at such a dramatic angle that I felt a breeze from below, where shirts left the underside of my belly—like the dark side of the moon—invisibly exposed. Each time I passed a window and caught a glimpse of myself I startled, then grinned helplessly, delighted.

In the second grade, I tried to find religion. We'd moved from a bohemian city neighborhood to a suburb where my Chinese neighbor extolled the virtues of a blonde, effeminate Jesus. The neighbor's name was Jenny, like every third girl in the country, and she was in my class at school. After hearing I wasn't a Christian, Jenny's father showed me an array of what looked like the yearbook photos of a school for the gruesomely disfigured. These were people who'd been sent to hell but—through some loophole that wasn't entirely clear—escaped. They'd been burned about the face with brimstone, yet their pain would be given meaning if it prompted me to accept God into my heart.

I liked the idea of God, but preferred a kindlier version—one whose policies resulted in less scar tissue. My mother sometimes read to us from a reference book on World Religions, and my younger brother had found a home for a time among the ancient Egyptians, worshipping the sun god Ra. I flipped through the pages in search of a creed of my own: I read about Buddhism, Hinduism—a host of isms. I waited to feel something, and told myself the millions of people in churches and temples had to be onto something. But as much as I wanted to, I couldn't convince myself that God was any more real than Santa Claus or the Easter Bunny.

When I was pregnant, I'd sometimes stand in the doorway of our apartment's second bedroom, trying again to reason myself into faith. The room was filled with unpacked boxes; we'd designated this the office, but never got around to setting it up, and now it would be the nursery. I had every intention of painting and hanging twee curtains, just as soon as I had both the energy and optimism necessary to do so. Genetic testing had estimated our risk of the most common chromosomal problems at 1 in 10,000, and after the first trimester, the likelihood of miscarriage was less than two percent. I had a greater chance of developing schizophrenia or ovarian cancer, and I wasn't padding the walls or scheduling myself for an oopherectomy anytime soon, but I always seemed to be too tired or sick to begin the process of cleaning and sorting. Instead I looked at fabric for a quilt I didn't know how to make and researched cribs and double strollers, in what felt more like indulging a rich fantasy life than it did undertaking preparations for an actual future.

A few years before, I'd started an online journal. The subject of infertility didn't lend itself to casual conversation, and it was lonely, being consumed by something I couldn't share. When my late-night Googling led me to a network of blackly humorous women chronicling the absurdity and grief of failing to conceive, I joined them, titling my website "Flotsam" because I planned to write about many things, once I had a baby and my reproduction fixation had waned. It would be a sort of public diary, giving me a place to vent my feelings about promotional stirrup covers, and also keeping me writing at a time when inspiration had absconded. I'd always planned to whittle a career from my writing, but lately this plan had been hobbled by the fact that I hadn't actually *written* in months. I figured the public nature of the Internet was a sufficient threat to vanity to keep my standards high, but that because I wasn't writing for publication, I'd avoid the paralyzing perfectionism that otherwise dogged me. It didn't occur to me that writing online was a form of publication itself—this "didn't count," as far as I was concerned, and that was part of its charm. I'd have sooner performed my own dentistry with common household tools than discuss cervical fluid with my mother, but my boundaries evaporated before the nebulous strangers of the Internet. Only—strangely enough—they ceased to be strangers, after a time. The relationship was difficult to explain to those unfamiliar with the online world. How do you explain that there are people you've never met who have seen more of you than most people have? My visitors weren't exclusively fertility patients, or, as their number climbed, exclusively anything. Some had websites of their own, and as a reciprocal audience I knew what scared them, and remembered the names of their children. Others only read, and I saw only as much as they revealed in their comments. Combined, my readers formed a virtual *kaffeeklatsch* of humor and support. Bad days became less so—transformed into slapstick by the prospect of their retelling, or at least made less lonely by the addition of company. It was like having an invisible entourage, this portable feeling of fellowship I carried with me everywhere, and these people became, in a way that wasn't virtual at all, my friends.

The day after my 3D ultrasound, I admitted to my assembled colleagues that I hadn't let myself go or developed an abdominal tumor. I smiled as the congratulations rang out, but still couldn't bring myself to refer to the future of the pregnancy without qualifiers, like "it's still early," "hopefully," and "if all the shoes stay up where they belong."

Online though, among my kin, I was braver. I decided to make a show of faith—even if I didn't have any. I began writing to the babies.

"*Dear Science Babies,*" the first letter began, "*I know this is a busy week for you, what with developing reflexes and all, so I won't take up much of your*

43

time. But they tell me you're each about the size of a lime now, and I think that is big enough to be talked to honestly."

Honestly? Sometimes I wasn't sure that they were in there at all. But I wrote to them anyway, every week or so, and I always ended with "*Love, Your Mother.*"

Six

The thing about living in an apartment is that when the telephone rings in the middle of the night, it's more likely to be a drunk calling for the previous tenant than it is to be anyone you know, personally. I speak from experience, and so the first time the phone rang at 4:30 on the morning before Thanksgiving, I registered it only vaguely before drifting back to sleep.

It stopped, and then started again. Drunk people can be very persistent.

The third time, I heaved myself out of bed to answer, and when I did I heard the voice of Jill, my mother's boss, telling me that there had been an accident. Someone had driven into my mother, carelessly flinging her 100-pound form into the air, and continuing on his way.

She hadn't dashed into traffic; she'd been in a crosswalk. Far from being neutral, Switzerland suddenly seemed like a terrible, sinister place. Was it really so much to expect, that motorists refrain from running people down in broad daylight? Isn't this something that translates into any language?

My mother was said to be in good spirits, and had been seen chatting in the back of an ambulance. She'd need surgery—she'd broken one ankle and the opposite knee, shattering the head of a tibia. The doctors hadn't realized the extent of her injuries until viewing the scans, because my mother had spent the five hours after her accident politely declining pain medication. I understood completely: medicine might make you sick to your stomach, or have some other unpleasant effect—better to endure the pain with which you were already acquainted than opt for the unknown.

"She's going to be fine," Jill was saying.

On medical shows, it's usually misleading when a person appears to be "fine" or "in good spirits" after blunt force trauma. In fact, this is usually a sign that things are about to go terribly wrong. The patient is talking and laughing in a hospital bed, and then their eyes roll back, and the music turns ominous and frenetic as people yell and open thoracotomy trays. *Tension pneumothorax! Cardiac tampenade!* Oh, I knew all about these things, about slow-bleeding spleen lacerations, about fat syringes jabbed into the pleural cavity.

"Are they sure there's no internal bleeding?" I asked.

Jill assured me they'd done a thorough ultrasound, and I wished I could see it for myself. I was an old hand at ultrasounds, and if the doctors all spoke German, how did anyone know what they were *really* saying, amongst themselves? I'd flown to London once on Icelandair, and on the return trip we hit a patch of turbulence. The captain came on and delivered a lengthy, emphatic monologue in Icelandic, and then, in English, said: *"Please fasten your seat belts."*

My mother would be in a hospital in Zug for two weeks, and then in a rehabilitation center for at least another two after that. Surgeons would harvest bone from her pelvis and mix it into slurry. There would be multiple pins and plates, two of which were being flown in from overseas. After they were removed, she'd keep the screws that had held her ankle together in a small specimen container to rattle proudly at visitors. Switzerland gets a lot of ski injuries, and my mother's orthopedic surgeon happened to be one of the best in the world.

"I suppose if you're going to break both your legs, this is the place to do it," she'd say to me, later.

"I have to use a *bedpan.*"

It was the next morning, and my mother's tone was understandably aggrieved. So far, the bedpans were her primary concern. Her nurses didn't speak English, and I imagined them as large and stalwart, clad in unforgiving foundation garments and impatient with her reluctance to pee in a basin. *"Ach, fraulein Amerikanische ist zu gut fur bettpfanne!"* they'd say, sneering. I'd sent a few relevant German phrases via email (*"Mehr Morphium, bitte." "Nicht amputieren!"*), and my mother replied with a small dispatch about her meals, as if she were on vacation: *"Had a lovely croissant and yogurt for breakfast. My lunch is some kind of turkey in a whiskey sauce."*

There didn't seem to be anything for me to do, and so I packed my body pillow and array of supplements to spend Thanksgiving with Scott's family in Iowa, as planned. I'd always liked them, my mother-in-law Kathy especially, but on this visit their every word and action rubbed me the wrong way. At dinner there was no butter, only margarine, and this seemed emblematic of a basic difference in our beliefs about childrearing that was suddenly of crucial importance—never mind that I hadn't known I *had* beliefs about childrearing until just that second. All weekend, reason fought a losing battle against insane hormonal petulance. When my mother in-law proclaimed her intention to buy a gigantic mechanical pony for the nursery, I blinked back tears. She'd *had* children to ply with false butter and robot animals. These babies were *mine*, and nobody had better forget it. My own mother couldn't travel until spring, meaning not only had her holiday visit been scuttled, but she'd probably never see my glorious belly. I couldn't do anything about that, or to ensure the Science Babies were born alive and healthy, but I was damn well going to be the one deciding what kind of cribs they'd sleep in and what they ate for breakfast.

My favorite bookstore was in Iowa City, and we'd been there more than an hour when Scott found me in the children's section, clutching a copy of *Corduroy* and looking tormented.

"Are you getting that?" he asked, his arms full of books.

"I don't know!"

I had yet to buy a single baby-related item, and looking down at the book, the letters of the title seemed to rearrange themselves to spell HUBRIS.

My husband led me—protesting weakly—toward the checkout counter. Afterward I felt drunk with triumph, and in another store that day picked up a green-and-white-striped sleeper, glancing around as if planning to slip the thing under my coat. I'd had one like it myself, as a baby, and it seemed perfect and necessary that my children have green-and-white-striped sleepers of their own. Which would be less likely to draw the Evil Eye, buying one sleeper or two? If I only bought *one*, I could pretend it was for *a* baby, but not necessarily these *specific* ones. Would I then be dooming the sleeper-less baby to nonexistence? I didn't actually believe in the Evil Eye, not with my brain, but reproduction had turned me into a woman with a constant stream of salt jetting over her left shoulder. In the end, I bought both sleepers, but didn't remove them from their packages.

It is tempting to view my mother's accident as the warning strike of a gong, an ominous, lingering harbinger of events to come. I know things don't work that way, but it can't be denied that Thanksgiving marked the beginning of a series of misfortunes. I became anemic, and contracted an infection associated with preterm labor. The antibiotics redoubled the nausea that in recent weeks had slightly abated, and my glucose tolerance test was a comedy of errors involving a fire alarm and a fainting spell, culminating in a diagnosis of gestational diabetes. The prescribed diabetic diet, far from feeling restrictive, required an absurd amount of food. For years I'd kept a mental list of the things I'd eat once pregnancy gave me an excuse to indulge my every gustatory whim: greasy diner cheeseburgers, cream cheese wontons, cartons of gooey Chinese takeout—but now that the time had come, all I could force down were a few "safe foods" like French fries and vegetarian baked beans, the latter of which I ate nightly for a while, like a pregnant hobo.

I made my first visit to Labor & Delivery triage at 16 weeks, convinced I was about to pop open like a coin purse and expel my babies into the world. An ultrasound showed their small round skulls turning next to one another on the screen, and I realized that despite my best efforts, I'd fallen for them with specificity, not just as babies qua babies, but whole beloved persons who were more than the sum of a pregnancy. The scan also revealed that Baby A's head, resting directly atop my cervix, was responsible for the sensation I'd had of a billiard ball lodged where no billiard ball ought to be. It wasn't an unfamiliar feeling, and when the nurse gave me a card listing the signs of preterm labor I saw it there under "pressure." Not only were they vague, these signs, but I had nearly all of them already. *Pressure?* Check. *Backache?* Check. *Cramping?* Check. I asked the nurse about it when she returned, and she told me not to worry.

"But feel free to come back if you feel like something is really wrong," she said, handing me the discharge papers.

I *always* felt like something was really wrong. The Science Babies had finished forming new organs and now were developing and fattening the existing framework. They'd been proven free of the most dramatic coding errors, and now it was my body that had the greatest potential for failure. What about that pain when rising from a sitting position? I'd never had a contraction, and doubted my ability to identify one correctly. Then there was what's called an "incompetent cervix," where the pressure of a growing baby causes it to dilate with no warning at all. The only real way to test a cervix is by putting a fetus atop it, so by the time its incompetence is discovered, it's usually too late—at least for the test baby. In future pregnancies they sew you up. I wished they'd sew me up prophylactically, as I couldn't see my cervix being any more competent than the rest of me. I became obsessed with grisly online accounts of twins born just before viability, at 22 or 23 weeks, and dying in their parents' arms. I don't know whether I was trying to prepare for the most likely catastrophe or looking for clues: Was there a symptom someone had overlooked? How had they felt the day before? I transferred to a perinatology clinic—the forty-minute drive to my obstetrician had begun to seem silly, even dangerous, especially when a group of high-risk pregnancy specialists practiced out of a hospital blocks from our apartment. This hospital even had the state's best neonatal intensive care unit, should my fears of bodily mutiny came to fruition. I'd been to triage twice by 20 weeks, and almost every day I debated whether to call the doctor, mediating a war between an embarrassed dread of overreaction and my fear of missing something important.

Seven

Christmas was cold and snowy and grey. My mother had been discharged from her rehab facility, still in a wheelchair, and my brother, Max, had flown off to spend a month with her in Switzerland. Scott and I were alone, with only the cats for company, unless you counted the two babies who'd recently begun to writhe within my abdomen. For a while all I'd felt was a muffled flickering, but by late December the sensations were forceful but formless—like the undulating of some internal parasite whose intentions were unclear.

I don't know why—maybe the weather, or the short, dark days, or the parasitic slithering—but I had begun nursing a constant, low-level anxiety. The more anxious I became, the less I could eat. Doctors are fanatical about the importance of weight gain in twin pregnancy, and the less I could eat, the worse my anxiety, particularly before meals, which were becoming tense affairs that made me feel like a *foie gras* goose.

For a month, Scott had been warring with the upstairs neighbors, a pair of recently graduated frat boys prone to drunk shirtless wrestling at 2:30 every morning. Just after the bars had closed for the night we'd hear them come tromping home, and then a series of great THUMPs commenced above our bedroom, causing the ceiling fan to tremble. It took weeks to figure out what they were *doing* up there, but an angry visit finally revealed the drunk, shirtless, wrestling truth. I found it annoying but livable, even amusing, but then I was a city dweller who'd lived in apartments for over ten years. I was comforted by the sounds of nearby strangers: hearing them move about or watch TV felt cozy, especially as I hated being the last one awake. But Scott was from Iowa. Iowans don't believe in apartments, and night is so unnaturally dark and silent there that on my first visit I couldn't sleep—it was like being locked in a trunk of a car, without the soothing traffic noise. Winters make my husband glum and crabby, and impending fatherhood had activated a primeval instinct to Protect the Family Unit, and all combined these factors resulted in irate phone calls—first to the landlord and then the police—and much middle of the night fuming about how we Couldn't Live Like This, and would have to move that summer, when our lease was up. Moving was highest on my list of personal stressors—all that change, you know—and the thought of being uprooted with two-month-old twins made me physically ill.

Any other time, I'd have snapped at Scott to pull himself together, or relentlessly joked him into a better mood, but in my weakened, pregnant state, this disruption of household equilibrium was too much for me. My anxiety fed off his anger, until I woke at the slightest wrestly sound and lay stiff, hoping he wouldn't hear it.

There was a long weekend for the holiday, and we were snowed in. I napped, and woke with a pounding heart, swathed in groggy despair. I rallied for my return to work, but then another long weekend came, and with it, a cluster (a herd? a coven? a quiver?) of panic attacks. At Target, a stop amongst the baby clothes forced me from the store at a run, and I hyperventilated, holding my vast, lurching belly. Babies! I couldn't take care of babies, feeling this way! I also couldn't stop crying, and Scott rushed home from work to tend to me. *I'm sorry,* I repeated over and over, to Scott, to the babies, to no one in particular, *I'm so sorry.*

The difference between panic and worry is that worry has an ABOUT. Sometimes this ABOUT is vague, but worry is related to circumstances. Whether or not the circumstances are imagined or your concerns justifiable, worry at least pretends to rationality. Panic, on the other hand, is senseless, a sudden storm that knocks out electricity and washes bridges away, foiling your plans of escape and felling the lines of communication between reason and...whatever *this* is, that has you convinced you'll live out your days in an asylum—assuming you can make it through the next fifteen minutes, which is far from a given. It's like a restless-leg syndrome of the soul, a desire to claw your way out of your own skin. Panic comes from nowhere, then worry follows and the panic becomes its ABOUT. *Surely you will feel like this forever,* the worry frets, *and what kind of life will that be? You can't possibly work/care for children/have a relationship. It would be too much for you, prone as you are to fits of madness.*

I had my first panic attack at eighteen. I woke with my heart racing and my hands clammy, enveloped by a crushing existential dread, and naturally assumed I was in the grip of stimulant psychosis. I had not recently consumed any amphetamine, but that didn't hinder my diagnosis, one I'd read about in a recent magazine article. You know that saying doctors are so fond of, that when you hear hoofbeats you ought to think horses rather than zebras? When I heard hoofbeats, I thought centaurs.

I'm not sure how I figured it out. I know I did research, but I can't remember how such research might have been conducted, pre-Internet. Did I just...read things? Were there card catalogues involved? Microfiche? Once I solved the mystery, I tried to deal with the problem on my own: with more research, in the form of a book about anxiety disorders. But my wee-hour episodes continued to wake me at 4:30 every morning, like Satan's alarm clock, and at last I haltingly suggested to my mother that I might need to "see someone." She's since revised her opinion, but back then my mother's view was that everyone had troubles and a psychiatrist couldn't tell you anything you didn't already know. Her family had been farmers, people who could be relied upon for a good "goat on the roof" story, who'd lived through the Depression and war, and done it all with a minimum of whining. I should have known that if my mother wouldn't permit store-bought piecrust—or even the use of a pastry cutter—a psychiatrist was out of the question. Instead she gave me a book called *The Art of*

Happiness, written by the Dalai Lama. When the jolly art didn't help, I visited my doctor, who wrote me a prescription himself.

Possessing a pill that could restore my sanity often removed the need to take it at all, and once the stress of leaving for college was behind me the panic attacks receded. They'd flare up every few years, during periods of unusual overwhelm. Once, an intractable week-long panic bloomed from a perfect storm of personal disaster and medication malfunction, earning me a weekend in the psychiatric ward, where my swivet was chemically broken, like an unruly horse. There were no open beds on the floor for ordinary neurotics, so I roomed with patients who pushed invisible vacuum cleaners and argued with invisible people in foreign languages. Some were chummy and gregarious, while others had well-defined personal boundaries—boundaries they were prepared to enforce with a cane. Most had been in and out of hospitals for years.

My parents divorced when I was young, and not long after, my father was diagnosed as bipolar, and he spent some time in locked wards himself. My youth likely kept me from noticing the rumbles preceding the avalanche, and so to me his downhill slide seemed chillingly sudden. I came to think of mental illness as a monster or act of God, something that with no warning. As far as I was concerned, every panic attack I had was the potential beginning of the potential end, and I feared nothing so keenly as losing my mind.

Almost a year after my time in the Nervous Hospital, I met Scott. He was funny, earnest, and calmed me as effectively as if he'd been dusted with Ativan. The severely anxious are a bit like animals, the way we react to people and settings. We're sensitive to vague qualities of atmosphere, to "just a feeling,"—what a hippie might refer to as "vibes." Usually new relationships made me nervous to the point of retching, but with Scott I was no more neurotic than usual, and often less so. I rarely panicked, and when I did the episode was never longer than a day or so—just long enough to remind me of my secret fear—that once you've gone cracked, you never go back.

Our 20-week anatomy ultrasound was the Monday after the weekend of panic, on the morning of New Year's Eve. The room was hot and close-feeling, like a closet, and my chest was tight with suppressed tears. I'd been eagerly anticipating this event for months, and now instead of enjoying it I felt oddly detached. I was relieved when I got into the spirit of things toward the end, laughing with Scott at Baby B's thrashing. Tiny feet pressed into view, and I wondered at the iconic perfection of them, like something you'd see on a shower invitation or birth announcement. The pad of each toe was like a tender pea.

After the ultrasound, a perinatologist we hadn't met before grinned as she flipped through the images.

"Everything looks *great*. You have…the ideal twins. Sometimes we do high-res scans more often with multiple pregnancy, but I don't see why you'd need another for six weeks."

I mentioned, casual-like, that I was having **cough** a bit of anxiety, and was relieved when the doctor's response was to snort loudly and scrawl me a chart of hormone levels through pregnancy, indicating with an emphatic X my place high on the upward slope. Despite propaganda portraying the second trimester as a Golden Time of peaceful belly-rubbing and frequent intercourse, it's also fraught with hormonal unrest and *oh-God-I'm-really-having-a-baby*-type realizations. Carrying twins turns gestation up to eleven, to say the least, and between continued morning sickness and measuring ten weeks vaster than my actual twenty, I'd piled on the worst of the first and third trimesters as well. It reassured me to hear that while I may have been crazy, I had ample excuse to be.

That evening the storm clouds regathered, and I slipped into the kitchen to look at the stills from the morning's ultrasound. I was hoping for perspective, something to help me regain the giddy gratitude of earlier weeks, but instead of warm maternal feelings, the sight of my children delivered a wallop of sickened terror.

Two distinct humans, *for whom I would be ever and entirely responsible,* were *living beneath my skin.* They felt as foreign to me as Jonah to the whale, a lash of aversion that made me shove the pictures back in their envelope. This was a mistake. What if I couldn't do this? What if I was too anxious and broken; what if they hated me, these foreign babies?

I didn't think I wanted them, anymore.

A wave of shame and self-hatred caused my knees to buckle. How could I be afraid of my own *children*, the children I'd longed for so intensely? What was *wrong* with me? Could they tell what I was feeling? What if they heard the fleeting thought of adoption, of time-travel to undo their existence? Sackcloth and ashes were too dignified: I ought to be tarred and feathered; they should bring back public stonings, just for me. Maybe my wronged fetal children could cast the first stones, from the inside. I didn't notice my ugly, anguished sobs until Scott was by my side.

"What is it?" he asked, and I shook my head, inside which a voice was hissing *Bad Mother! Bad Mother!*

"I can't tell you," I choked. "I *can't.*"

It was hours before I could, and then I mumbled, whispering the worst of it: *for a second, I didn't want them.*

I was afraid to meet my husband's eyes. My own were swollen nearly shut, but tears wedged their way through. Scott let them dampen his shoulder, saying all the right things.

"Of course you didn't mean it. Of course I know. It's just the awful winter. You'll be fine by the time the babies are born, and if not, I'll just take care of them myself until you are. You don't have to worry about that. You don't have to worry about anything. It's okay. Everything is going to be okay."

The preterm labor paranoia, the drama of diabetes, anemia, and panic—all of this began after Thanksgiving, as the days grew colder and shorter and I had progressively more to lose. I pricked my finger four times a day to check my blood sugar, bringing the number of needles involved in the conception and gestation of my children into the realm of higher math. I vomited and counted carbs and sat in the evenings with my hand between my legs, sure my pelvis would snap and drop my innards to the floor. Throw in the pathetic fallacy of the changing season, give the convenient narrative nudge of a car crash, and is it any wonder my mind wants to see my mother's accident as the first slip down a lubricated slope?

To do so, though, you'd have to ignore a raft of conflicting data points. It was the best of times, it was the worst of times, and all that. The lows may have been subterranean, but the highs were somewhere in the stratosphere. Take our first appointment at the perinatology clinic, when I was 17 weeks: during the ultrasound portion, Baby A sat directly upon the camera—as if it were a photocopier, and he a drunken temp at a Christmas Party.

"That is definitely a boy," said the doctor.

It definitely was. I couldn't stop giggling. It was a boy! It was a baby!

Scott and I clutched each other's hands while the doctor tried to get a look at the other set of genitals I'd cooked up. Baby B took exception to our prying, and tried to scoot away until, sensing our determination, she grudgingly revealed her girlhood for a fleet moment before re-crossing her legs. We were ecstatic. A girl! A boy and a girl! A girl and a boy! I'd have been happy with any combination—I could see myself as a mother of boys, languid and amused, or laughing with my clan of daughters, but there was something satisfying and right about having one of each. We'd chosen exactly two names thus far, our favorites: one for a boy, and one for a girl. Our babies would be Ames and Simone, though I was far too fearful go public with the announcement. Still, once named they seemed more corporeal. *Ames!* I imagined calling from the imaginary doorstep of my imaginary house, into the imaginary yard where my children were playing, *Simone! Time for dinner!* I saw myself putting on mittens, sliding backpack straps over tiny shoulders. *My children.*

Even after the New Year's Eve of My Discontent, it wasn't all gloom and misfiring adrenaline. I went back to work the next day, and the distraction gave my mind less time for its long, fretful monologues. When an ad for high chairs made my chest tighten—*High chairs! I forgot about high chairs! Oh God, feeding: what if I'm too nervous to manage even that? How will I feed both at once? What if they tire of my incompetence and fling their bowls to the ground in synchronized protest?*—I reminded myself that babies are just babies, and they like their mothers, because they don't know any better. Just because I'd have two didn't mean they'd form a judgmental cabal to critique my performance. Then would come another bad patch, as when Scott dragged me to the Expecting Multiples class I'd signed us up for before the holidays. It was taught by a bubbly woman about five feet tall—probably no more than the height of her toddler twins stacked atop one another—who struck me as someone who owned multiple pairs of overalls. Mid-class I bolted from the room to violently expel baked beans all over a bathroom stall, and then I went home and had a panic attack. A day or two later the mood had swung again, and I basked in the happiest moment of my pregnancy, when Scott first felt a kick from the outside. We spent that evening tapping my belly and laughing when we felt an answering thump.

"I wish you could have seen his face," I wrote online, *"it lit up like a flare in the dark. This particular kick was courtesy of my dear boy, who is head down on my left side and has taken up the study of Morse code. His sister, on the other hand, has positioned her placenta between herself and the outside world, for privacy (I forsee a surfeit of poorly-lettered KEeP OUT! signs in my future). Since that first startling thump I have been able to feel movement in a more organized and baby-appropriate way—that is to say distinct kicks rather than the vague impression of subterranean scurrying I had before. This seems more congenial somehow, and less like I am housing a sneaky, abnormally large tapeworm instead of two human babies. Feeling my children, whom I will presumably one day assist with homework and entreat to put on a jacket, for heaven's sake, kick me with their ACTUAL FEET defeats all superlatives. I have been told the novelty will wear off, but I don't see that happening anytime soon."*

On Friday we noticed that one of our cats, Lennie, was repeatedly slipping into the litter box and out again. He'd lick his penis industriously before marching back inside, grim and determined, looking just as Churchill must have before the Battle of Britain. When we called, the vet pronounced it an emergency, and we raced to the Animal ER, where a waiting technician snatched the yowling carrier from our hands and whisked Lennie to a back room. They thought it was a urinary blockage—fatal if not caught before the bladder reaches capacity. Scott and I had been preparing to leave for a movie before we noticed Lennie's behavior, and once he was safely in the care of professionals we stood in the waiting room, whispering *what ifs*. What if we'd left for our movie a few minutes earlier? What if we'd returned, full of popcorn and Junior Mints, to a dead cat?

Lennie was quickly mended and sentenced to an hour of observation, while Scott and I sat reading outdated magazines that smelled of wet dog. Ames—whom I'd started calling "Stampy" for his love of uterine Flamenco—was kicking hard enough for the movement to be visible. I'd seen his kicks from outside before, but never this vehement, and only while staring hawk-eyed at my naked belly. Now you could see them through my clothes, from across the room, possibly from space. *Shiver! Flup!* went my maternity shirt, leaping about as if possessed. I giggled. A family was waiting nearby for news of their dog, and I tried to stifle my amusement, to no avail.

"Did you *see* that?" I whispered every few minutes, poking Scott with my elbow. "Are you *seeing* this?

Shiver! Flup!

CHAPTER

Eight

There I am, leaving work for my fortnightly clinic appointment. I am 22 weeks and 2 days pregnant. I think it is about noon, and I waddle through the icy parking lot, glad I took the whole afternoon off. It's a grey day, with the flat, dingy light of a northern January.

Some details are very clear. I am wearing my coat from the winter before; the top button is the only one I can still fasten, and the rest of the material falls around me like a cape. It's all of five degrees, but pregnancy has stripped me of the ability to feel cold, and my belly juts into the air. The shirt covering it is my favorite, all in shades of brown, with wide horizontal stripes over a pattern of thinner horizontal lines. The pregnant can wear such things without fear of looking wide, a fact of which I take advantage at every opportunity.

After the parking lot, there is a period of time populated by conjecture. I suppose I drove to the hospital via my usual route, and parked in my usual place. I imagine I checked in at the desk, and produced a urine sample in the bathroom while staring at the poster about fetal fibronectin testing. I am sure I was weighed, and ran through my medications and dosages with the nurse. These actions are absent from my memory of that day, but they are the things I did at every appointment. Maybe my brain failed to take their impressions because they were routine and multiple.

Then it is clear again. I am sitting in an exam room, across from a cloying framed poster—black and white with certain details hand-colored—of a boy in a news cap kissing a little girl with a bow in her hair. The nurse with me is older, with a small serious mouth, a cap of curly brown hair, and glasses. I could probably draw her face for you now, if you gave me a pencil. She takes my blood pressure and asks when I last felt movement, and I answer with my standard uncertainty. I don't keep track—the distinct kicks and thumps are still new and random, and as for the squirming and popping, who can tell what is baby and what is bowel? Anyway, with twins I get an ultrasound at every appointment, and I am still talking as I climb onto the table and lie back, lifting my shirt. I tell her how painful walking has become, and that I think it might be time to curtail my work schedule. *You've gotten so* BIG *overnight!* she says, squeezing a ribbon of gel onto the transducer. *I know!* I laugh, and I see a flash of kicking legs as she slides it across my belly. She moves down to look at Ames, who is curled low with his shoulder against my cervix and an arm crooked over his head. His position makes it hard to see him clearly, so we pan up to Simone, and then back again, where Ames is still sleeping, and the nurse makes a little puffing sound of good-natured frustration, saying she's having a hard time getting a good shot of cardiac activity. (Babies! So uncooperative!) That's all the nurses check—the doctor always finishes the ultrasound.

"I'll let him find it when he comes in," she says.

When she leaves to get the doctor, I lay there for a moment—smiling, stupid—before I know. I think I know. My eyes begin to feel hot and my own cardiac activity picks up. The nurse is gone for a long time, and when she returns with the doctor she takes a position at my side. The doctor picks up the transducer.

"I was looking at the records of your 20-week ultrasound to see if there were any indications," he says nonsensically, and then he points: "There. I'm sorry. You can see clearly that Baby A is *demised.*"

It's so hard to remember the details. The harder I look, the more they skitter away, some solicitous, maternal part of my brain rushing to obscure my memory, holding it back from the scene of the crime the way policemen restrain relatives who return to find their driveways full of lights and sirens. I know tears slide down my cheeks and the nurse takes my hand, the purpose of her new position now evident. The doctor points to fluid accumulating in my son's chest, the thickening of the dura of his brain, the way the umbilical cord has become swollen. I remember thinking it looked like link sausage, or DNA. The doctor explains that these signs mean that it— the *demise*—happened more than a day ago. He cocks his head, looks at the screen: *maybe three.*

Friday, I think. Three days ago was Friday, the night we took Lennie to the Animal ER. It must have happened then. Maybe the last time I felt him was in that waiting room, with muddy paw prints on the linoleum. Assuming Ames was the one kicking me then, which I am at once sickeningly aware that I can't know, not for sure.

I don't scream or become hysterical. I don't roll around on the floor and wail. I just cry and cry, without making any noise. I cry and cry and cry.

I want to know what happened, but there is no tiny smoking gun to be seen. I am told that while they will analyze the placenta and check the chromosomes, in two-thirds of cases the cause remains "a mystery." Still, I'm assured his death wasn't caused by anything I did, which seems at odds with the previous statement. If it's such a mystery, how do they know? They seem to be willfully ignoring a pattern even I can see: I get pregnant; my babies die.

I am not wild about the word choice, either: "Mystery" implies intrigue, as if to add a thrilling veneer to something that, personally, I don't find thrilling at all. They should be saying *we don't know* instead of *in 2/3 of cases, the cause remains a mystery*, as if my baby were being willfully obtuse.

There is another word I take issue with: babies should not just *die* two weeks after having every bodily system inventoried and pronounced *ideal*. That's not what "ideal" means. In fact, look:

1. *Conceived as constituting a standard of perfection or excellence: ideal beauty.*
2. *Regarded as perfect of its kind: an ideal spot for a home.*
3. *Existing only in the imagination; not real or actual: Nature is real; beauty is ideal.*

Ahh, number three. There it is. *Existing only in the imagination.* In grainy, shiny pictures in a folder in my closet. In a small bag of ashes.

The doctor moves on, looking at Baby B; Simone is flipping around, indecently enjoying the extra space. Ames is still and crooked at the edge of the screen, but Simone is waving, showing us her eyeball and tiny chin. I stare at her desperately. I need her to live. I wonder what it is like for her in there, what she knows.

I am left alone to call Scott at work, and I tell him to come right away. *One of the babies died.* Later I realize I didn't tell him which one, and that for the drive from the bookstore to the hospital they are both equally dead, and equally alive. Schrödinger again, damn him.

It was already over as I walked through the parking lot from my office and drove away, had been over for days. Isn't it strange, how that works? The morning after my first kiss, I remember being struck by the way one's After is so unexpectedly visited upon Before. I'd woken the previous morning kiss-less, with no kiss prospects or plans, and there I was 24 hours later, kissed, worldly, a girl who had *touched a penis.* Almost as striking is the distance that can exist within what should be a sudden event. One Saturday I spent three hours of that distance doing laundry, only unaware that my current relationship was over because I hadn't yet gotten the phone call. I was already in my After, as I sorted whites from colors, I just didn't know it yet.

At my wedding, I walked down the makeshift aisle to "What a

Difference a Day Makes," by Dinah Washington. That song had been a comfort to me during the year before Scott and I met, when the knowledge that nothing lasts forever was sometimes all that propelled me through my days. After we fell in love, the lyrics served as a reminder of the wonder that could be right around the corner—though of course it goes both ways. It is still one of my favorite songs.

Scott arrives and sits dumbly next to me while we wait for the perinatologist to return. I try to think of questions. I know there are questions that need asking, but my head feels stuffed with cotton batting and wind-up toys. When the doctor appears, he offers his condolences again, and explains to Scott about the mystery.

"These things happen," he says—irrelevantly, as by then we've figured this out.

The pains I've been having the past few days are likely contractions that began when Ames died. Because he is closest to my cervix, there is a risk of preterm labor, or infection.

"It's better when the upper baby is affected," admits the doctor, and I want to slap him.

Carrying so much "non-living tissue" presents another problem, and the nurse takes my blood to check for clotting factors that might indicate danger for me or Simone. These levels will be followed for six to eight weeks, after which the risk is minimal. Six to eight weeks is a long wait for minimal risk, but nothing compared to the wait if all goes well: I'm told the furthest I'll be allowed to carry Simone is 36 weeks, but though that's a full month earlier than my due date, it seems impossibly distant. Weekly fetal checkups begin at 28 weeks, and the doctor promises that Simone will be delivered at the first sign of trouble.

"There's an excellent chance she'll be just fine," he assures us, and I wonder how he knows, what with all the *mystery*.

When we enter our silent apartment that afternoon, I realize it is January 14th, almost a year to the day since we were told our second pregnancy was doomed. Our first miscarriage was two Januarys before that. Simone will be viable outside the womb on January 26th. Twelve days to go; I am terrified the evil month of January will steal her from me before we get there.

Thanks to the focus commanded by having something real to worry about, my ABOUT-less panic has vanished. I hate that losing Ames is what banished it. I feel ill knowing that two weeks before, I hadn't wanted to be pregnant at all. I wonder if it means something that in my sole dream about the babies they'd appeared as two white rats, scampering about the kitchen while I tried to corral them with a broom, or that the only other baby dream I'd had featured just one baby—a girl, curly-haired and nearly a toddler, upon a changing table.

It's simpler to relate to a single baby, maybe because the logistics are more manageable and easier to visualize, or because in the pinkly-lit and iconic tableaux of motherhood, it is always *one* baby per mother. Two babies can seem less individualized, splitting the mother/baby relationship in half or slipping once in a while into a unit—*The Twins*. This is what I tell myself when, after the ultrasound, I imagine holding my sleeping newborn Simone in a sling, and it brings a rush of warmth and yearning stronger than anything I'd felt for either baby, before.

Long before, pre-IVF, Scott wanted a girl. He'd teased that girls are closer to their fathers, while boys prefer their mothers, and offered example after example to bolster his argument. Already aware that I was unlikely to be the good-time parent, this led me to mournful fantasies of my husband and daughter laughing together—probably at my expense—while I shambled pathetically after them, like a younger sibling desperate to be included. I'd secretly hoped for a boy, to give me at least a fighting chance, and in the weeks before he died, I'd grown especially attached to Ames— my Stampy—because his kicks were the ones I felt most often. I'd tapped my popping, jolting belly and whispered to him during moments when my panic had cleared.

In retrospect (which, by the way, is pretty useless—try selling a crystal ball that only looks backwards) it's obvious to me that the doctor from my 20-week ultrasound was right: hormones *were* responsible for my mid-pregnancy anxiety. She was wrong, though, about the direction they were headed. After every previous miscarriage, their precipitous drop had led to a bout of panic. On this last occasion, my mental unmooring was almost certainly due to the beginning failure of Ames' placenta, the organ responsible not only for production of pregnancy hormones, but for providing him with sustenance, and the organ that had—about that time, we'd later learn—begun to deprive him of it.

On my website the next day, I would begin an entry with the thought that had swarmed and circled and buzzed in my head, ever since the word "*demised*" left the doctor's lips:

"*It is always something, but rarely the something you expect. Don't you find that to be true? I expected another first trimester miscarriage, and when that didn't happen, I shifted my morbid focus to preterm labor. I read studies and memorized statistics. Now I keep thinking 'I prepared for the wrong thing. I didn't prepare for this.'*"

CHAPTER

Nine

When my mother picked up the phone, I could hear Max and my uncle laughing boisterously in the background. I forced the news from my cracking throat.

"One of the babies died." My brother's jovial shouting soared over my voice.

"What?"

I made myself say it again. A booming laugh rose from beyond.

"SHHHHHHHH! QUIET!" hissed my mother, with a terrible ferocity. She must have given a look to match, because the silence that followed was complete and instantaneous.

There it was: Before. After.

When Scott told his mother, I could hear the wail through the phone.

"I don't want to talk to anyone," I warned him dully, from my spot on the couch. I had no room for the sorrow of others. Their tears made me feel obliged to assume a cheerful and reassuring demeanor, as if there were room for only one sad person at a time. It had always been this way, and when I was a kid and my parents fought or my father slipped into a depression, I'd resort to puns and impromptu limericks, inappropriate sarcasm and even mime to raise the collective spirits. This dogged hilarity made me a delight at cocktail hour, but it also meant my misery played against type, and abhorred company.

We got a few phone calls ourselves. One was from the teacher of our Expecting Multiples class, wondering where we were—it was Monday; I'd forgotten. I almost laughed at the horror in her voice when I explained why we were missing the lesson on tandem breastfeeding. Then a grief counselor—she'd been notified by my doctor, per the protocol that lurches into effect after an Intrauterine Fetal Demise. It was startling, that first realization that this was part of a script, an event commonplace enough to have standard operating procedures. The counselor wanted to make an appointment to discuss our "birth plan."

"I don't understand," I said, and truer words were never spoken. She voiced a gentle reminder that I'd be delivering both babies, though Ames would be smaller, and would have undergone euphemistic Changes. This would be a delicate event, with birth and death on top of one another in such an improper way. There were decisions to be made.

"You might like to start thinking about whether you'd prefer to have your son buried or cremated," said the counselor, and though I knew it was simply a matter of poor word choice, I wanted to snap that I would like no such thing, that there were few things I'd like LESS to think about.

We met her a few days later, in a dim, closet-sized room at the hospital, a room with a box of Kleenex, a few soft chairs, and a book of quotes by Mother Teresa. The counselor was tall and sympathetic, and came bearing brochures. She'd had a stillbirth herself, years ago, and it inspired her to leave her job as a nurse to work with People Like Us—members of a club no one wants to join, like lepers or amputees. Scott and I belonged to several of these now: infertility, miscarriage, *Intrauterine Fetal Demise*. We should have been collecting merit badges.

The counselor mentioned her other children, and I wondered aloud how we'd approach the subject of Ames with Simone. I wished I could pass her a note, later, maybe slip it under the door of her room—*You had a twin brother, but he died before you were born.* I was adamant that Ames not be treated like a shameful family secret, but I didn't want his death casting a grisly pall over our every milestone, his ghost hovering behind us in vacation photographs. It would have been ideal for Simone to be born knowing the whole story, thus removing the impossible task of choosing an appropriate time for the news. It would be taken for granted, not a shocking discovery at thirteen, used as an excuse for months of tiresome brooding.

"Our children know they have a sister who died," said the counselor, "We even throw her a birthday party every year."

Scott and I exchanged a silent agreement never to do such a thing. Ames and Simone would share a birthday, and I could think of no surer way to ruin a celebration than emerging from the kitchen with a cake in honor of the birthday girl and her long-dead brother.

There were brochures—for stillbirth photographers and bereavement retreats. The counselor gave us a primer on grief, opining that eventually we would find a way to extract some meaning from our loss. *Everyone takes something different from the experience*, she said, as if it were a buffet. A buffet of death!

I was revolted at the thought of finding meaning in the loss of a baby. How grotesquely solipsistic, to reduce an existence to a single Teachable Moment, as if Ames' demise were really about *me,* merely a way to impart wisdom I could glean only by losing him.

"I don't believe in that," I told the counselor, "Ames' death doesn't have to have meaning. It doesn't have to be anything other than what it is, a terrible thing. Maybe it will change me or teach me something, but a good thing can come from something terrible without that being its *meaning*." For the first of many times during our sojourn in the underworld of pediatric death and disaster, I was grateful for my atheism. It was comforting to believe that this horror was, if not entirely random, at least nothing personal. It demanded nothing of me. It was not a riddle or a code. It was not part of some celestial puppetmaster's master plan.

I'd been more vehement than I intended, but the counselor was used to People Like Us, and moved smoothly to the main event. What was our original birth plan? she wanted to know. How did we envision the experience?

"We can incorporate some of these things into your new plan," she explained, and I didn't know what to say. I hadn't had an *old* plan. I'd had a birth *preference*, and it was simple: both babies born alive, by whatever means was deemed safest. I'd thought I might like to use the Jacuzzi tub during labor, if I wasn't having a C-section. Maybe even if I was—I was a big fan of baths.

Now the bar had been lowered considerably. My goal was a modest one: to get 50% of the babies out alive. At this juncture, it seemed absurd to be picky about the details. I would have liked a birth without any death in it, but failing that, candles and Jacuzzi tubs weren't going to fool anyone.

Still, we went dutifully through the questions in the standard plan, and the counselor recorded our answers. I told her I found the smell of lavender relaxing. Dim lighting and music? Fine. Pain medicine? Yes, with something to stave off nausea. Popsicle flavors? No grape.

"Can you put in there that I want to know what is going on at all times?" I interrupted. "I want the nurse to be around for questions. And put down that I don't care about anything except getting Simone out alive. If there is even the suggestion of trouble, I want them to get her out right then."

"Yes," the counselor said, gently, "We'll put all of that in here. They'll know."

"And it would be good if the nurses are ones who have done this sort of thing before. Stillbirths. We don't know what...condition Ames will be in. I don't want to upset anyone."

"Oh, honey. You won't upset anyone."

"Well, good." Oh, hell. Now I was going to cry.

"We should talk about your son," she said, nudging the tissues in my direction, "Do you want to see him right away?"

"Yes," I said, without hesitation.

"*Mom wants to hold,*" murmured the counselor, writing it down.

"The nurse can clean him up first," I amended.

The counselor silently made another note.

"Mom wants nurse to ameliorate obvious putrefaction, fluids," I imagined it said.

"Who else will hold him?"

"No one," I said, just as Scott said:

"My parents."

We looked at one another. The counselor leaned back in her chair.

"I don't want a lot of *sobbing*," I said, fifteen minutes later, "by other people. It will be a sad day, but it's also the day Simone will be born. She deserves a happy birth."

"They're going to be *upset*," Scott said, exasperated.

"I know that." This was so complicated. It shouldn't be so complicated. There should be two separate events, one per baby. This was like having a double wedding, only one of the weddings was a divorce. The new bride's beaming would be painful to the ex-bride, and the dour flock of lawyers would spoil the vows. "I know it will be sad, and awful. It's just...I want there to be joy, too."

I'd seen those shows, the ones that follow a happy, moderately unat- tractive couple through pregnancy and the birth of their child. We see them tempting fate by decorating the nursery and having baby showers, and then one night they leave for the hospital with a duffel bag, and after a lot of lying around and a commercial break, the yelling begins, the woman is entreated to push, and voilà! The rapturous tinkling of a piano.

Even during my first pregnancy, the inevitable happy conclusion sur- prised me. I watched the wives complaining about paint colors and thought *Oh hubris, you wily bastard!* but nothing ever happened. I won- dered if there were episodes that never made it onto the air, episodes with ultrasounds like mine, or cord accidents during labor: episodes shelved in a box somewhere, unfinished. I was unaware of my faulty assumption— that these lost episodes would be uniformly tragic. Happy ending; sad ending. It never occurred to me that there was a third option, a space between the other two.

But this was the space we were mapping, in the first two weeks after the Bad Ultrasound. My bedrest became indefinite after three days, when my contractions increased and I landed in Labor & Delivery for four hours with a fetal heart monitor strapped to my stomach, a monitor Simone kicked irritably before skittering out of range. The nurses grew competitive and took turns pursuing her: they pinned a receiver disk in place on my belly by stacking rolls of tape upon it, stretching the elastic monitor girdle over the lot. The doctor on call from my clinic was new to me, with a soft Indian accent and a musical laugh that burst unexpected from her studious expression. She performed an ultrasound, and in the moment before the image cleared I had a wild hope that it would show Ames alive. I'd sob with relief, and we'd all joke about what trouble he was for scaring us so. *You're grounded!* I'd quip, wagging a finger at my belly—but I wouldn't mean it.

Alas, the blur resolved to show Ames still *demised*, cramped and crumpled while Simone stretched her long legs above him. He'd sunk so low that my uterine wall was bulging from the weight of his body, and my cervix had softened. So bedrest it was, or couchrest, for the foreseeable future.

In the mornings I watched television, mostly *What Not to Wear*—an odd choice, as I myself no longer bothered with pants, lounging in my underwear and an oversized *Cramps* T-shirt of Scott's. It seemed appropriate, as contractions—while never over my prescribed threshold of six an hour—were a reliable feature of my days. The worst took my breath away, literally, beginning with the sudden departure of all air from my lungs. Then my stomach would clench in a steady, relentless seizing, while I bowed my head and Scott looked frightened. The frequency didn't pick up until afternoon, which I spent Googling and brooding, desperate for information on probable outcomes. In the evening my contractions were at their worst, which is why the twilight hours were spent weighing whether or not to call the hospital. The doctor's orders were always the same—drink lots of water, keep your bladder empty, and remain horizontal: an exasperating triad of requirements that I worked at like a puzzle.

71

Emotionally, we slipped in and out of a strange anesthesia. You expect, after something terrible has happened, that your ability to laugh will be excised entirely. But Scott and I did laugh, at small things even, like lines of television dialogue. We laughed as my stomach bounced with Simone's increasingly strong kicks. The democratic primaries were in full swing, and we watched hours of debates and coverage, squabbling over heath care policy and electoral math.

And then one or both of us would be bereft, the change abrupt as a bucket of water upended over our heads. We'd sit in silence, our eyes as thickly glazed as hams. One ordinary night, after an ordinary evening, lying in bed in my ordinary fashion, I was accosted by a violent weeping. It was sudden and unstoppable, as if a grenade pin had been pulled, and the sobs piled atop one another and deprived me of breath. Scott appeared and held me tight against his chest, while I gasped and clutched at his arms.

"My baby! My baby! My poor baby!" I cried, and part of me floated up at a remove, observing my melodrama with alarm. It was like a scene from an old movie, the way I moaned and wailed and carried on, finally sobbing my way into sleep.

When I was a teenager, we visited relatives in Colorado, and I was struck by the bizarrely regular irregularity of their weather. Every afternoon around two, clouds materialized in what had been a clear sky, and there was a flare of rain and thunder. An hour later the sun would be fierce again and the sky returned to oceanic clarity, with none of the atmospheric moistness that usually follows a storm. This was what my moods were like, after the Bad Ultrasound. The anesthetic veil would be drawn back for a searing moment, and then would mercifully fall. I might be hopeful leaving an appointment, then gripped with fury as I passed through the waiting room, where a heavily pregnant woman complained about her C-section date. Some hours I regarded my belly fondly, thinking only of Simone kicking inside, and other times I was overwhelmed by nausea at the physical fact of a dead baby and a live one floating inside its skin-stretched globe.

The only constant was fear. Every moment that Simone was not kicking, I wondered whether she was dead. Even the weak voice that normally chided my irrationality was silent—because after all, it wasn't so irrational to wonder. Compared to my usual fever dreams, this was as solid as Newton's first law. A body in motion tends to stay in motion, and my body was obviously engaged in the process of ending its pregnancy, one baby at a time. Part of me wanted her extracted from my murderous womb *tout de suite*. What if she made it to viability, and afterwards succumbed to whatever mysterious baby-killing mechanism had claimed my son?

My world had grown very small, and I lost track of things Out There, Beyond the Couch, Where People Wore Pants. If I'd lost track of the world, however, the world took pains to make it clear that it hadn't lost track of me.

The first thing I'd done, when I arrived home after the Bad Ultrasound, was post the news on my website:

22 weeks, 2 days, I wrote, *No heartbeat on Baby A.*

The comments and email messages began as a trickle and swelled to scores by the next evening. I checked for them compulsively, and read with a needy gratitude, just as I did the cards that arrived from friends and family, and even people I hardly knew. Some said only "I'm sorry," others bore long, heartfelt paragraphs spilling over all available space. Phone calls we didn't answer—we were too spent for conversation—but the cards were just right.

I'd never been a card person. Too disorganized and lazy. It was something grown-ups did, sending thank-you notes and Christmas wishes. I bought cards—boxes of them—and then they sat disapprovingly in my closet, judgment seeping from them like a noxious gas.

I never sent thank-you cards for my wedding gifts, and I felt guilty about this at least once a month. I'd kept a careful accounting of what I'd received and from whom I'd received it, and I purchased cards in our wedding colors, to add to my Judgmental Stationery Closet. But, as always happened with these things, I put it off, and the longer I did, the more egregious my lateness seemed, until some invisible line was crossed and it was too late to send them at all. Lots of people forget to send thank you cards, I told myself. In Modern Times, this was acceptable. Ladies wore pants now, for heaven's sake—it was time we threw off the tyranny of forcible correspondence. People wore white after Labor Day, prepositions proudly ended sentences, and my beloved subjunctive was going the way of the hoop skirt. Maybe my lack of formalized gratitude wasn't correct, but surely it was a small, easily forgivable transgression.

When Ames died, I revised my position. Cards weren't communication's equivalent of the doily; they were as necessary and useful as spatulas. I waited for the mail like a lovesick Victorian, and after reading the day's epistles I kept them next to me in a stack on the sofa. They were my tether, planks of the bridge that would carry me out of my remote and lonely place. Each one ignited a brief, welcome conflagration, causing the pain to flare up for a moment in a way that was ultimately cleansing.

Sometimes, under my anesthetic veil, I thought I might have imagined it all—Ames or his death, both, everything—just made it up, accidentally even, and slipped into a living fable. The cards and flowers, the comments from far away strangers, all reassured me I hadn't: that Ames had been real, and that something real had been lost.

After this, I told myself one afternoon, freshly wrung of tears, *I will be a Card Person.* As soon my ordeal was behind me I'd buy stamps, the lack of which had often tripped me up in the past. I'd keep a variety of stationery on hand—there was quite a bit in the closet already—so that I would be ready at the merest suggestion of tragedy. I'd send cards for holidays and congratulations, and as thanks, but I knew that times of affliction were when Card People were needed most, and having realized its value, I would never again fail to give the comfort that others had given to me. During sickness or marital strife, after death or traumatic medical procedure, I would be there, via envelope.

This is what I would take from our counselor's grisly death buffet, though I wouldn't be narcissistic or unimaginative enough to construe it as meaning. It would be only a fortunate corollary, like the whittling skills you might pick up in prison.

It has been two years since Ames died, and I have sent only one card in all that time. Technically, I didn't even send it—it was hand-delivered by my husband as part of a baby gift. I never bought stamps, and couldn't tell you how much they cost these days. I've hoarded all the cards and messages I received during those bleak long-ago days. My sloth feels uncomfortably like betrayal, though I'm not sure of whom: the senders of the cards? My son? Our kind, hopeful grief counselor? The broken, determined me of 24 months ago?

Two years! Oh, my. I suppose there's still time for things to change.

The morning after I reached the hallowed 24 weeks of viability, I woke up and walked to the kitchen for my milk and saltines, and felt a sudden dampness. I pulled down my underwear right there, next to the sink, and squinted in the dim dawning light. Had my water broken? Had I maybe *peed* a little, as pregnant women were reported to do? Was this normal, dead-baby-related...discharge?

"Scott," I said, a moment later, shaking him awake, "I think we have to go in." We'd been to Labor & Delivery so many times by then that it had become an ordinary inconvenience. We pulled on clothes and stumbled sleepily from the building.

When we arrived they put a strip of paper between my legs and determined that whatever I'd thought was amniotic fluid, wasn't. The strips aren't always accurate when it comes to fluid that differs from the norm (which is as nice a way as I can think of to say "has a dead baby in it"). Still, it was enough to convince me that I had overreacted yet again, and I was embarrassed and annoyed at myself for ruining a perfectly good Sunday morning. I had an exam that showed my cervix short and soft but closed, and I was installed in a bed for monitoring, feeling silly. The nurse came in with an IV bag.

"What's that for?" I asked.

"The doctor thinks she might start you on magnesium and fluids, so I thought I'd get the IV going."

"Oh! Oh *no no no!* I'm sure that's not necessary. I'm fine, really!"

Magnesium Sulfate—"The Mag," they call it—is a drug with a reputation, and I'd read about it often while poring over high-risk pregnancy forums online. It is used to stop contractions, and ostensibly it works by affecting the body's calcium, which is needed for muscles to contract. Plausible, but from those with experience I'd gleaned that The Mag's *primary* mechanism of action was to deprive every cell in one's body of the will to live. These cells become so overwhelmed with ennui that they can't be bothered to move at all, whether to contract the uterus or perform other, less problematic tasks, like lifting an arm or *focusing the eyes.* The Mag imparts a boneless, full-body malaise, and I balked at being administered a drug deemed unbearable by women far more stalwart than I—all because I'd peed myself and leapt to conclusions.

The nurse agreed to wait for a final ruling on The Mag, and start with IV fluids. I love IV fluids. In fact, I'd go so far as to say IV fluids are my drug of choice. Saline run into my veins gives me a euphoric, well-rested feeling. I'd assume this relates to the frequency with which I reach evening before realizing I've forgotten to drink anything that day, but mere water guzzling doesn't produce the same effect, so who knows. Whatever the reason, not long after the IV was flowing I became chatty and saturated with *joie de vivre.* My nurse laughed at my jokes and put me on the monitor before leaving the room to talk to my doctor.

"I'm sorry," I said, turning to Scott with a rueful smile, "I can't believe I dragged us in here for nothing." Before he could respond, the door opened. The nurse entered looking regretful.

"Well," she sighed, "It looks like we need The Mag after all. Your fetal fibronectin was positive."

When they'd swabbed me to check for amniotic fluid, they'd also tested for fetal fibronectin, a substance present when labor is imminent. A negative test virtually guarantees you won't deliver within two weeks. A positive test isn't half as reliable, but to be safe I'd get a pair of steroid shots to mature

Simone's lungs. They had to be given 24 hours apart, and reached full effectiveness 24 hours after the last dose—Tuesday. My doctor had decided that, to ensure I remained pregnant that long, I'd be staying in the hospital—in bed and on The Mag. Which, by the way, required I consume only clear liquids (on account of the risk of vomiting) but not much in liquid form (on account of the risk of my LUNGS FILLING WITH FLUID). I supposed I'd make a hearty Sunday dinner of popsicles and ice chips.

The nurse drew up a syringe of steroid and warned me that it was an intramuscular shot, and might be painful. I rolled to my side to expose my ever-popular upper outer quadrant, and offered to do the shot myself. She marveled at my battle lumps—a term that doesn't have quite the ring of battle scars, does it?—and stuck me. The steroids burned going in.

Then she brandished a small IV bag with a warning label on it. The Mag.

"We start with a loading dose," she apologized, "It's not pleasant, but once we finish that you'll be on maintenance dosing, and it won't be so bad." She strapped an automatic blood pressure cuff on my non-IV arm, and dragged a fan in from the hallway.

"The Mag can make you feel..." the nurse paused, as if considering her description carefully, "...kind of like you're burning from the inside out."

My eyes shot wide.

"The fan should help. And I'll get you some ice chips. What flavors of popsicle do you like?"

"Anything but grape," I said. Look at that! My birth plan was coming in handy already.

"Burning from the inside out" is an apt description of The Mag's effects. It seared the length of my arm where it entered the vein; the capillaries on my eyeballs seemed to sizzle like strips of bacon. My face felt hot, but that was nothing compared to the...other locus of heat.

Scott had been tending to me with cold wet washcloths, which became hot after a shockingly short tenure on my forehead or the back of my neck. When the nurse left to get another bucket of ice, he stood at the sink wringing a washcloth dry. I motioned desperately for him to come closer.

"Do you need more ice chips?" he asked. I thought for a moment. No, ice chips wouldn't work at all.

"No, it's just—" (I lowered my voice) "—I'm pretty sure that my vagina is *on fire*."

Scott looked alarmed.

"I'm talking *Backdraft*, here."

"You should tell the nurse."

"I'd rather not," I replied stiffly, with as much dignity as a girl can muster while discussing her flaming labia.

"Why? It's not like she hasn't been all up in there already."

"Thank you for that," I said drily, "But I'm sure it's just a *feeling*. The nurse said 'from the inside out,' after all. I'm sure they wouldn't give me something that could actually scorch my...tissues."

"Alexa—"

"*Shh!* It's FINE!" I said, flapping my hand at him as the door opened.

"What's fine?" the nurse asked.

Scott gave me a stern look.

"Oh! Well. Nothing, really. I just noticed that it seems to be especially, uh, *hot* in—"

"Your groin? Oh, that's normal. I'll get you an icepack. We put them in the armpits sometimes too. Do you want three?"

"Just one, thank you," I said in a small voice.

The nurse was right—it was better after the loading dose. My vagina emerged unscathed, and I found I didn't mind The Mag, except for the continuing sizzling of my eyeballs and the need for cool washcloths upon my neck. I think my natural agitation blunted its effects—it didn't even stop my contractions, though they became sparse and irregular; it was almost relaxing. I was simply disinclined to move, a little weak and hot and tired. Simone was disinclined to move as well, which meant that she was easy to keep on the monitors, and we listened to the hoofbeats of her heart as day turned into afternoon. We called our families, and Scott's mother made plans to drive up from Iowa the next morning. Scott went home to get some of my things.

When he returned, we watched television while the light faded outside the window, and the darker it got, the more nervous I became at the prospect of a night in the hospital. In theory, it sounds like a neurotic's dream— omnipresent doctors! Obsessive monitoring of my symptoms! Constant vigilance!—but pregnancy paranoia was temporarily overcome by my horror of sleeping away from home. I'd been an insomniac for ten years, and rest was hard enough to come by without adding an unfamiliar setting and IV leash.

Every hour or so, I pressed the nurse for a promise that I'd be allowed to go home on Tuesday, and every hour or so, she allowed that barring complications, I would. The shift changed, and the night nurse, Jenna, introduced herself. At 10:00 she gave me something to help me sleep, and Scott nested in an uncomfortable-looking vinyl chair that folded out to be covered with a sheet. I curled in bed, trying to make the best of it.

A month before, as anxiety tightened its grip, I'd made a soothing playlist to listen to as I drifted off at night. Blossom Dearie, Astrud Gilberto, that sort of thing. Every night I lay with my earbuds in my ears and a lavender-filled pillow lain over my eyes. That first night in the hospital, my contractions picked up as they always did. In the dark, a new song started: Hadda Brooks, singing "All Night Long," in her dusky languorous way. I had a strong, clenching contraction, and felt a popping, like a bubble squeezed and broken, and a gush of warm wetness splashed onto my thighs.

I buzzed the nurses' station on my intercom.

"Could you send my nurse in, whenever she has a minute?"

"I'm pretty sure my water just broke," I said when Jenna entered. It was 11 PM. She turned on a light and lifted my sheet to look. When she lowered it and spoke again, it was with a careful calm.

"Based upon what I am seeing, here, I think you are right." Health care professionals abandon grammatical contractions in times of crisis.

"I'm not going anywhere on Tuesday, am I?" I asked, and then I started to shake.

Eleven

I'd always thought of shock as stillness. Shock was a woman setting down a telegram and silently folding the socks of her now-dead husband, a cool and mechanical absence from reality. For me, though, it was electric and literal. My cognitive circuits blew, and I couldn't stop the shaking that turned my body into a set of chattering teeth. It took ages—Jenna and Scott each holding one of my trembling, jerking legs—to administer an amniotic fluid test. Negative still, but there was no longer any doubt it was mistaken. Or, based upon its appearance (Jenna's delicate skirting), that the fluid belonged to Ames. With my water broken, I couldn't leave the hospital pregnant; those were the rules, I knew. The contractions were stronger, Mag be damned, and adrenaline slid over me like a cold, damp sheet. I couldn't deliver babies. I didn't know how to deliver babies. I had to go home.

An unholy hybrid of physical pain and mental panic rose from within my back, and all at once I needed desperately to turn on my side, but there were wires and cables. I arched into a writhe; I was hot, so hot! I tore at my gown; I retched into the pink comma of an emesis basin. Jenna applied cold washcloths to my forehead while I babbled and cried and apologized—polite even in shock. *I can't*, I pleaded, then: *I'm so sorry*, then: *please keep talking to me, just talk about anything.*

Jenna's calm voice floated at me like the beam of a lighthouse. Simone's heartbeat was strong and loud. Scott stroked my hair and turned the TV to CNN, so that I could stare fixedly at the face of Hilary Clinton, and slowly I returned from wherever I had gone, arriving sweaty and spent at a more commonplace panic. Scott emailed my mother, and I managed to tap out an SOS via four sentences posted to my website:

"Ames' water broke an hour ago. I will not be leaving the hospital until I deliver both babies. I am having contractions. I am losing my mind."

At my bedside, Jenna moved about, adjusting IV tubing and entering information into my chart. I'd never had a full-fledged anxiety attack in front of a stranger. In the grip of panic, even the presence of those you love can be abrasive, but Jenna was patient and tender, without giving the impression that it was anything *you* were doing that *required* these qualities. After my hysteria had ended, she returned so smoothly to the tasks of normalcy that I forgot to be embarrassed. Quite a feat, as one of these tasks was to divest me of underwear. Underwear is *verboten*, once your water is broken, because it increases the risk of infection. Infection is the hobgoblin of ruptured amniotic membranes, or so the saying goes, and antibiotics had been added to my IV pole in a roundel of alternating formulas. The contractions slowed at last. Simone kicked me. My IV dripped on. Jenna proffered Vistaril, an antihistamine that in the past had knocked me out so thoroughly I struggled with my eyelids the following day. Alas, after eight doses were swatted away by the powerful backhand of my terror, it became clear that nothing short of lobotomy would sedate me. There was nothing to do but wait for morning. Scott was asleep in his clothes. He looked like a teenager, with the hood of his sweatshirt obscuring his face. I focused on the screen that showed the CNN newsroom, its inhabitants cozily awake. I dozed in brief snatches, my eyes opening to Anderson Cooper's reassuring concern, then again to the familiar electoral map, and finally, the last time, to morning.

Not long after I awoke for good, I was revisited by the panic-inducing back pain I'd had the night before. It passed more quickly this time, but not before I retched into yet another pink plastic comma, this one held by my new nurse, a skeptical-seeming older woman who wrinkled her nose at me.

"What's wrong with you?" she asked.

I let the many sharp answers to that question pass, and explained that I hadn't had my usual 4 AM Zofran, milk, and saltines, and that I was experiencing a bit of *anxiety*, for whatever reason. Whether it was the dead baby, the preterm labor, my water breaking, or the indefinite hospitalization was hard to say.

When I got up to go to the bathroom, I found my right leg had gone out on me, thanks to the low-riding babies separating my pelvis. I could not lift my foot from the ground, and any attempt to do so was met with swift retribution in the form of searing sciatic pain. The nurse found this even more peculiar than my nausea and anxiety, and regarded me with suspicious alarm as Scott helped me drag my bulk and IV pole to the toilet. When I returned, my beleaguered upper-outer quadrant was assaulted with my final steroid shot, and the nurse checked my blood sugar with the hospital's diabetic kit, the stout needle deployed with the force of a crossbow.

"You weren't approved for a breakfast tray, because of The Mag," she said. "I'll get you some more ice chips."

So began my first day on hospital bedrest.

At noon I was transferred via wheelchair to my new home: a small sunny room with a wall of windows overlooking a rooftop near the helipad. A deep ledge ran the length of the wall, and on it went my recently delivered bouquets of consolatory flowers. The unit was mostly women on long-term bedrest, with a few low-risk delivery and postpartum suites scattered along the edge. It was brighter than Labor & Delivery, but decorated in grey rather than pink—a nod, maybe, to the neither here-nor-there-ness of our situation.

Outside my door hung a purple card strung on a ribbon, depicting a fallen leaf upon which rested a bead of water—probably, God help me, meant to be a teardrop. The card had been placed there by the hospital; its purpose was to alert anyone entering that death had kindly stopped for the room's occupant. It ensured that no unwitting medical personnel would enter with congratulations. I was not just any pregnant woman; I was marked by tragedy, like the house of a plague victim. We called it the Grief Leaf, but of course a card—even one with a teardrop upon it—couldn't tell the whole story. It should have been the tragedy/comedy masks, which would at least have been closer to accuracy. There was no international sign for "clusterfuck," for preterm labor and broken waters in a pregnancy that already comprised multitudinous pills and injections, intractable nausea and vomiting, gestational diabetes, infection, anemia, pubic bone separation, and stillbirth. I was in a teaching hospital, and as I recounted my history to a parade of student nurses and residents, it became increasingly hard not to giggle as they struggled to retain professional composure. Really, who could blame them?

My friend Jenni sent me an email that on each rereading made me laugh, again, at the absurdity of my situation. It was probably the single most helpful piece of mail I received. It was certainly the most apt:

"This is turning into the zombie movie of pregnancies," she began, *"You know how it is, where one by one, the lights go out, and the furnaces click off, and shit continues to go wrong, and pretty soon, you're all, 'Remember when we were holed up in the mall, enjoying grim survivalist camaraderie while eating our dinners out of cans? God, that was so great.* WE STILL HAD FLASHLIGHTS THEN. *And no one had eaten Bob.'"*

"It's not if—it's when," said the doctor, sounding both grim and blithe, a combination I would not have thought possible. He'd appeared to discuss our newly revised plan: to attempt to stave off infection long enough to buy Simone more time to grow. It helped that her membranes weren't the ones that had broken, though I assumed that what we'd been told the day of the Bad Ultrasound still applied: *it is better when the upper baby is affected.*

The plan was simple: antibiotics, lots of them, in a preemptive deluge. Later, when the IV was discontinued and I was given my first dose in pill form, I'd recoil from the paper cup holding the capsules, shocked by the same sweet awful scent that had cloaked me for days. I'd been certain the smell came from the leaking trickle of death-muddied amniotic fluid. What a relief to find it was only the antibiotics oozing from my pores, so potent I could have marketed my blood as a hand sanitizer (Lady Macbeth Brand!).

I'd remain on The Mag until the next morning, when the steroids reached full effectiveness. After that the only thing keeping my contractions at bay would be bedrest and fluids. If I went into honest-to-goodness labor, no one would try to stop me. My mouth fell open, hearing this. Why hospitalize a girl because it's too early for her baby to be born and then stand around letting her give birth willy-nilly?

"Labor can be a sign of infection," the doctor explained, "and once the broken sac is infected, it can spread to the other baby and the rest of the uterus. These infections progress very quickly, and they can be deadly both to you and the baby. We can't afford to mask the warning signs." Not that they'd be looking too closely—infection risk meant my vagina had a NONE SHALL PASS policy, and that included ultrasound wands and cervical exams. My cervix could shorten in privacy, but they'd monitor Simone for an hour three times a day, and they'd monitor my contractions then as well. For kicks, I suppose. And that would be that, until 34 weeks, the latest they wait to deliver after your water has broken.

"We just...wait?" I asked. That couldn't be right. This was a hospital! Surely there was another needle or pill or radioactive scan they could utilize?

"We wait," confirmed the doctor.

I digested this, or tried to.

"So, I could be here all the way until the end. At 34 weeks."

"Well. Yes. That is one possibility. We'd certainly *like* you to make 34 weeks." The doctor paused. "Honestly, though, I'll be surprised if you make it to 28."

In medicine, waiting is called "expectant management." This is what they were doing with me, though as no one could tell me what to expect, it didn't feel much like they were managing anything. "They" was an amorphous medical entity with which I was becoming increasingly famil-iar: "They" concluded in studies, "They" hadn't found a treatment to be effective, "They" recommended so and so. "They" would follow me even-tually to the NICU, visiting Their vague pronouncements upon my daugh-ter. I was dependent upon Their judgment. There was no Internet access unless I pressed my laptop flat against the window, which required me to get out of bed, a luxury I was allowed only in order to use the bathroom. It seemed cruel to supply wireless Internet to the patients in Labor & Delivery (who surely had more pressing matters to which to attend) while withholding it from those of us subject to the tyranny of long-term confinement.

Scott's mother arrived the day after my water broke, and I was so happy to see her I almost cried. Kathy was an enveloping maternal pres-ence, ferreting out extra pillows and letting me spool away my nervous energy by talking. She went with me to an appointment at my clinic—only a hallway away, one of the perks of patronizing the practice that staffs the hospital. This meant the doctor doing rounds or on call was always one of my own, and though I don't recommend my method, it was quite an effi-cient way to meet those in the practice I hadn't before. I was wheeled through the clinic's back door, either to protect my vanity or the waiting room full of pregnant Normals. I adored my clinic's nurses, and they greeted me like a hero.

In the dark ultrasound chamber I'd visited at 20 weeks (*ideal,* I thought bitterly, remembering), the scan confirmed Simone's water was intact. Even Ames had quite a bit of fluid remaining, which was why my bed featured an absorbent pad of the sort used to housetrain puppies. The room was as stifling as before, and I was broiling from The Mag, my face a moist scar-let. Kathy went in search of cool washcloths for the back of my neck, and when she returned we watched while a nurse measured Simone and observed her movements. My mother-in-law's awe helped me recapture my own: I'd had so many ultrasounds I'd nearly forgotten how strange and miraculous it was, to see my baby's face before she was born.

The ultrasound was part of a fetal test. There are four sections to this test, each worth two points. The nurse explained that Simone had gotten a six out of eight, meaning she passed.

"What were the two points she missed?" I asked, failing to suppress my test-related competitiveness.

"She didn't get any for breathing."

"None? For *breathing*? Isn't that kind of...important?" I laughed, nervously. One would think missing breathing would be an automatic failure, like hitting a pole during your driver's test.

"Don't worry," the nurse assured me, "she's still a little young to be practicing her breathing much."

Well, she should probably get right on that, under the circumstances, I thought to myself.

Kathy helped me off the table and into my wheelchair, solicitous and dear. She'd been a Labor & Delivery nurse herself, though in her day they'd treated preterm labor patients with IVs of alcohol to slow their contractions.

"It made the women so sick they'd throw up," she told me, as we made our way back to my room. "The whole ward smelled like vomit and ethanol. And cigarette smoke. Because of course smoking was allowed in hospitals, then."

I imagined spending my bedrest in something like hell's dive bar, rows of blitzed pregnant patients wiping bile from their chins and brushing ash from their sheets as alcohol drip, drip, dripped into their veins. You'd think the practice belonged alongside blood-letting, or the arsenic face powder that prettied the faces of the Elizabethan court, but it was common only 30 years ago. God bless expectant management.

I woke hot and sweaty three days after I was admitted. My temperature was up to 100.4 from my customary 97. Probably, I thought, because my bed was in the sun. I closed the shades and applied cold cloths, but the thermometer was stubborn. Now I was flushed and feeling unwell. I kicked myself free of the covers.

Even before the monitors showed I was contracting every two to four minutes, I knew it was the beginning of something unpleasant. I was 24 weeks and 4 days pregnant. My nurse was an older woman with glasses, who bore a strong resemblance to the one who'd held my hand the day of the Bad Ultrasound. She returned from calling the doctor, wearing a look of deep pity. This was it, then. I had an infection, and would have to deliver. I called Scott at work. I was sweaty and scared, and the nurse and a medical assistant offered to give me a sponge bath.

"You'll feel better," they said, and silently gathered rags, a clean gown and sheets. I was embarrassed, at first—I hadn't been allowed to shower since admission, and was mortified by the smell I still believed was decay, seeping from me in fluid drips. But the women were tender, ignoring my apologies and running their washcloths up my back and legs, the soapy water sloshing quietly back and forth in its bucket, until I stopped protesting and lay still and grateful. There were very few sounds in the room; their gentle ministrations felt like a ritual preparing of my body. That sponge bath was one of the kindest things I have ever known.

I was back on the monitors when the doctor arrived. He was a bit of a legend, this doctor, commuting from his home in Laguna Beach, California to work 10-day shifts here in the frozen North, sleeping in the hospital or a hotel. LAGUNA BEACH, CALIFORNIA: that was how the nurses said it, never merely "Laguna Beach," and always pronounced as if in caps or italics. His presence generated considerable excitement, and when he entered, I immediately understood why. He was about fifty, with close-shorn silvering hair and a slight mustache and goatee. He looked as if he'd just come from kayaking or catching fish with his bare hands, all tanned muscular arms and gleaming, perfect teeth. I saw those teeth a lot, because he grinned easily, and gamely laughed at my feeble gallows humor. He was warm and empathetic and his eyes actually *twinkled*, and the whole package came wrapped in an uncommonly flattering set of scrubs. I suspected he wasn't really a doctor at all, but an actor who played one on television. He'd have slipped seamlessly into the cast of *Grey's Anatomy*—McGleamy, I called him, for his teeth.

"Look for a hidden camera," my brother advised when he called. "This is probably just an attempt to create drama, for ratings."

McGleamy and I were discussing what seemed to be my fast-approaching C-section when nurses stormed the room, pushed me onto my side and clasped an oxygen mask over my face. Scott stumbled into the maelstrom, his face drained a fearful beige. The monitor at the nurse's station had revealed Simone's heart rate plummeting. I breathed my oxygen and felt tears leaking from my eyes.

Her heart sped up again, and stabilized. McGleamy rolled in a portable ultrasound machine: Simone had turned head down, so the C-section was off—my vagina was being called up to the majors.

My belongings and bed were wheeled back to the pink rooms of Labor & Delivery. Simone was now on continuous monitoring, and I was tethered uncomfortably by wires. The television had terrible reception, and we watched *Law & Order* with Mr. McCoy's eyebrows just visible through the static. I couldn't have an epidural, because I had an infection. When I asked about other options for pain relief, the nurse told me there was a shot called Nubain. It didn't do much, she admitted, and I could only have it twice.

"The second shot doesn't work as well as the first, so I'd wait on the Nubain until you really need it."

I also couldn't eat, in case I turned out to need a C-section after all. I was starving, and for some reason the food embargo was the last straw. I complained ceaselessly, bitterly to Scott until he snapped. How could I care about *food* at a time like this? Our daughter was about to be born four months early. What was *wrong* with me? I was shamed into silence, and started to cry. In truth, the problem wasn't food. It was the tension created by contrast between the drama of the situation and its glacial pace. I hadn't expected labor to involve so much tedium. The nurse rarely checked on me. My contractions hurt, but weren't distracting; I had no desire to scream obscenities or shout YOU DID THIS TO ME! at my husband. I didn't know what to expect, or where in the process I was. What should I be feeling? What would happen next, and when?

What happened was that my contractions got further apart, and my temperature fell, along with my white blood count. I was allowed a cup of broth, which I drank greedily. McGleamy reappeared to tell me that I'd had an infection in my blood, but it had cleared: the Swiss efficiency of my immune system had bought my daughter more time. She might still be born the next day, or two weeks later. There was no way to know.

"We are in a data-free zone," McGleamy said. I'm sure I needn't tell you how little I liked the sound of that.

Twelve

"Bedrest," to me, conjured a scene out of 1930s-era Hollywood: Ginger Rogers atop an expanse of satin sheets, wearing marabou slippers and a bedjacket, pawing through a box of chocolates or lazily ringing a large, tasseled bell-pull. The reality, transferred back to my old room on the antepartum unit, was less glamorous. I didn't even own a bedjacket, though as the days wore on I thought it might be time for a bedjacket renaissance. I'd seen the garment for the first time in a vintage shop when I was eleven or so, a delicate satin creation I'd held up to my mother with a puzzled look.

"Oh, that's a bedjacket," she'd said, and I'd been instantly enthralled. As one so devoted to the custom of breakfast in bed that I would often get up and prepare it myself—crawling back under the covers with my be-legged tray holding teapot, china, and egg cup—it was only natural that this cosmopolitan cousin to the housecoat should fascinate me. In the age of telecommuting and home offices, I could see the fashion reviving among freelancers. Like the smoking jacket, the bedjacket was an article that lent an aura of sophistication to sloth. Perhaps it would counteract the indignity of my lack of underpants.

In what was becoming a pregnancy tradition of combining the incompatible, I was simultaneously bored and perched on the edge of my seat—not literally, as I wasn't allowed to sit upright, much less perch on the edge of anything. "Reclining on the edge of my seat" lacks the drama of the original, but this might make it the perfect metaphor for the emotional hybrid of hospital bedrest: on the one hand, the knowledge that I could deliver at any time bathed me in blind, terrified anticipation. On the other, prisoners had more freedom, and there are only so many crossword puzzles a girl can do before she begins to view the diversion of mess hall conversation as worth the potential shanking. This volatile psychological cocktail was garnished with a twist of guilt for the moments when I wished it would all be over, moments when—for a few, shameful seconds—something, ANYTHING happening seemed preferable to continued limbo.

Of course things did happen. Waiting is seldom one's solitary occupation, and it's not like I lay stock still in my hospital bed, waiting for the sword of Damocles to fall—again. There may not have been places to go, but there were still things to do and people to see, and I had a routine that I recall easily even now:

4:00 AM: I am awakened by a nurse bearing Zofran, a packet of saltines, and a small carton of 2% milk, per the instructions I requested be added to my chart. I return to sleep.

6:39 AM: Sensing the approach of the breakfast cart—long before it becomes audible to the human ear—I wake again, this time for good. I buzz the nurse to tell her I am ready for my glucose reading.

6:41 AM: Bed adjusted into semi-upright position, light on. Scott wakes up and leaves for work. Nurse arrives with pills and glucose strip.

6:45 AM: The breakfast cart! It's coming closer!

6:47 AM: I can hear the food service woman talking and laughing *right outside my room.* I'm pretty sure my insurance company isn't paying her to gossip. I turn on CNN.

6:50 AM: Breakfast! At last! Oatmeal, tea, milk, and two sausage links. The sausage links are the source of much controversy during my stay. I campaign, via the unit's Care Coordinator, for more, but am barred because of my assignment to the Diabetic track of the hospital diet, which seems to differ from the norm only in the reduction of portion size and the inclusion of revolting artificial butter and sweeteners. I explain that I am HUNGRY; I try to make them see that allowing me the option of a

FRUIT CUP while denying my request for extra protein is nothing but dietetic madness. One day, I uncover my breakfast plate to see only one piece of sausage—a 50% reduction!—and I stab at my call light, hissing tearfully into the speaker that part of my breakfast was *omitted*, and could they send someone up with my allotted pork product? Near the end of my stay, I finally win the battle to be granted a third link.

7:50 AM: I call the nurse to perform my post-breakfast glucose reading—normal, as are they all. The nurse takes my temperature, and hooks me up to the monitors.

7:51 AM: Simone wakes up, gives the monitoring disk a hearty kick, and scuttles away.

7:52 AM to 8:55 AM: The nurse returns every few minutes to chase after my daughter, sliding the gooey probes about my belly, in a vain attempt to get one solid 20-minute strip of Simone's heart rate. I do crossword puzzles.

9:00 AM: A giant scale is wheeled into my room and I step upon it. My lack of weight gain is noted. I mutter darkly about sausage.

9:10 AM: Visit from doctor, checking to see that I am still pregnant. Or social worker, wondering whether I have called funeral homes, or grief counselor, offering to answer questions about labor, or hospital masseuse (!), providing much needed kneading of sore hips and back.

9:40 AM: Shower—at least after the first four days, when I am finally granted the privilege. In the past, I'd been strictly a bath person. Showers seemed unduly violent, the way the water just comes *at* you, and getting up the nerve to step into the spray reminded me of entering the whirling ropes in double dutch. But apparently baths were almost as dangerous as underwear, and after four days marinating in my own literal juices, I wasn't feeling picky. As it happens, showers are second only to breakfast and visitors in the joy they bring me. My IV-arm is wrapped in plastic, and I sit on a stool in the bathtub wielding a handheld nozzle and slathering myself with margarita-scented body wash. I shampoo my hair. I emerge reborn. Outside the bathroom door, nurses change my sheets.

10:00 AM: I comb my hair and put on lotion, then sit up in bed with my iPod. Sometimes I begin with "Superstitious," and its deeply pleasing bass line. Without fail, daily, I listen to "What's My Name?" by Snoop Dogg, and Biggie singing "Juicy." I feel bolstered and hardcore, ready for whatever may come, my loins girded with fierce bravado. The volume is loud enough, I am certain, that the beat travels my bloodstream, and I imagine Simone dancing inside me as she throws her fetal hands in the motherfucking air, and waves those tiny motherfuckers like she just don't care.

10:30 AM: More visits. (See **9:10 AM**)

11:00 AM: I do a crossword puzzle or watch CNN, listening for lunch.

11:20 AM: Lunch! Hotly anticipated, perpetually disappointing. Lunch and Dinner are virtually interchangeable: limp iceberg lettuce with revolting fat free dressing, low-sugar cake/Jell-O concoction, roll—for which I will have to repeatedly request actual butter in place of the provided chemical facsimile. Milk, sometimes tea. Main course featuring vegetable, nearly inedible meat product, precious smear of gravy, and woefully skimpy mashed potato portion. Sometimes, for variety, main course instead featuring tiny serving of pasta/pizza/casserole, this last containing bits of obviously leftover nearly inedible meat product that must be painstakingly removed. As usual, I am left unsatisfied by the questionable diabetic protocol that includes dinner roll and dessert with every meal while failing to provide adequate, edible protein. I take to ordering broth as a beverage. I am a terrible brat about the situation, and am eventually allowed to order from the a la carte menu, after which I have a fish sandwich every day.

12:20 PM: I buzz nurse to obtain post-lunch glucose reading.

12:30 PM: Still more visits. This time, additional possibilities include clinic appointment or visit from NICU personnel to discuss the odds of Simone's survival, should she be born that day. I adore the latter, as the doctor comes bearing sheets of hospital outcome statistics. These are much more encouraging than general statistics found on the Internet, which paint an unremittingly grim picture. As it happens, our NICU is third for outcomes worldwide, and the doctor waves aside the question of whether they treat many 25-weekers with a gesture that suggests 25-weekers are old hat. Why, in *their* NICU, they routinely treat *23*-weekers, and 28 weeks, my goal gestation, is practically term. Of course every week makes a difference, particularly early, particularly between weeks 25 and 26. *Just get her to 26 weeks,* the doctor says. 26 weeks is the new 28. After 26 weeks, chances of survival are near 90%. I tentatively ask whether they see 24 or 25 weekers go on to live and flourish in all the precious, ordinary ways—performing in tedious elementary school pageants and spelling bees, running fleetly after classmates, talking back to elders, and reading surreptitiously at the dinner table. I am assured that they do. Some babies do well, and some don't, in ways that can be hard to predict. *It's good she's a girl, though,* they tell me. *Girls do better.*

1:00 PM: Happy Hour! Sometimes it is one of my mother's tightly bound group of friends: Julie brings me stacks of crossword puzzles, Todd fights tears, Bill braves his obvious hospital discomfort. Rick, whom I've always secretly viewed as my surrogate father, marvels over my bravery, which baffles and delights me. He brings me the best milkshake I have ever had. Sometimes my friend Eloise comes, to argue over whether Jessica or Elizabeth was the most annoying Wakefield, making me laugh until I begin to contract. Sometimes it is my cousin Michelle, bearing fashion magazines and making plans for later shopping excursions—reminding me helpfully that there will *be* a later. My cousin Amy brings me her quilt, made by her mother. It transforms my hospital room into a home. It's on my bed now— she let me keep it, and not just because of the wee bloodstain on the edge. When my brother Max comes, he brings cold spicy Szechuan noodles, or a fat cheeseburger. My brother is mysterious in many ways, but feels as familiar as my own limbs. We tell terrible, inappropriate jokes, and never a serious word is spoken, because it needn't be. He never fails to appreciate my puns, and he is my favorite visitor of all.

All my visitors deplore the lack of a hospital bar, though I'm granted a snack of dry popcorn in a baggie, and we make do. Sometimes I think it's a shame that it took bedrest to fill my social calendar so pleasantly.

2:00 PM: A nurse hooks me to the monitors, managing, with considerable difficulty, to get a steady rhythm from Simone with the aid of props.

2:04 PM: Simone scuttles away in a burst of static.

2:07 PM to 3:20 PM: Nurse pursues baby at intervals. (See **7:52 AM to 8:55 AM**) I have sporadic contractions.

3:30 PM: Scott arrives, after checking on the cats. He reports that they are distressed. He looks rather distressed himself, and I wonder when he last changed clothes. Scott downloads my email, and I savor it like pornography.

4:30 PM: Dinner. I don't want to talk about it.

5:30 PM: Post-dinner glucose reading. Scott and I watch CNN, or episodes of a show we began on DVD a few weeks before Ames died. Though I never did finish season three, I haven't watched an episode since I left the hospital.

7:30 PM: Nurse hooks me up to the monitors. You can intuit the rest.

9:00 PM: Evening medications, saltines, milk. I lie on my side and arrange my pillows (one in front of me, one wedged behind my back, one between my legs, two beneath my head). I turn out the lights, drape my lavender sachet over my eyes, and insert my earbuds. I peek out from time to time at the lights of passing cars beyond the window. I sleep.

And so it went. I spoke to my mother via telephone, I wrote a little, I read. By 25 weeks I had the belly of a woman a month or so past her due date, or one who'd had an ill-advised affair with a circus elephant, doomed to gestate for 21 months. Naked I was comical, like a snake that had swallowed a Buick. My tent of a hospital gown only made matters worse, creating an unmistakable resemblance to something that at first I couldn't place, but eventually identified as a Weeble. Simone had another test, and this time got full marks for breathing. The nurse got a good shot of her face, one where she looked like a real baby instead of something out of Georgia O'Keefe's bony period. I could see her eyeball and her forehead: she looked wild and stubborn. It made me laugh. I propped the photo on the ledge beside my bed, next to a small goat figurine my mother had sent me for Christmas. I'd always wanted a pet goat, and he was as close as I'd gotten, with his real white hair and tiny perfect horns. He watched over me in the rare stretches that found me alone in my silent room, floating between reality and another place, tallying the perforations in the ceiling tiles. My math teachers would have been proud—rather than simply counting, I arrived at the total using a series of equations and multipliers, dividing the room into sections to accommodate its irregular shape.

(5,733, in case you were wondering.)

The strangest part of my Zombie Movie Pregnancy was that despite the fear and boredom and fleeting guilt, hospital bedrest agreed with me. I was surprisingly calm for a girl carrying one dead baby and one who might not make it out alive, probably calmer than I'd been at any point since the pregnancy began. Maybe it was because I was so thoroughly monitored and cared for, or perhaps my anxiety abated because there was nothing left for me to do, and my usually excitable amygdala figured that with the water rising so fast, it made more sense to float than continue emptying buckets.

Thirteen

After I was admitted to the hospital, one of my readers sent me a clinical study that surveyed the median time between preterm rupture of membranes and delivery. They call this period for which the inevitable is delayed "latency"—a nice little way to refer to borrowed time. The results of the study varied according to how far along subjects were when their waters broke, and the median latency for women like me, who ruptured between 20 and 25 weeks, was 12 days.

At 12:30 PM on February 7th, otherwise known as day eleven of my latency, I was 25 weeks and 5 days pregnant. My schedule was unusually clear; I propped myself on pillows to attend to my neglected website. As I typed, I noticed that my pelvis felt remarkably like it did the first day of a period—silly, because of course pregnant women don't get periods, a state of affairs that helps make up for all that vomiting. I'd completed my ceiling tile perforation tally the night before, so I thought I might mention that, or begin my campaign for the resurrection of the bedjacket. But one of my readers had asked why I wasn't getting medication to prevent contractions, so before I got into the algebra of boredom or the revival of leisure garments I explained about infection risk, and masking labor, and all the antibiotics I'd been extruding through my pores.

"They are certainly trying to prevent infection, just not contractions," I wrote, in the last sentence I typed that day.

An hour later, I was in labor.

When the nurse stopped in at 12:45, I set aside my laptop and mentioned the pelvic unrest.

"Contractions?" she asked.

"No, just a generalized crampy feeling. Like I'm about to get my period." I laughed. Oh ho ho!

"Call me if it gets worse, or you start to notice contractions," said the nurse. When she entered, 45 minutes later, I was leaning into a pillow, wincing.

"How are you feeling?"

"Not great, actually."

It can be tricky to pick up the contractions of women well before term. I didn't see why this should apply to me, given my belly's gigantism, but it did, and this nurse was one of the few who could consistently record my womb's gymnastics. That day, the monitor showed I was contracting every three or four minutes, the stylus tracing distinctly mountainous formations as the paper spooled outward.

Looking concerned, the nurse left to call the doctor on duty—McGleamy again. She returned a moment later, a sterile wrapped speculum in her hand.

"The doctor wants me to check your cervix," she said, spreading a fresh puppy pad on the bed. I was shocked. My cervix had been unmolested since my water broke.

As usual, my unusual anatomy made my cervix unusually hard to locate. I tried not to arch away from her as she muttered and dug about and frowned. Finally she sighed and removed her gloves.

"I'm pretty sure that was it," she said, failing to inspire my confidence. "You're not dilated at all, so that's good." She left again to report. When she reentered she bore a package of stick-on heating pads, the same ones I'd often used for menstrual cramps.

"Since your cervix isn't changed, the doctor wants to wait and see whether this turns into actual labor," she told me. I tried not to be offended at the implication that mine were substandard contractions. "Until then, we'll try to keep you as comfortable as possible." She unwrapped the heating pads and handed them to me.

I stared at them, and then at her. This was how they were going to keep me comfortable? With something I could buy at Walgreens? Was she kidding?

"Stick one on your back and one in front—that should help."

She wasn't kidding. I put on the pads.

"Baby's transverse, so if it turns out that this is it, the doctor wants you to know you'll be headed for a C-section."

No dinner, I thought, mournfully.

The heating pads did help, though they didn't stop the contractions. Around 2:30 the massage therapist stopped by, with her magical fingers and the bottle of Lavender essential oil she'd promised. I tried to relax as she did her work, but every three minutes, I seized up and felt her hands pause over me.

Mid-massage, Scott arrived. I tried to relax, but I kept shifting around, distracted by the pain, opening my eyes to peer at him. I was reminded of the long-ago acupuncture appointment before our embryo transfer. Not so long-ago, really: only a fraction more than five months had passed. .

A new shift started at 3:00, and with it a new nurse, a small, sturdy, gray-haired woman with a perpetual harried expression. She put me back on the monitors, slipping one disk in place to detect contractions and chasing Simone's heartbeat with the other. Rushes of static burst from the speaker as Simone twisted away. Scott and I grinned. The nurse moved the disk over my belly impatiently, then stopped to heave a great, exasperated sigh.

"Is she *always* like this?"

I frowned at the nurse's sour face. The appropriate response was amusement, however grudging. What, was she angry at my *fetus*?

"Yes," I said, "I'm afraid she is."

Simone was located at last, and the tracing showed my contractions two minutes apart. The monitoring hardly seemed necessary at this point, as the pain was hard to miss. The nurse left, and Simone was off again in a snarl of static. I slid the disk around until I found her myself.

The next time she disappeared, I was too busy gripping my bedrail to care. The nurse came back.

"Sorry," I said.

"This one really doesn't like to stay put, does she?"

I shook my head, managing a tight smile. She found the galloping of the heartbeat and moved to tear off the completed tracing and scroll through it.

"At least those contractions are under control."

"What?" I asked, "No, they've been the same—every two or three minutes."

"I'm not showing any for the last fifteen."

"Sometimes the monitor doesn't pick them up."

"It *should*. It was before."

"Well, I don't know what to tell you."

We stared at each other. Scott stood awkwardly between us. Then I began to wince through another contraction, and the nurse left, returning with a dose of Vistaril—the antihistamine I'd been given the night my water broke.

"To help you relax," she said, obviously referring to my friable mental state, "and it might slow the contractions."

"I thought we weren't supposed to interfere with labor," I said.

Her mouth twisted, enigmatic.

"Oh, if you're in labor, *Vistaril* won't stop it."

And she was gone.

"The pain feels grinding and insistent, like some efficient German industrial process."

Originally, I'd planned to take notes during labor, so that I could remember it later. I giggle just typing that. So stupid it's almost adorable, like a dog running confidently into a glass door. Needless to say, no notes were taken, but I composed the above quoted sentence in my head around 5:00, thinking I'd write it down, after the next contraction. Then it was after the next, and then the next, and then I gave up on the idea altogether, but the words lodged in my skull, because of their horrible accuracy. The Vistaril had spaced my contractions to five minutes apart, but it was only an hour before they wound back up again. When dinner arrived I asked the nurse if I should eat, figuring I knew the answer. These were not dilettante contractions, and at some point I'd need that C-section. The nurse seemed surprised by the question, as if I were getting rather ahead of myself, but she said she'd check with the doctor and disappeared. My fish sandwich languished on my plate.

"I'm pretty sure this is it," I said to Scott, in a low voice. We looked at each other, seriously. I swallowed. "I'm pretty sure," I said again. I held the bed frame with both hands.

The nurse hadn't returned, and Scott's intercom calls to the nursing station were becoming increasingly furious.

"I'm going out there," he said.

"Don't," I begged, desperate not to be a nuisance. But eventually I didn't care. I was starving, and sick to my stomach. He went and returned, twice. Over an hour passed; our nurse never appeared. *Fuck it*, we decided, and I ate half of my dinner, one bite at a time, stopping after each to bend under the force of the pain.

The nurse returned. The doctor had said not to eat, just in case.

"*Oh*," she said, when she saw the partially eaten sandwich, "I hope that's okay."

When a contraction began, I'd give Scott a hunted look. He'd watch the monitor in order to tell me when the numbers stopped rising, which meant the worst was over. The TV was on, and I half watched, hoping the distraction would keep me calm and focused. But after a while the pain obscured everything else. The contractions were relentless and unceasing, one after another after another after another. It was hard to tell whether they were more painful because they were stronger or because my uterine muscles were sore from hours of brutal involuntary exercise. Even breathing hurt.

The pain scale goes from zero to ten, with zero being no pain at all, a state in which the round face on the illustrative chart is smiling. In fact, that smile doesn't disappear until the scale reaches four (Moderate Pain), and then it transforms into a neutral line. At Severe Pain, a six, the face wears what could scarcely be called a frown, more an expression of slight ennui. The Very Severe eight looks pretty miserable, and by ten, tears are running down the poor bastard's cheeks. Ten is supposed to be Worst Possible Pain, which I'd always figured should be saved for being cheese-grated to near death and then sprayed with lemon juice, or maybe fed feet first through a woodchipper. Also a ten: slow mauling by bear (speedier death would merit a lower integer), or being dipped repeatedly, like a teabag, into a vat of hydrochloric acid.

I had a vivid enough imagination to be certain of one thing: whatever Worst Possible Pain was, it didn't include bowel control or the ability to speak, both of which I still possessed.

When they'd asked, I'd rated my contractions a six. I'd never used my six, and on the day of the almost-labor a week earlier, my pain had hovered at threes and fours. The highest number I'd ever deployed was an eight, and that was during my first kidney stone, which brought me literally to my knees—and then down further still, until I was curled on the floor waiting for death. To me, a six was serious. I was on edge, inching toward desperation, and I needed information. When would they check my cervix? Would they move me to Labor & Delivery? What was the *plan*? They'd said they'd keep me comfortable, and it was time for them to put some pharmaceuticals where their mouths were. We asked the nurse to call the doctor, and she disappeared again, into the ether.

One of the medical assistants stopped by as my nurse was leaving. She watched her go, and then warned me not to let her check my cervix, if I could help it.

"She has really stubby fingers," she said.

An hour passed? More? It was dark.

"The doctor ordered some Demerol, but the pharmacy hasn't sent it up," said the nurse when she arrived at last, having conquered whatever presumably Odyssean obstacle course lay outside our door. After failing to answer our questions she left again, and I waved both my middle fingers, wildly, at her departing back, in an impotent rage that would have been funny if it hadn't been so pathetic. That gesture—my spindly fingers brandished in frustration at the sightless, retreating form of a medical professional—sums up the entirety of my labor experience, *just*ely.

My memory is foggy here, and gaps. I had started passing gobs of blood and unpleasantness. I asked, again, about The Plan. A new doctor was on call.

"I think she wants to wait and see how you are in the morning," said the nurse.

"I don't think I'm going to make it that long."

"Well, you weren't dilated at all when they checked you."

I looked at the clock. It was nearly 10:00, which meant my cervix check had been eight hours before. I asked whether things mightn't have changed, since then—could I be checked again now, stubby fingers or no?

No. I couldn't—because of the risk of infection.

"How will you know I'm in labor, then?" I asked, meaning *how else will I convince you?* The nurse didn't have an answer. She left. I hated her.

The next day that same nurse would appear in my room, where I was recovering from birth. Near tears, she'd tell me how sorry she was: she'd *known* I was headed for delivery, she'd *tried* and *tried* to get the night doctor to listen, she'd hounded the pharmacy and stayed after her shift had ended, *determined* to get me my shot of Demerol. It was *unforgivable*, that they'd left me in pain for so long. She'd grasp both my hands and

I'd goggle at her wide, wet eyes, my piecemeal memories of that night shifting vertiginously.

More pain, for I don't know how long. I'd started shaking. My mind was blank with focus. I was resigned to helplessness, retreating into myself like a telescoping thing. It was clear to me that I was on my own. There wasn't anything to be done, or that would be done, by anyone. I told Scott to go to bed, and he did; it must have been very late. I finally got my shot of Demerol, rolling desperately to my side to expose the relevant quadrant, nearly slapping the nurse when she warned me the needle might hurt. The Demerol did nothing. I threw up. I was given more Vistaril—I should try to sleep, They said, and I lay facing the window, grasping the bedrail.

Eventually I'd drift off for the few seconds between contractions, then wake in dread as I began to be seized in that dire, uncontrollable way. It was one undulating wave, with tiny pinpricks of unconsciousness punctuating a pain that would never, ever end. I could feel a pushing and leaking with each spasm. I wondered if I might give birth to Ames in bed. I was terrified he'd come out in pieces, his soft body broken by the violence of my own body's mechanics. What would he feel like? Would I feel a leg, a face?

I made noise. Like an animal, I thought, though Scott later told me it was more like a porn soundtrack, and that you could hear me in the hallway. The sounds were unintentional and necessary. I was aware of very little, only the pain, like a sea.

There had been a shift change, and my moaning roused the new nurse. She entered and told me, sternly, to *breathe*. I wanted to scream at her—standing in her clean scrubs, starting an ordinary night of ordinary work—that I was long past breathing. I begged her to call the doctor.

"It's an EIGHT," I wheezed.

At some point I went to the bathroom, and more unpleasantness passed from me, a bloody goop, and I contracted and fainted, pulling the emergency cord as I fell. Then I was surrounded by nurses, who scraped me onto a rolling chair and helped me back to bed. They *all* told me to breathe. I wanted to kill every last one of them, but was too tired.

It was after 4:00 AM when the doctor appeared. I recognized her as the one who'd pronounced my babies "ideal."

"So." She sat on a chair by my bed. Someone had turned on a light. "I think you're probably in early labor."

Scott was awake. Why had the doctor finally come? I couldn't remember. I tried to focus, now. Help was here, and she was saying that because of Simone's position, we had to decide whether to do a C-section or attempt to stop the contractions with another round of The Mag. Wait. What?

She was looking at me, expectantly. Everyone was, and I realized they were waiting for me to decide.

"I thought..." I said. It started, and I made a small noise.

"Contraction?" the doctor asked, and I nodded. They waited. I realized as I bent sideways that I'd been sitting up. We were all up, with the lights on, ready for the doctor. When she'd entered she'd asked how I was, and I'd said *Well, I'm in a lot of pain.* I'd told her about the eight.

"I'm confused," I said, when the contraction was over. "I thought we weren't supposed to stop labor, because it might be a sign of infection."

The doctor tilted her head and nodded, thoughtfully. "It could be."

"So..."

"Well, you don't really *seem* like a woman in labor. But it's hard to know." Ah. That's what the problem was: I wasn't screaming. Even at an Eight, I felt compelled to prop myself upon a pillow, to attempt to speak within the bounds of grammar and propriety: I may have been in a hospital, but I was still in *public*. Did my moaning count for nothing?

Everyone was waiting for me to reach a conclusion. I didn't want to reach any conclusions. I didn't want to decide whether to deliver my daughter three and a half months early. It couldn't be up to me, surely. It shouldn't. Delivery seemed inevitable, but what if it wasn't? I'd never know if it was me deciding, or the pain. I wanted this to be over; it had been 15 hours.

Premature babies die; Simone could be among them. It couldn't be me.

"Do *you* think this is real?" I asked, "Do *you* think The Mag would stop it? What do you think? What would *you* do?"

I had another contraction. I could feel the doctor watching me.

"I think it might be time to get this baby out."

I was flooded with relief, colored with shame.

Everything began to move quickly; Scott was whisked away. I was given a shot of something foul to drink, and briefed by an anesthesiologist who read the consent form so rapidly that at the end I half expected him to shout "*SOLD! One C-section to the lady in the hospital johnny!*" Nurses from Labor & Delivery came to prep me, and one of them was Jenna, from the night my water broke. I exclaimed when I saw her, and she smiled at me. It was all like a dream I was having, and then I was wheeled to the OR.

I'd always worried about epidurals—not because of the pain, but because sticking a needle into one's spine is only asking for trouble. However, once on the table I assumed the position eagerly, exposing my back to be swabbed with Betadine.

I had another contraction, and Jenna told me to lean into her. I draped myself over her shoulders and shook and moaned while the anesthesiologist waited. Then it was over, and the needle was in, and as they swung my legs onto the table I began to babble gratefully.

"I can't feel a thing! No more contractions! I can't feel anything at all!"

I felt like sobbing and laughing and kissing each and every person in the OR, with tongue. I felt like seizing my lifeless legs and waggling them in a happy dance.

Scott entered, wearing scrubs. He looked handsome and doctorly, except for the expression of terror.

"You look so *nice!*" I told him. He held my hand. We stared at one another, printing the moment like a picture. The caption would have read: *This is really happening.* I heard someone call "time of incision," and realized that the incision had been made, right on into my belly. Oh, anesthesia, you lovable old so and so!

Later, Scott told me he made the mistake of looking over the drape once, where he saw my blood bubbling into a suction vat. Then something happened with my blood pressure, and I threw up for the last time in my pregnancy, retching almost cheerfully. This was worse for Scott than for me, as he was made to hold the emesis basin while the doctors pushed drugs into my IV with apparent urgency.

Scott's terror of vomit is legendary, almost as legendary as his terrible memory, and to this day his clearest memories of my bedrest, labor, and delivery are the times I threw up. If you ever meet my husband, ask him about the delivery of our daughter. If the first thing he mentions is not the horror of holding that receptacle, I will personally pay you fifty American dollars. As I began to write this chapter, I myself asked what he remembered about my C-section.

"You threw up," he said, in an accusatory tone.

"That's it?"

"I had to hold the bucket!"

He also remembers the blood in the suction vat, of course, but apparently my roiling wifely blood was not disturbing enough to warrant first mention. Usually, this is when I bring up the fact that he slept through the worst of my labor, and he reminds me that I told him to, adding darkly that he woke enough to hear me throwing up after the Demerol. I didn't know he was awake for that, and will always assume he feigned continued slumber to keep the nurse from foisting my bucket upon him.

My blood pressure recovered. I felt a rolling and an improperly internal rummaging.

"Poor little thing," the doctor said. Ames was out. I felt a pang. I saw a nurse carry something to the side.

It was 5:35 AM, and there was a heavy pulling. Then, gloved hands held something aloft: a wormy purple-red bundle. I saw a leg—it was *moving*, oh my God it was MOVING, it was a whole, live *person*! I gasped and laughed and gasped and cried and nothing had ever surprised me more.

I watched them hand her away and then turned my face to Scott.

"We have a baby!" I said, "We have a daughter!"

I repeated it over and over, my grin soaring through jubilant, astounded tears. Scott stroked my wrist, and we stared at one another to photograph another moment—this one uncaptionable.

"Oh, I *love* it," the doctor was saying, about her new staple gun. I heard the interested murmur of a surgical nurse, and the *KaCHUNK! KaCHUNK!* of the doctor's pleased and efficient staples. It was odd to have such a clear aural picture of myself being put back together again—like Humpty Dumpty, now, in more than just silhouette. Scott was off, checking on our freshly born daughter. Someone came to stand with Jenna, ready to take me to recovery. It was the nurse who'd started The Mag, the first nurse I'd had in the hospital.

"You!" I said, delighted, "*Both* of my favorite nurses!"

People were bustling brightly, cleaning up, making certain no one had left a retractor next to my spleen. I'd been the first delivery of the day, and there was an air of celebration. Or maybe it was the customary early buoyancy of an as yet unsullied day, and the celebration was all my own. After all, I'd had a baby! And probably some morphine, by then.

I love C-sections, I thought, looking around the clean, bright room where my daughter had been born, alive, with the help of these swell, cheerful people. The doctor appeared by my head and I beamed at her, benevolently.

"Your uterus was *completely* thinned out," she told me.

"Oh?" I said, politely. My uterus was old news. It was the Year of the Baby! Let everyone rejoice!

"It means that you'd been having productive contractions for some time," she explained, "The Mag wouldn't have bought us more than a couple hours."

What she was saying reached me, and I felt a sharp rush of vindication, my uterus pumping its fallopian tube into the air in triumph. *I TOLD you so,* it shrilled. My eyes swam with absolution.

"I was shocked, actually," the doctor continued, "You didn't seem like

a woman in active labor, when I saw you. You were sitting up, and talking...but then I watched you have a contraction, and I thought *hmmm*."

Hmmm!

"And I'm so sorry for the loss of your little boy. It will be in my report
of course, but I thought you'd like to know: his cord was the width of den-
tal floss, at one point. It began normally, and then got very thin." She held
her fingers half an inch apart, and compressed them, like she was squeezing the life out of something.

They were ready for me now, a raft of warm air inflated beneath my
numb body, lifted from table to bed. My limbs were arranged and pillows
adjusted, and I was shepherded into another After by the kind hands of my
nurses. In a few hours fever would bloom, and my IV pole would once
again be festooned with antibiotics. *Probably,* they'd tell me, *we got her out
just in time.*

Part II

HANG ON LITTLE TOMATO

CHAPTER

Fourteen

I am awakened by a rustling. A woman is changing the trash bags in my room, and I recognize her as a member of the housekeeping staff.

"Hi!" I say, brightly, scooting myself up in bed, "Guess what? I had my baby!"

I am burbling like an insane person, beaming at a small Hispanic woman to whom I have never spoken before. I am vaguely conscious that perhaps I ought to be less effusive, under the circumstances—namely that the baby I birthed yesterday (at least, the one who isn't *dead*) is still in critical condition—but this is impossible. I feel as though I *invented* babies. Not entirely unjustified, as I made one from scratch, with organs and everything, and she's *alive*. How clever and lucky am I!

The woman congratulates me, but I can see her looking around, surreptitiously, for a bassinet.

"She was only 25 weeks, so she's in the NICU," I explain.

"Oh!" says the woman, her eyes stretching themselves wide. She lowers her voice, tentative, "But...she is good?"

"She's *wonderful*," I say, grinning like an idiot. I am fairly shimmering with a cocktail of postpartum hormones and the wild glee that grips those who have come through a terrible ordeal. Of course I have another ordeal ahead of me, but that hasn't sunk in yet. I am Paris after the liberation! I am that amorous sailor on 42nd Street! My Zombie Movie Pregnancy is over, and I have staggered, finally, into the sunlight.

The morning before, I'd been wheeled from the operating room into recovery, covered with warm blankets and hooked to a morphine pump. My baby was down the hall with the NICU team, being assessed and stabilized. I knew they'd be sliding a ventilator tube down her throat and administering surfactant, a slippery substance to coat her lungs and keep them from collapsing. A nurse told me she'd heard that Simone cried before she was intubated: some preemies are too weak to make the effort, and I was relieved that my daughter had been pulled out wriggling and ornery. I pressed for details—how much did she weigh? What were her Apgars?—but no one knew anything yet. I was impatient. I had known no healthy infant covered in what always reminds me of chèvre was going to be transferred directly from my womb to my chest for a tender post-birth moment. But I wanted, at least, the traditional reading of statistics. Simone Lee, born February 8th, 2008, at 5:35 AM X pounds, X ounces. X inches long.

In elementary school they'd impressed upon us the importance of learning the metric system: we'd need it when America converted, an eventuality that was said to be fast approaching. We memorized the various meters—centi, milli, deci—but the metric revolution never came to pass. However, these lessons were good practice for the metric-centric NICU, where a baby's weight is measured in grams, her length in centimeters, her input and output in milliliters. Oddly, it seems that the closer you get to discharge, the further you get from the metric system: milliliters become ounces, grams become ounces and pounds. I would become very adept at converting these units in my head, but the day Simone was born I was still rusty, remembering only a few metric tidbits from my youth, like the fact that an inch is 2.5 centimeters, and that speed and cocaine are measured in grams, while marijuana is measured in ounces. So when someone finally arrived in recovery with a card bearing my daughter's birth length and weight—33 centimeters and 760 grams—I needed a nurse to translate: Simone was 13 ½ inches long, and she weighed one pound, 10 ¾ ounces.

(I always round up to eleven.)

There was a commotion in the hallway, and a team of masked nurses, gloved and gowned and be-hatted in blue, wheeled Simone's isolette into the recovery room. It was bigger than I'd expected, or maybe it just looked that way because my baby (my baby!) was only a small ruddy spot in the middle. She was wrapped in plastic, to conserve her body heat, and someone had covered her head with a makeshift hat made from what looked like a sock and a rubber band. There were no *actual* hats small enough for her tiny head, which was the exact size of the bulb syringe lying next to her on the blanket. Her skin was bright pink and raw-looking, her eyes still fused shut, like those of a baby animal.

When Max and I were young, we found a newborn sparrow that had fallen from its nest and lay—fetal and featherless, sticky pieces of egg nearby—in the dirt. We waited to see whether the mother would return, but when she didn't we named him Squeaky Barrow and kept him in a check box, attempting, futilely, to nurse him to health. He's probably still buried in the garden behind the house we lived in at the time. Like my baby daughter, he'd looked pink and uncooked, and his fused eyelids had the same plump, swollen look that Simone's did the day she was born.

But even wrapped in plastic and dwarfed by tubes, the weight of a six-week-old kitten, my baby was beautiful. All mothers say that, you're thinking, but I assure you I've done ample research, and feel qualified to state that mine was the fairest of them all. She was long and delicate, her waving limbs as slender as fingers, her fingers like anemone tentacles. I was propped upon a pillow while Scott stood touching my shoulders, and when they halted the isolette by my side I reached, tentatively, through the open porthole, toward my new, familiar daughter. A hand the size of a dime wrapped around my finger, and my heart liquefied and dribbled out of me with the rest of my postbirth fluids.

It was less than a minute—a quick stop on their way to the NICU—but on film it appears as an eternity. We have a yellowish Polaroid of that moment: a nurse with her blue cap like a halo around her head, my gowned husband at my side. I am pale and smiling, my face shining with awe as my arm reaches out, finger extended, gripped by a tiny scarlet hand in a plexiglass fortress. Everyone in the photo is focusing upon that point of connection. It is our own tableau of Michelangelo's *Creation of Adam*, the fleeting touch of the miraculous. I am welcoming her to the world.

And here we are at a strange juncture, an impossible transition for which there is no segue. Simone is off to the NICU, and it is time, now, to see Ames. It seems as though the scenery should be changed—at the very least, a curtain ought to fall and rise again: *Long Live the Queen! The King is Dead!*

In reality nothing changed, except the expressions on the faces of the nurses. It must have been jarring for them too, this sharp juxtaposition of birth and death, but they handled it smoothly, quiet with sympathy as they carried in the body of our son.

They'd dressed him, which I hadn't expected, and I instantly wished they hadn't. He was wearing a pale blue cloak with a hood, tied with a satin ribbon under his chin. The contrast between his body—pickled for a month after death—and the frou-frou gown was grotesque, like a macabre Little Red Riding Hood. On the day of the Bad Ultrasound, the doctor had explained that Ames' condition at birth would depend upon how long he remained inside while I tried to bring Simone to term. He would *macerate*, the doctor said, and I remember thinking of my margarita recipe—*macerate* was what you did to the fruit, overnight, to soften it and release its juices.

I held him with both my hands. Ames was much smaller than Simone, his skin colored a nut brown. His body was attenuated, close to the bone. I had wanted to survey and memorize every part of him, but sensed that with rough handling he might come apart entirely. He gave the impression of being both desiccated and moist; he was sticky and, in places, gelatinous.

In my desire to describe and thus hopefully remember, I am assailed by adjectives. Attenuated, desiccated, gelatinous. Dwindled, diminished, distilled. *Demised.* They are too much and insufficient—I want you to see him clearly; I want to shield him from view. I soften the glare of examination with a veil of syllables. "In places, gelatinous" is kinder than the bald, simple truth that my son's belly was bloated and squashed; that it had the glistening surface and consistency of a freshly set custard.

It's true that his features were faintly smudged, the eyes little more than slight hollows. But Ames's hands and feet were long and graceful, perfectly formed. His lips were bracketed by a pointed chin and elegant nose, and his ears and fingernails carved with improbable delicacy, like writing on the head of a pin. He was obviously a baby—my baby—oh, what had become of him?

"I'm sorry," I whispered, sadly. We took a few pictures, and I waited to cry, but never did. I was queerly removed from the scene. Tears rolled appropriately down Scott's tired, pale cheeks, and I felt much as I had since Simone was pulled from me an hour before: high on morphine and new motherhood, limp from the release of physical pain and anxiety. All I could think, looking at the corpse of my tiny son in his blue hood, was that he looked like Skeletor. Scott held him, tenderly, and I sat staring into Ames' inscrutable face, wondering what was wrong with me.

They wheeled me back to the antepartum unit via the NICU. I had an impression of soft beeping and labyrinthine hallways, and I peered at Simone from my horizontal vantage point in the doorway. Back in my room, the nurses wanted to know about my pain, which they would track for the next few days with a fervor bordering upon obsession—insisting I assign it numbers, popping in at intervals to ask whether I was having any. It seemed a safe bet that I was, seeing as how I'd recently been de-babied with the aid of a scalpel, yet my answer was always "But no contractions!" delivered with a sincere, amazed gratitude. For years I'd gone along, living my life, not having contractions. I'd taken it for granted, but never again. It was enough to get me through the other unpleasantries of recovery, including the part where they put a basin under your bottom and push on your sore belly so that blood gushes from your nethers. It's an excruciating and startlingly barbaric procedure, and yet during it I simply gritted my teeth and thought *No contractions!* The pain of my incision was throbbing and constant, but this seemed hardly worth complaining about, given the lack of you-know-whats. When I finally slept, some 30 hours after labor had begun, I dreamed they were back, this time in my legs—*LEG contractions, God help me!*—but woke to discover it was only the rhythmic squeezing of my post-surgical compression boots.

Scott returned to the NICU to check on Simone and fill out paperwork, and I asked a nurse to bring me a breast pump, eager to get this motherhood show on the road. Instead she urged me to sleep, which I dismissed as ridiculous, like taking a nap after being awarded the Nobel Prize. Did she not know about the baby? *My* baby, who was alive? I had a child! I was a *mother*! It was the happiest I had been in months.

As soon as it was light outside, I called my friend Becky, at the office, to gurgle my news and ask that she send an email to our coworkers, announcing Simone's arrival and vital statistics. "One pound, eleven ounces," I told her, proudly. Later I would laugh, imagining the horror on the faces of my colleagues, but in the moment it didn't occur to me that reading this weight would inspire anything but the same joy I felt at the birth of my daughter. Visitors came, bearing flowers, and I beamed, told jokes, and showed them the Polaroids of Simone. In the pictures she's barely visible, on a ventilator and wrapped in plastic, her arm bruised from delivery. I couldn't see those things, not really—I saw only her (relatively) big nose and adorable chin. I asked the nurses to switch me from morphine to something lighter, because the opiates were interfering with my ability to chat.

All I wanted, it is obvious to me now, was to be treated like any other new mother. Why shouldn't I have had that? I had already given up so much—little things, like a baby shower, and bigger ones I needn't enumerate. For a few hours of unadulterated revelry I forgot the cremation arrangements still to be made, and that Simone was about to have her first blood transfusion. I paddled in my pool of post-birth oxytocin, and my brain took pity on me, obscuring the context.

My in-laws arrived, bearing packages. Soft lounge clothes, and an amethyst necklace—"Because your children were born in February," Kathy explained. It was early afternoon, and I wondered how they'd had time to shop before making the five-hour drive.

My sister-in-law, Laura, had gifts for Simone. There were preemie-sized sleepers our preemie was too small to wear yet, with matching hats that just fit my fist. She'd also brought a floppy stuffed frog, long-limbed, soft, and about the size of its new owner. To me—in a backwards, materialistic rejiggering of *The Velveteen Rabbit*—this faux amphibian proclaimed my baby real. Simone may not have been in the room with us, fat and swaddled and cooed over, but she was a real baby, one who had *things*. The frog was faith made plush, and I was grateful to Laura, both for the gesture of normalcy and believing enough to make it. Of course, I never did send her a thank you card.

Fifteen

H ad I checked my email the day after Simone was born, I'd have seen a message from a pregnancy newsletter I'd subscribed to in a fit of optimism, months before.

"*Congratulations!*" the message read, "*Welcome to your third trimester!*"

It turns out this wasn't entirely accurate. Most sources place the start of the third trimester at 27 weeks, a full eight days after Simone was born. But whatever the calendars said, this was certainly the start of something— we'd been told that if she survived we could expect to take our baby home around her due date, just as if she'd been born full term. This was the beginning of Simone's last phase of development, the part that would take place in a carefully constructed limbo between the womb and the world.

On the mock first day of my mock third trimester, I was finally able to hoist myself out of bed and into a wheelchair, to visit the NICU. I'd tried to stand up the night before, but though the spirit was willing, the flesh was weak. I hadn't slept in 36 hours; 16 of those were spent in labor. A month of bedrest had left my already paltry physical strength diminished, and once your abdominal muscles have been sliced asunder, you become acutely aware of how necessary they are for almost any movement at all. I felt like a marionette whose strings had been cut.

The next morning, I was refreshed and determined. We'd finally procured a breast pump, and a nurse had helped me assemble the pieces and clap the cones to my bosoms, while Scott watched, intrigued.

I don't know what I'd imagined would happen, exactly, when we turned it on, but I had failed to appreciate how literal was the "pump" portion of the device's name. I do know I hadn't expected to see my nipples to stretch and retract and stretch again with such...zeal. And *flexibility*. Neither, as was evident from his expression, had Scott. We stared, fascinated, and a little disturbed.

As a result of my areolas' calisthenics, though, when Scott pushed me through the hallways to the NICU I clutched two specimen cups, each containing a few drops of colostrum, the first milk produced after birth. It's yellow in color and so full of magical baby-saving properties that it's known—hand-to-God—as "liquid gold." I don't know its street value, but I'd produced only a teaspoon or two, and even this small quantity prompted reverence from the nurses. I knew it would be days before Simone was strong enough for milk, but still I bore my specimen cups as proudly as if they contained frankincense and myrrh, gifts for my baby in her high-tech manger.

Simone was on her back, bathed in blue anti-jaundice lights and wearing tiny foam sunglasses. Her skin already looked less red and sticky than it had the day before, and the nurse explained that exposure to light and air would toughen it up quickly. This made me think of taxidermy or curing meats, but I kept these thoughts to myself.

Each of the NICU's private rooms had a couch that folded out to become a bed, a small refrigerator, a desk, a phone, a breast pump, and a privacy curtain. The nurses had decorated Simone's cupboards with a calendar and signs bearing her name, her hand and footprints, and a collage of pictures they must have taken the night before. Her weight was listed as 1lb, 10 oz (*and three-quarters!* I thought to myself). On the calendar, the day of her birth was outlined thickly with marker, and inside it said *5:35 AM on Friday, February 8th: A little miracle is born!*

"I can't believe you did all this," I marveled, touching one of the handprints. The fingers were surprisingly long. Scott had helped me out of my wheelchair to look at the decorations, and now I hobbled to the isolette to peer more closely at Simone. Her hair was dark, almost black, like Scott's, and I'd been right about the nose. She didn't look like me, which was a shock somehow, but thrilling—she was distinctly herself, foreign and mine.

"Would you like to touch her?"

"Oh, yes! Can I?"

"She's stable, so sure. You're her mom! It will comfort her; she'll recognize your smell. Sometimes you'll see that heart slow right down on the monitor, and sats go way up. Don't *stroke*, though; no light, feathery touching. I know it's the first instinct, but it's not soothing for preemies—*way* too over-stimulating. Simone's skin is still a little tacky, so remember it tears pretty easily, kind of like wet tissue paper."

This "touching the baby" thing was sounding less appealing by the second. The possibility of stroking my daughter's skin off, while certainly enough to give one pause, wasn't what worried me most: What if my touch *didn't* comfort her? A monitor was tracking Simone's oxygen saturation and heart rate, and recording her breathing pattern. When her oxygen dipped out of range, it prompted a series of ominous bells. Sure, the screen could show Simone improving, lulled by my maternal presence—or it could show her going swiftly downhill as soon as I made contact. Then the alarms would sound, and everyone would know that my baby didn't like me. She might as well be connected to a polygraph machine. This was a bad idea.

When I was still pregnant, my friend Becky brought her newborn son into the office. Everyone took turns holding him, but I declined, for fear he'd start crying and my coworkers would look from the squalling infant to my rounded belly with concern. How much more damning would it be if it were my *own* baby rejecting me, making it clear that I had no business being anyone's mother? I wouldn't have blamed Simone for failing to find me calming, given my poor nurturing track record—I'd only managed to gestate her two-thirds of the way to completion.

The nurse must have sensed my hesitation, and possibly possessed some psychic ability.

"If she gets agitated and I have to stop you, it doesn't mean anything.

It doesn't mean she doesn't like you. Preemies are touchy. Her nervous system is easily overloaded, and she can only handle so much."

I nodded. My nervous system was easily overloaded as well. This I understood. I washed my hands and the nurse opened the two portholes on my side of the isolette.

"The idea is containment," she explained. "If they were still inside they'd be contained by fluid, so preemies like consistent positive pressure. Gentle but firm. It helps them feel safe. Just cup her head, and then gather her feet up to hold the other end."

I reached in through one porthole and palmed my daughter's plum-sized head. Her hair was soft and downy. My other arm slipped through the second porthole, and I bent her splayed, frog-like legs at the knees until I could cup her bottom. I held her between my two hands, each curved like a parentheses. Simone pressed a foot against my palm.

"Oh!" I said. It was the first time I'd felt one from the outside.

"She likes it," said the nurse, looking at the monitor.

On NPR a few years before, I'd heard an interview with Temple Grandin, an autistic woman who refined a chute to calm cows on their way to slaughter. It worked by gently squeezing them, a technique that had comforted her as an autistic child, when overwhelmed by sensory input. Listening to the interview I'd thought it made perfect sense, and wondered where I could procure such a chute for myself—without the slaughter component, naturally. I'd always liked nooks and crannies, beds tucked into alcoves, small spaces where I could feel pleasantly cocooned. Babies in the womb are curled inside their flesh water balloons, and at birth preemies find themselves suddenly flailing. All at once they're subject to gravity: splayed on their backs, shoulders and knees rotated outward, butterflied like shrimp. It's the opposite of the fetal position, the position all humans resume in degrees when under stress. To comfort ourselves we cross our arms and roll our shoulders forward; we bow our heads and tuck up our legs; we protect our vulnerable underbellies. There's a reason the phrase "curl up and cry" is common. Who ever heard of someone stretching out on her back to cry?

Simone's favorite position, for as long as stayed in the NICU, was the same—on her belly, knees bent beneath her, hands by her face. In this position she needed less oxygen and her heart rate was steady. This was partly because breathing is easier when you aren't expanding your chest wall against gravity, but the simpler reason was that were it not for her premature evacuation, she'd have been that way still.

I cupped Simone for ten minutes, as long as I was allowed. By then I'd begun to sweat and shake from the exertion of remaining upright, and my incision was furious. I sank into my wheelchair and the nurse offered Scott a turn, but he shook his head, looking fearful. I'd brought the stuffed frog along, pale green and kindly looking, because I'd read that small beanbags and stuffed animals were often used for positioning. I'd hoped to put him in the isolette.

"I suppose you *could*," said the nurse when I told her. "Any outside object increases the risk of infection, so *I* wouldn't, probably. But it's up to you." I blushed, mortified. It seemed clear that what she meant was *"Sure! As long as you don't mind your daughter becoming SEPTIC, dying as HER ORGANS FAIL in quick succession!"* and I thought it was a good thing there were professionals taking care of my baby. Obviously, I wasn't quite up to it yet.

Tara—the neonatology fellow who'd visited me on bedrest—arrived to give us an update. She held our daughter's chart: not one of the slim metal clipboards you see on television, but a vast aqua binder that could have stopped a bullet.

"Simone's doing extremely well so far," she told us, "but we're still in the honeymoon period." The "honeymoon period" is what neonatologists call the few days or a week after birth, when preemies are full of vim and haven't yet exhausted their limited reserves. For now, the breaths being puffed into Simone's lungs via ventilator were only 21% oxygen, the same as ordinary room air, but this wouldn't last. She'd wear herself out, and the honeymoon would be over.

I understood the principle, but objected to the terminology. The night before, they'd drawn Simone's blood—twice, because the technician slipped and sent the first sample spurting to the floor, as my husband watched in horror. Simone had little blood to begin with, and so along with her first transfusion she'd received drugs to raise her blood pressure by constricting peripheral vessels, and as collateral damage, a few of her fingers and toes turned black from lack of blood flow. Scott had returned from the NICU with news of a possible amputation—not the whole hand, but maybe one or two miniature fingers, a procedure that might easily have been performed with an ordinary nail clipper. Thus we'd spent the evening of our daughter's birth reassuring one another that amputation was "no big deal." Four fingers, three—what's a digit between friends? At least Simone was alive, and there were worse things to live without. The crisis had passed by morning, leaving her extremities intact, but still: it didn't seem like much of a honeymoon, to me. Maybe it's different for neonatologists, but on *my* honeymoon, I don't believe the word "amputation" came up even once.

On the way out, I noticed the Grief Leaf hanging by the door to Simone's room. I was confused for a moment, and then I realized it was there for Ames, though he'd never been in the NICU. That leaf seemed to follow us wherever we went, and I wondered if, after Simone was discharged, they'd give me one to wear around my neck.

They did, in a way: on all of Simone's paperwork and the hospital wristband around her foot, her name appeared as "Wisgerhof, Simone 2 Lee." The "2" stood for the fact that she was the second born of twins, and it remains that way in her medical records. A year later during a visit for an ear infection, the triage nurse saw her name on the screen, "Simone 2 Lee," and remarked upon it in what would become a familiar exchange.

"Oh, she's a twin?"

"No. I mean—she was. Her brother didn't make it."

Now that I think of it, I'm pretty sure Scott stole the Grief Leaf when we left. It's probably sitting in a bag of assorted artifacts, deep in one of our closets.

The day before, as we'd held Ames in the recovery room, the nurses told us we could see him as often as we liked during our four-day stay in the hospital. He would be kept in the forgiving coolness of the morgue, but they'd bring him up at our request, a terribly sad sort of room service.

Scott had wanted to say our good-byes then, but I lobbied to have Ames brought back to us the next day—when, I hoped, some of the numbness would have worn away and I could feel more than detached disbelief at the sight of him. I arranged for a photographer from an organization that takes pictures of stillborn babies, because I thought it would be important to me later, to have photographs other than the few blurry shots we'd managed in the recovery room.

The next afternoon, after our visit to the NICU, we waited. We'd asked that morning to have Ames brought to us at four, and when he wasn't there at quarter-to-five, my husband and mother-in-law went in search of explanation.

Scott kept this from me for more than a year, but while he and his mother were waiting near the nurses' station to ask whither our baby, my nurse—a new one, young and brunette, with an air of being perpetually inconvenienced by her job—walked over to a bassinet by the side of the hallway and lifted the blanket that covered its contents.

"What are we supposed to do with *this*?" she asked, with audible disgust.

Of course, it was Ames.

Nursing is, I think, the most intimate profession. I said this to Scott once, and he insisted that surely that distinction belonged to prostitutes, but I disagree. The night my water broke, Jenna held a cool washcloth to my head as I heaved and panicked, and it was her body I draped myself over two weeks later, contracting as I waited for my spinal. Nurses witness and care for us at our most vulnerable. They clean up our fluids; they give us sponge baths. They see us when we are afraid, and when we are dying. They hold our emesis basins, and they are the ones who remain after the doctor who has given bad news is gone. They listen to our stories and answer our questions. They take the footprints of tiny corpses, and help newborns latch onto their mothers for the first time. They are there when there is nothing medical left to be done, to remove now superfluous wires, to watch as tired breathing slows and stops—and the aftermath, too, is left to them. Even to me, an atheist, it seems like a sacred job. But it can't be an easy one, and I would imagine that the constant, helpless intimacy is exhausting.

It couldn't have been the first stillborn preterm baby this nurse had seen, working on a unit with a mix of postpartum women and those on extended bedrest. According to Scott, disgust was only the second most evident quality of her tone, the first being annoyance. It is hard to excuse a lack of empathy profound enough to allow for annoyance at someone's stillborn baby. It might have been easier if she weren't so young: after 20 years, maybe you'd need to be numb to obstetric tragedy in order to continue working, but she wasn't old enough for that. I suppose that's silly, because what *would* be old enough? What would be the magic number of stillborn babies a person must see before the bodies reduce to items on a to-do list? 100? 20?

I wonder about that nurse sometimes, what she's up to. Giving unduly brisk cervical exams? Complaining about the tiresome weeping from the lady in 2012? I can't help but feel her high school guidance counselor ought to have guided her in a different direction, perhaps toward working the beak-clipping station at a chicken farm.

Meanwhile, I was waiting in my room with the photographer, sitting in uncomfortable silence.

"Thank you for being so patient," I said, finally.

"Oh, please, don't worry about it."

More silence. I was a pitiful hostess.

"So...do you like...doing this sort of thing?"

It's awkward to talk to the stranger about to take pictures of your dead child, which is probably why I was reduced to asking whether she enjoyed corpse portraiture. I found myself blurting a warning about Ames' appearance, reminding her, apologetically, that he had died long before he was born. I wanted to ensure that her face betrayed no negative reaction to the body of my son, of whom I felt fiercely, guiltily protective.

As it turns out, I've only looked at those pictures a handful of times and Scott never has. Months later I'd argue with him over whether his family ought to be allowed to display a photograph of Ames, taken in the recovery room. The idea horrified me. None of us would be at our best, a month after death, and that was not how I wanted him remembered. They may have been the only photographs we had, but he was not his corpse. He grew for five months inside of me, doing ordinary fetal things; when Scott or I tapped my belly, he returned an agreeable kick. I felt obligated to protect him from the eyes of those who would, through no fault of their own, see only the macabre.

When they finally wheeled him in, Ames was in a plastic bassinet lined with Koala-themed blankets—the same kind the hospital used to house full-term babies. This was the only contact we'd have with such a bassinet, which made me want to laugh, or cry, or possibly both at once. Ames was naked this time, and wrapped in a white felt-like cloth. He'd softened even from the day before: I'd planned to request a picture of his perfect feet, remembering that these, at least, looked no different from those of a living baby, but now that was no longer true.

The photographer and Scott's parents had stepped outside to give us privacy, and I was crying at long last. For the first time in weeks, really, and it was a savage relief. We examined our erstwhile baby, touching him with a ginger tenderness. He looked like me, we decided. He had my chin, and I gave him my middle name, Michel. I was too self-conscious or fearful to separate his legs and the gummy umbilical cord that lay stuck to them (*what kind of pervert wants to see her dead baby's penis?* a voice chided), so I never was able to see for myself that he was a boy. My nurse—the piqued brunette from the hallway—barged in after ten minutes, irritated to find we weren't *finished,* intent upon changing my IV bags and giving me a stool softener right that very instant. For a moment, I thought Scott was going to hit her, or worse, but she lived to be annoyed another day.

Scott's parents stepped in for a brief and tearful audience. I'd been against this—afraid, I think, that if they saw Ames they'd think of him less like a real baby, as illogical as that sounds—but later was glad I'd relented. The photographer entered after they'd gone, moving around the room with her camera. From some angles, it was easy to imagine the boy who would have materialized given different events. Mostly it was like discerning figures in a cloud, but "Here," we said, "Look!" and the photographer dutifully snapped the frame. Without the farcical blue cloak and my morphine haze, I could see him so clearly—my *if only* son. What I saw never made it onto film, though I search there fruitlessly for it once in a while.

After the photographer left, I held Ames cradled in my arms. I think I even sang him a song, the one about a fly that my mother sang when I was little, and that I'd later sing to Simone. I know I gave him a kiss, though I was afraid at first to do so.

The worst part of the hospital protocol after a stillbirth is that the time you have is open-ended. It is up to parents to tell a nurse when they are "ready" to have their baby taken away for good—in our case, to be autopsied. I understand the reasoning, and the alternative would be as cruel. But "ready" feels like the worst kind of betrayal. How can you be? I handed Ames to Scott to return to the bassinet, and then wailed for him back, arms outstretched. But eventually we did it: we wrapped him up and called the nurse, and he was gone.

Amy Bloom said "*Everyone has two memories. The one you can tell and the one that is stuck to the underside of that, the dark, tarry smear of what happened.*" My dark, tarry smear is this: I thought of Ames very little in the next months. In truth, almost never. People assumed I mourned in private, but I did not, and when others mentioned him while Simone was in the hospital, I grew impatient. Couldn't they see I had a live baby to worry about? When Simone was doing well, I was so grateful it seemed improper to ask for anything more, greedy to mourn for an extra baby, and when she was doing badly, there was no room in my head for anything else. Sympathy expressed for a grief I rarely felt made me feel bewildered and judged. Ames hardly seemed real—I wasn't sure I even considered him my son, at least not the way Simone was my daughter.

If Ames had been a singleton, his death would have left me incapacitated. Three years before, after a miscarriage at seven weeks, I'd quit my job to better accommodate my recreational sobbing, and obsessively tracked the progress of my ghost pregnancy. I'd thought of nothing but when and how I might get pregnant again. That time, I hadn't seen a baby waving onscreen, or even heard a heartbeat. I'd never felt kicks and punches, much less held a body, and yet when it ended I all but fell into a Victorian decline. If Ames had been a singleton, when his small form was rolled away to the morgue, my insides would have howled with a feral emptiness. If Ames had been a singleton, my heavy, leaking breasts would have been a hideous physical mockery. But instead, I had Simone to think of, and it was time to pump.

Sixteen

The day before my discharge, Scott and I visited the hospital's breastfeeding supply store, so that I could be fitted with a nursing bra. I may not have been nursing *per se,* but I was pumping eight times a day, and besides lacking convenient cup-opening clasps, the bra I'd worn on admission now provided all the coverage of a pair of pasties. Nursing bras are an undeniably mother-specific purchase, and I'd been looking forward to this expedition, intent on procuring the supplies necessary to my new job. In my eagerness, I delivered us to the store a few minutes before it was due to open, and we waited in the hallway outside the door.

Conveniently for most, the shop is located across from the newborn nursery, in the postpartum unit. I'd never seen a newborn nursery before, but they are easy to recognize from their appearances on television and in the movies: a glass wall with bassinets beyond it, dotted with relatives cooing in happy clusters. Scott and I feigned disinterest, but our eyes couldn't help but slide in that direction. Here, everything seemed to be brighter, and the walls were covered with decorations. Doors stood open along the hallway, and the atmosphere was less that of a hospital than of a convivial rest home. Women in robes winced slowly by, with an air of exhausted accomplishment. I felt acutely displaced. We were interlopers in a foreign country.

As we stood there, a father came out of the nursery, rolling a swaddled baby in a bassinet. I nudged Scott as my eyes widened. My God, I thought, look at that baby, just *out in the air* like that! The customary bassinets are really no more than square plastic buckets, and this baby was completely untethered—being whisked down the hall, open to the elements.

As the pair came closer, I realized we weren't just in foreign surroundings, amid foreign customs—*Babies! Just out in the air!*—we were among a foreign species as well. I don't know whether it was an especially large infant in reality, but to me, after three days of the NICU, he looked grotesque. Huge and doughy, like bread that had been left too long to rise, his eyes were barely visible in the folds of his face. He was all cheeks and smooshed, pouty lips, wrapped in a blanket and topped with a hat.

We watched the pair disappear down the hall and into a room as the shop opened its doors and we entered. Inside, a lactation consultant introduced me to a rarefied section of the brassiere alphabet: the letters in which, coincidentally, all began synonyms for "large." F for Fearsome, G for Gigantic, H for Humongous—any of these adjectives could have applied to my newly engorged bosom, which I wrestled into a remarkable piece of industrial engineering with straps the width of a sturdy belt, the kind a cowboy might wear. A woman entered the shop while I was in the dressing room, and through a gap in the curtain I could see that she was wearing a hospital gown. There was talk of latches and feedings. A third woman arrived, and I emerged to see Scott standing by a display of nipple creams, looking uneasy. I paid for my purchases and we scurried outside.

As we made our way through the maze leading back to my room, Scott and I marveled over the baby we'd seen earlier, rolled along by his father—Fat Hallway Baby, as he'd henceforth be known. Fat, we agreed, and frankly, ugly. Nothing like our lovely daughter, with her long limbs and finely articulated features. Full term newborns were monstrous and indecently plump: how had we never noticed this before?

"They look like...." I searched for the appropriate simile, "...*like shaved Sharpeis!*"

"They really do!" said Scott. We walked for a moment in silence. "Of course," he allowed, "I wish Simone hadn't been born so early. But she *is* much prettier than a regular baby. More elegant."

"Oh, I agree," I said, nodding vigorously. "*Much!*"

Before we could leave the hospital, we had to watch a video about Baby Shaking. The video takes the *Anti* position, in case you were wondering, and the nurse had been pestering us about it for days, ever since I'd returned from surgery.

We couldn't even hold our baby and the lecture seemed redundant. For some reason, we found the whole thing hilarious.

"We can't get *close* enough to shake her," I whispered to Scott, giggling. Simone was housed in a protective plexiglass case with only small, circular openings. She was attached via wires and tubing to a variety of machines, and watched over, 24-hours a day, by nurses. The Pope would be easier to shake—just let him think you were kneeling to kiss his ring, then reach up and give his shoulders a good rattle.

"I'm pretty sure she's safe," I told the nurse, the third time the video was offered. As she left the room, I murmured darkly, "*For now.*"

Oh, I know, it wasn't really funny. It's serious business, baby shaking, and for the record, nurses are quite humorless on the matter, like airport security when you make perfectly innocent jokes about nice Arab men handing you packages. But it helped to revel in the absurdity. We were desperate to find humor in our situation, even if it was black as pitch, and so when we finally did watch the video on the morning of discharge, we laughed at that as well. A clearly tortured woman told her story, and we howled at the dramatic reenactment, like ghouls. The official slogan of the hospital's baby shaking prevention program was "NEVER, NEVER, NEVER SHAKE A BABY!!!" and this sent us into further fits.

"Because one 'NEVER' just isn't enough," intoned my husband.

I nodded, with false solemnity: "Yet four would be too many."

If we were wicked for laughing, at least our levity was quickly quashed by our final visit to the NICU. Parents are allowed to sleep in their baby's room, but Simone's nurses had all but insisted we go home. It might have been different were we out-of-towners—our baby flown in from a smaller, less equipped hospital, as was often the case—but our apartment was technically within walking distance. By car we could get from the door of our building to the door of Simone's room in five minutes or less. The fold-out couch was barely a twin, and the nurses assured us that constant beeping and the coming and going of medical staff would make it impossible to get any rest. And we'd need it, because Simone would be in the hospital for at least three more months.

"You have to take care of yourselves," said a sweet-faced nurse named Maura. "You can always call to check in, any time, night or day. Just say you're Simone's mom and you want to talk to her nurse. And if anything happens, we'll call you."

"Anything at *all*," I emphasized.

"Anything at all."

It had been almost three weeks since I'd slept in my own bed, and it was calling to me. I'd return first thing the next day, and everyone seemed to agree it was the right thing to do, leaving. It wasn't as if I'd slept in the NICU those past few nights in the hospital. I'd be further away at home, but not by much. Still, it felt *wrong*—so rendingly wrong it seemed to pulse in each of my bodily cells—to leave the hospital without my baby. I whispered goodbye to Simone, and told her I'd be back in the morning. I fought the desire to scoop her from the isolette. I reluctantly returned to my wheelchair, but once Scott was pushing me down the hall, away from the NICU, I broke into panicked weeping. He was only taking me to my room to pack: I wouldn't leave the hospital for more than an hour, when my brother arrived to ferry me home. But it didn't matter, and logic did nothing to dissuade me from the conviction that I'd just abandoned my baby.

Back in my room I got dressed as best I could, what with all the crying. Scott was wheeling carts of my accumulated belongings to the parking garage; he'd drop them off at the apartment before he went to work. He returned from his last trip to the car to find me sodden and unable to catch my breath.

"Are you going to be all right?" he asked, looking worried. I nodded, gulping, and he hugged me and left, setting off a fresh wave of weeping. As

I cried, I stood limply in the center of the room, my hands clutching at my garments. I heard the brisk knock that indicates a medical professional is about to enter unbidden, and darted into the bathroom.

"I found that birth certificate form," said the voice of the discharge nurse I'd met that morning.

"Great!" I hiccupped from behind the door. "Thanks!"

There was a pause.

"Are you ok?"

"Oh, I'm *fine!*" I lied, with an extravagant vocal wobble. *Don't mind me! I'm just hiding behind an open door, having a nice, cleansing nervous breakdown!*

"Well...I can wait, if you want to go over this. When you're done in there."

I have one of those unfortunate complexions that blotches with crying, ugly strawberry-colored patches dotting my pale skin around the mouth and eyes. I knew that if the nurse saw me, the jig was up. What the jig might be—that I *wasn't* a hormonal postpartum woman who'd just left her baby in the NICU?—was unclear. What *was* clear was that the nurse wasn't leaving anytime soon, and so I fanned my face dry and flushed the toilet before strolling out of the bathroom, casual-like, avoiding her gaze.

"Thanks for waiting! Sorry about that! Just let me find a pen!" I bent over, pretending to be rifling through my bag.

"It must be hard to leave, with your baby still in the hospital." The nurse's voice was gentle. "They'll take good care of her, though."

"Oh, *I* know," I said when I straightened to face her at last, lips wrenched smile-ward. I waved my hands at my mottled face. "It's just the hormones!" I gave what was meant to be a Gay Little Laugh, but it came out strangled.

It's traditional, the new mother being wheeled from the birth center to the hospital entrance. I'd seen it plenty of times when I arrived for appointments at the clinic. Usually, the father leapt from a car idling at the curb, but sometimes he was following the wheelchair, carrying flowers or balloons. The baby was cradled by the mother, or strapped into a car seat.

I wasn't holding any baby, myself, just my purse and a plastic hospital bag. I made cheerful conversation with the nurse pushing me, trying to look conspicuously happy so that people wouldn't see my deflating stomach and wonder what had happened—*had my baby DIED?* How would I answer *that* one? *Yes, and No. Or, Only one, so far!*

We waited by the window until Max's familiar car entered the drive, and I felt a surge of relief as I was rolled into the cold air. I hadn't been outside in eighteen days, and there was my dapper redheaded brother, leaping out to help me into the front seat. He asked after Simone and we drove the rest of the way cracking wise about serious subjects. Why, I had all of the tax benefits of a new baby, with none of the work! A prescription for Percocet and no one to wake me from my narcotic slumber with wearisome demands for "food" or "affection." I was free of the ball-and-chain that usually accompanies new motherhood. Except, of course, one couldn't really call Simone a "ball-and-chain," as she wasn't nearly heavy enough.

You're less likely to cry when you're laughing, and I was glad for Max's company. He helped me up the stairs and into the apartment. After he was gone I called the NICU to check on Simone, and then I sat on the couch, alone.

I was home. I was home, and I didn't have even the faintest idea what to do with myself.

CHAPTER

Seventeen

L ong before premature babies were treated in hospitals, they were treated in sideshows, beginning with an exhibit at the 1896 Berlin Exposition, called "*Kinderbrutanstalt,*" or "child hatchery." The "child hatchery" was meant to publicize the newly invented incubator, and to this end tiny babies in what amounted to tiny convection ovens were placed on display next to *Conga Village.* This was long before preemies were known as such, back when the technical term was "congenital weakling," and an advertisement for the event hailed the incubator as "An Artificial Foster Mother."

The exhibit outsold both the skyrides and the Tyrolean yodelers, and its success prompted Dr. Martin Couney to take the show on the road. He went first to London and then the United States, where his exhibits of Incubator Babies became a fixture of amusement parks and expos, including the World's Fairs in Chicago and New York. A young Cary Grant worked as a barker for one of these exhibits, enticing passersby to come and see the miniature infants, kept alive through the wonders of technology. Parents offered their weaklings into Couney's care because there were few other options, and the incubator exhibit had a permanent home on Coney Island until 1944, when New York opened its first hospital unit designed to treat premature babies.

An illustration from 1906 shows a jostling crowd kept back by a railing, and beyond it a nurse bending over an incubator with a baby inside. Below the scene is a caption: "*...dozens of faces peered at her curiously.*" Back then, most of the preemies who survived to be exhibited were larger and older than Simone, resembling regular newborns writ small. Babies born at Simone's size and gestation are different creatures entirely, still fetal in appearance, as alien as any bearded lady and nearly impossible to describe without resorting to size comparisons involving produce and small mammals. Simone had a head the circumference of a clementine, legs like spears of asparagus. Her skin was dark and bright, the color of meat. Thin, with visible veins, it hung wrinkly on her frame, which had yet to develop insulating fat. Her knees resembled those of an elephant; her eyes were fused. Nipples wouldn't form until the 34th gestational week. The plates in the front half of her skull were so soft still that when Simone lay on her back, they seemed to sink out of sight, leaving a ridge where they met the more solid rear of her head, and giving the impression that she lacked half a skull.

Once, I convinced Scott that babies were born without ears. "Okay," I conceded finally, as if he were splitting hairs, "*technically* they have ears, but they're not developed. At birth it's just a little flap, with a hole—sort of like a lizard might have." He lingered in suspicious belief for 15 minutes, and I'd mocked him for weeks. Yet there we were, in the NICU, two years later, faced with an earless baby. Oh, she *had* ears, all right, but at her age they were still devoid of cartilage: just malleable flaps of skin that could be folded and crumpled, and often required reshaping after they'd been slept upon. Her ears were smaller than my thumbnail, her thumbnails half the size of a grain of rice.

I tell you all this because now that the exhibit halls are long closed, it must be hard to picture what a baby weighing a pound and a half looks like, if you've never seen one. You'll start from the reference point of a full term baby, picture it smaller and thinner, but this isn't quite right. Micropreemies—babies born under two-ish pounds—aren't like toy poodles or the runt of a litter; they're not smaller-scale versions of an original, nor do they simply need time and fattening. In addition to the visible lacks, like ear cartilage and nipples, Simone lacked a developed nervous system and functioning lungs. She was not just small but incomplete, and would be completed in an environment very unlike the one in which most of us grew.

We'd cleverly chosen to live blocks from one of the first NICUs to have private rooms. In most units elsewhere, babies were still clustered in incubator dormitories, multiplying the number of alarm bells ringing, the lights switched on for procedures, the voices and footsteps, the sounds of drawers and crinkling plastic wrappers being opened. In contrast, Simone's room was kept dark, to better mimic the womb. A sliding glass door was closed to muffle noise, its accompanying curtain drawn to repel the hall-way's brightness. In case a stray watt should penetrate the gloom, Simone's incubator was covered with a quilt, like a parrot's cage. Through a window, nurses watched the monitors from their desks in the hall. All who entered lowered their voices to a whisper, and even the phone rang with a soft blinking light instead of a bell. You know how in movies, the importance of leaving the past unchanged is urgently impressed upon time-travelers, because as they technically haven't been born yet and aren't supposed to be there, the innocent adjustment of a picture frame could change the course of history?

Well, our NICU operated under a similar principle. Its patients weren't supposed to be born yet, either.

Every NICU, even ours, is full of sounds. A symphony of beeps—the *bong, bong* of Simone's monitors when something was wrong, the more cheerful *bing, bing* of the same monitors when her oxygen could be turned down. Then there was the shrieking of the ventilator alarm, the beeping of empty IV pumps, the sliding of doors and swishing of curtains, the low voices of nurses and the trilling sounds of their phone pagers, the rolling of cart wheels, the *whuh-shuh, whuh-shuh* of my breast pump, the occasional cry of a baby without a tube down its throat—an older, lustier baby than mine. There was a constant, ambient hum of machinery, the slight buzz of fluorescent lights that you hear in quiet places, like libraries.

The loudest part of the day was rounds. Each morning, shortly after I arrived, a cluster of professionals trundled into view. There were about a dozen: several pushed carts bearing computers, with heavy three-ring binders of reference material hanging from the sides. They wore scrubs or white coats over sweaters; they all had hospital phones clipped to their waistbands. I'd slip outside to join them and stand against Simone's door, holding a cup of tea. For a long time, as one of the sickest babies on the unit, Simone was among the first stops on the route. They rounded on the healthier babies later—I suppose because they knew they'd still be there when they got to them.

"Simone is a 26 week, 5 day infant, day ten of life."

The nurse practitioner assigned to Simone presented her case, beginning with gestational and actual age, the latter measured in days. The rhythm of the sentence was so familiar it felt like an opening benediction (*"Simone is a 26 week, 5 day infant, day ten of life—Lord, hear our prayer."*) Sometimes the number surprised me (had it only been 10 days?) Sometimes, after a bad night before, it felt like a hard-fought victory. Later it would inspire exhaustion, or a shot of grim pride.

The practitioner rattled off lab values, prescriptions, feedings, and weight. She reported on oxygen settings and chest X-rays, and proposed her plan. More of this medication, less of that electrolyte. An increase in vent pressure (boo!). Or feedings (hooray!). The position of Simone's ventilator tube perpetually needed adjusting—she'd been pulling on it, or perhaps it moved when a nurse turned her over, which they did every few hours to keep her from developing a flattened head.

I'd follow the neonatologist into our room, and we'd talk as she examined Simone. When she stepped out again, everyone snapped to attention for discussion, and final decisions were made. Calculators emerged. Some people paged through the well-thumbed reference books they kept in their sagging coat pockets. The nutritionist calculated fluids and calories and sodium balance while the pharmacist calculated dosages, and there was math in various meters and grams. Then the neonatologist would cross to a phone on the wall to dictate her notes, and I'd ask the fellow about anything that remained unclear as the others chatted amongst themselves. The respiratory therapists rolled their laptop stand through Simone's door, to press ventilator buttons and type numbers in mysterious respiratory spreadsheets. Then the dictation was finished, and the herd moved on down the hall with a low rumble of wheels and conversation, Simone's nurse sitting to chart the day's orders.

It took a village, and at the beginning I seemed to be its monarch: a ceremonial figurehead of ostensible importance, but with little ability to effect change. I may have been the Mother, but my role was mostly symbolic and my job description unclear. Simone had two central lines sewn in immediately following delivery—one in her umbilical vein, and the other in her umbilical artery. Transfusions, medications, and at first, all her nutrients were delivered through these catheters. They flowed from her bellybutton in a shameful parody of the cord that ought to have connected us for another few months, at least.

A little less than a week after she was born, Simone was strong enough to begin digesting my milk. It was drawn up in a syringe and delivered directly down her throat to her stomach, via a tube the diameter of spaghetti. She didn't get much—one milliliter every two hours, or a bit less than a tablespoon a day—and most of her nutritional needs were still met by the cocktail of electrolytes, vitamins, and lipids administered through her umbilical line. But I was happy to have something to add to my mothering repertoire, previously limited to hovering and hand wringing—though my hand wringing, it should be noted, was above the par—and it didn't hurt that this something practically counted as medicine. All the usual boons of breast milk are magnified in importance for preemies. For Simone, it wasn't simply a matter of a few dubiously alleged IQ points, but a roadblock for deadly infections. In the case of NEC (necrotizing enterocolitis, to you), one of the most dreaded complications of prematurity, breast milk was the *best available preventative treatment*. No pill or shot or bracing dose of radioactivity had been proven as effective as my own teat, and this gave me immense satisfaction. Suck it, doctors!

I'd never had particularly strong feelings about breastfeeding. Well, that's not entirely true. I felt strongly that breast was best, but that a mother without postpartum depression was better still. I was well aware of the health benefits of breast milk, and I liked the idea of being able to stumble from bed in the night and slap a squalling baby to my bosom, no equipment or dishwashing required. The supposed aid to parental attachment was especially appealing to me: by the time my children grew up and realized I wasn't the fun parent—probably as they were looking down on me literally and figuratively, from atop a carnival ride where they sat with their father while I stood nervously on the sidelines—it would be too late. We'd have already bonded during all that breastfeeding, and they'd have to love me anyway. With twins, I knew breastfeeding might be a struggle. My plan was to give it the old college try (though as I never did finish college, that may be an imperfect metaphor), but I wasn't going to cry over milk, spilt or otherwise.

That was before I gave birth to a baby who weighed less than my own liver. I'd begun to research preemies while on bedrest, in order to draw up a revised list of possible catastrophes. NEC was described as a poorly understood, sudden, and often fatal disease of the intestines, and unsurprisingly, it was the "poorly understood" part that frightened me most. It was *thought* to be some sort of infection, or maybe not. Discussion of treatment relied heavily on the phrase "supportive care"—doctor-speak for "hope for the best." My medical dictionary defines "supportive care" as "treatment given to prevent, control, or relieve complications and side effects and to improve the patient's comfort and quality of life," but you will notice the absence of words like "cure," and "fix," and that the primary disease is missing, in favor of "complications," "side effects" and "quality of life." Once a doctor is concerned mostly with side effects, and your quality of life, you might as well put your affairs in order.

I'd hoped my information was outdated, but grilling neonatologists only confirmed my fears: NEC is a monster that descends without warning, to eat the bowels of premature babies. It's disease as imagined by Stan Lee, and when I learned that formula-fed preemies have ten times the risk, I promptly abandoned my doveish stance on breastfeeding. Once Simone was born, I began to wring myself dry with the aid of a rented $1200 hospital-grade pump that could have easily sucked blood from a stone.

NEC aside, pumping helped assuage the helpless guilt I felt, watching Simone's alarms sound and her oxygen dive as she pushed her spindly arms over her head in distress. I'd always had trouble with follow-through. There were the countless aborted writing projects, the magazine I'd folded after four issues, my partially-achieved college degree. And now, here I was, with an unfinished baby. I'd ejected her early, forcing her to do work far above her pay grade, like breathing, and meanwhile *my* workload remained unnaturally light.

As penance, I spent many an hour attached to Pumpy, my demanding electronic baby (*YOU* try not naming something that touches your breasts every night for months). I poured the milk into bottles, and labeled them with Simone's name and the date. In the mornings I ferried the night's haul to the hospital, where my section of the NICU freezer was soon overflowing. Simone's feedings would increase, milliliter by milliliter; someday my milk would be her sole source of nourishment, and so help me God, I was going to feed my *own damn baby*. It was the least I could do. Sadly, it was often the most I could do as well.

Sometimes, late at night, Pumpy's rhythmic wheezing began to sound like speech: *Let's go! Let's go!* she'd say, as my milk began its steady drip into the bottles. Other times she sounded tired, and desperate: *Help me! Help me! Help me!*

The day after I was discharged from the hospital, Scott and I went out for breakfast. It was sunny as we drove to the restaurant; cars sped along, traffic lights passed blithely through their customary routine of green, yellow, red. It was such a cliché, I thought to myself, to be startled at the realization that the world went on in the face of one's personal tragedy, but I was startled, all the same. It was disorienting to pull into the parking lot and be seated in the same booth, when the last time I'd been to this place—any place, really—I'd been heavily pregnant with twins. A slim month later, there I was, not pregnant at all, one baby in the hospital and one whose ashes we were planning to pick up after we ate. I couldn't stomach my breakfast, and Scott couldn't finish his fast enough to suit me. I had to get out of there—out of everywhere that was not the NICU, out of the outside world in general. The contrast was too great, particularly in places I'd been Before, which remained heartlessly unchanged, After.

We ran our woeful errand, driving across town to retrieve Ames' ashes from the funeral home recommended by the hospital social worker. "We send them a lot of our stillbirths," she'd said, and the home had waived most of our costs. At the front desk, an unobtrusively solemn woman handled our paperwork, and we signed for the small velvet pouch that contained the "cremains"—a horrible term, by the way, funeral industry. Is that really necessary? Isn't "remains" bad enough, without your gruesome prefix? Can't you say "ashes" like everyone else?

Walking back to our car, we were bathed in inappropriate winter sunlight. We'd planned to run other errands before visiting Simone, but instead I insisted Scott drop me at the hospital. Inside I strode swiftly to the NICU, and felt my muscles relax and my mind quiet, once I was back where I belonged.

I made it a point to be present every day: I felt it was my duty to be there for Simone during procedures, and to gather information and monitor the monitors. Scott, like many parents, left or averted his eyes for the blood draws and echocardiograms and difficult IVs, but I stood up and crowded close, offering to help, if only by cupping Simone's feet to keep her calm. When I couldn't help I watched, hawk-like.

As with pumping, my motives were not entirely unselfish. I showed up because it soothed me to be near Simone, and it gave me a dubious but necessary sense that I was doing something constructive. I needed the routine, and a place where I didn't feel like an anachronism, and was recognized for what I was—a mother, sort of. Even on days when Simone was too fragile to be touched, sitting in her room made me make sense.

I suffered the customary hormonal crash a week after discharge, and on a particularly bleak morning after a particularly hysterical night, Scott took one look at my face and ordered me back to bed. I slept for another three hours, until the phone rang at eleven. It was the hospital. They suspected that Simone had an infection, and had started Baby's First Septic Work-Up.

I hadn't been there when her blood sugar spiked, or her X-ray came back ominous. No, I was the absentee parent they had to call at nearly noon, and trying to avoid that feeling in the future gave me another reason for attendance. Guilt, however, didn't require a concrete event like that one—guilt was a constant. I could have been with Simone 24 hours a day, and yet I wasn't. Even when I was present I wondered whether I was present *enough*. Should I have been touching her more? Reading to her more often?

I left the hospital at four or five each afternoon, and when I didn't go straight home, I shopped. Near my apartment there was a gift and stationery store, where I'd often bought overpriced notebooks I didn't need, and while pregnant I'd planned to buy a plush creature there for each of the twins. Maybe a lamb for Ames and a long-eared bunny for Simone, I'd thought, though I never grew brave enough to do so. On that first day after discharge, the afternoon after the morning of the breakfast and grim errand, I stopped there on my way home from the NICU. There was an elephant, pale grey, as soft as a chinchilla, and I bought it for Simone. I kept it in its paper bag, high on a shelf in her empty closet, for when she came home.

The rest of my shopping was practical. Isolettes are lined with flannel receiving blankets, and parents were allowed, even encouraged, to provide their own. So one evening I stood in the baby section at Target, carefully choosing package upon package of the prettiest and softest I could find. Each week the nurses gave me a bag of laundry to take home, and I'd wash my daughter's blankets with baby detergent and return them, folded, to her hospital drawer. I'd also purchased a set of baby washcloths at the suggestion of Simone's nurse, and every night I slept with one tucked into my bra, out of the way of my leaking nipples. Babies are allegedly calmed by the scent of their mothers, and the next morning a nurse would slip the washcloth under Simone's head, against her cheek. I liked being able to insert myself directly into the isolette, in a guise that was present even when the rest of me was not. I hoped that babies, unlike horses, could not smell fear.

I thought a lot, during the early days, of Harry Harlow's Wire Mother. You've heard of his experiment: baby monkeys, separated from their mothers after birth, were each given two artificial substitutes, one made of chicken wire, and one of terrycloth. Harlow found that even when the wire mother was the one providing food—via a bottle of milk mounted upon the metal crosshatching of her chest—the babies preferred the cloth mother. They clung to her for comfort, while the wire mother stood alone with her bottle, shunned.

When the monkeys were given only one mother, wire or cloth, their behavior differed dramatically. Place a baby monkey in an unfamiliar environment with the cloth mother who raised him, and he would cleave to her for a bit before beginning to explore, then return every once in a while for the reassuring touch of terrycloth. Babies placed in that environment *without* their cloth mothers rocked fretfully back and forth, screamed in terror and clutched themselves, or crouched close to the ground and cried. Subjected to the same environment, baby monkeys raised by wire mothers responded identically regardless of whether their mother accompanied them. They *all* cried, and rocked, and cowered. For monkeys raised by wire mothers, her presence provided no comfort, and none clung to her cold, wiry bosom for reassurance. A wire mother was no better than no mother at all.

It wasn't the same thing, of course, but the experiment popped into my head at odd moments, watching Simone sleep with her hands curled around the ventilator tube for comfort. She had my cleavage-scented washcloth beneath her—made of terry, even—and I did touch her from time to time, as did the nurses, though they wore gloves. Her bedding was soft and warm, not a wire in sight. I'd been told Simone could sense my presence and reminded that she'd recognize my voice, but I had trouble believing this was true. Babies grow to know their parents' voices in the womb, and Simone's womb time had been truncated. Who knew whether she'd heard enough to identify me with any degree of certainty? *A baby knows her mother*, I was assured, but how? How does she know? And if she does, what does she think when she wakes in the night? Where does she think I have gone?

A wise friend who'd had a baby in the NICU swore that Simone would remember none of her time there. I repeated this like a mantra: *she won't remember*, I promised myself, and I hoped that this was so. Though if it was, what was I doing, sitting there in the dark?

Eighteen

When Simone was a few days old, a neonatologist stood before the isolette, arms folded, and regarded it with a frown. Simone, she explained, with her fused eyes and gelatinous skin, seemed less developed than they'd have expected for an almost 26-weeker.

"She behaves more like a baby born at the end of the 24th week than the end of the 25th," she said, leaving me to wonder just what that might mean: preemie behavior was limited to reclining, with the occasional wave of a limb. "I just wanted to know whether you were sure of your dates."

I laughed the laugh of the reluctantly knowing.

"We did IVF," I said. "I can pinpoint her conception within a six-hour window."

I'd get this question a few times in Simone's first week, followed by another frown and a request for the date of my embryo transfer. I'd explain, patiently, that what they wanted was the date of *retrieval*, three days before—the equivalent of ovulation in an ordinary conception, and the point at which I was gestationally two-weeks pregnant. I liked giving these little IVF primers. It was a relief to be on familiar ground, because for the first time in all my medical adventures, I was otherwise thoroughly out of my league.

My usual Internet searches produced little in the way of useful information, giving me only the same broad strokes I'd gleaned from

PREEMIES: The Essential Guide, the book I'd ordered on bedrest and pored over in the evenings. The survival of micropreemies was a fairly recent phenomenon, and there were few long-term studies. More importantly, the intricacies of Simone's care, of the care of all babies small and early enough to warrant the *micro* prefix, were maddeningly individual. Her doctors were tasked with balancing electrolytes and fluids, managing anemia while encouraging the spontaneous production of blood cells, walking the line between enough oxygen to regulate CO^2 and pH, but not enough to cause eye damage; the line between vent settings high enough to keep the lungs expanded, but only just, to minimize damage to fragile alveoli.

There was more balancing still, like the need for diuretics with the risk of bone loss, and the need for steroids with the risk of brain damage. There was keeping blood pressure sufficient for fluid balance, but not so high as to increase the risk of brain hemorrhage. The variables differed from baby to baby, and worse, each of them—blood pressure, diuretics, electrolytes, respiratory function—related to the others in a series of delicate systemic connections. Even the equipment required a balancing act: the position of a ventilator tube has a margin of error as slight as the baby in which it resides. Too high in the throat and one loses ventilator pressure, but slide it too far and the tube is forced into one lung or the other, where the trachea branches.

Usually, when something is bodily amiss, it confines itself to a pathology or two: your baby has a concussion, or your sister has cancer. Neonatology was aimed less at treating disease than it was at successfully taking over the functions of an entire organism, one too underdeveloped to manage them on its own. It was like complicated puppetry, or a game of Shoot the Moon: tiny adjustments and careful control meant to keep the ball rolling without upsetting equilibrium. Compared to concussions or cancer, neonatology has no history at all, no long-standing precedent to fall back upon. Much of it is experimental, too new to be anything but.

It didn't take much time in the NICU to make it painfully clear that I had not, in fact, attended medical school. I understood the vocabulary and was familiar with the basic procedures and general problems—like anemia, and the whole not being able to breathe thing—but (at least in the beginning) I was uncomfortably reliant on the neonatologists and nurse practitioners for information about Simone's day-to-day care.

And information—the good stuff, the hard stuff, with numbers and acronyms and Latinate names—was hard to come by, at first.

A week into our NICU stay, I was standing near Simone's isolette when the nurse practitioner arrived. The neonatologists came by once a day, but nearly all of the prescribing and planning and proceduring was done by neonatal nurse practitioners, who were like creatures out of Greek mythology—an ideal and impossible-seeming combination of the knowledge and power of a doctor with the accessibility and communication skills of a nurse. Simone's regular, non-mythical nurse sidled over to the practitioner and began talking in low tones, glancing in my direction and keeping her voice studiously soft. I'd asked only moments before how Simone was doing, and received vague, non-medical generalities. "Pretty well" is not a technical term, thank you very much.

I watched the professionals murmuring over Simone's chart, and then I strode—ok, shuffled: my incision had yet to heal—over to interrupt their conference.

"Look," I said. "I really want you to tell me everything. I'm not going to break *down*, or *cry*, I promise. I can handle it. It helps me to know the details. I heard you mention a 'gas.' That's a blood gas, right? What were the results?"

The nurse seemed taken aback, but the nurse practitioner—a petite, sporty-looking woman wearing a fleece jacket over her scrubs—regarded me for a moment, and then opened Simone's chart to show me the lab reports. She explained the reference ranges for Ph and carbon dioxide, and the difference between arterial and venous measurements. Then she took me to the computer outside Simone's room, and for the first of many times, showed me my daughter's chest X-ray.

"See, there?" she said, pointing out the heart borders and areas of cloudiness. "Here, let me show you her X-ray from yesterday; you'll be able to see the difference."

Her name was Wendy. She was tan, with glasses and a dark blond bob. She had a brisk, buttery southern accent and laughed easily. She didn't do platitudes, but she was deeply kind. She had kind eyes, kind hands, and a kind, worried brow above her grin. She'd answer any question I asked, and answer it fully and without condescension, explaining patiently when my repertoire of *House* episodes and Internet searches failed me. I tried to adhere to a Tear-Free policy around the nurses and doctors, for fear that a display of emotion might spook them back to paternalistic generalization and head-patting. Actually, I tried to adhere to said policy among the public in general, to avoid humiliation and pity, and because of the previously mentioned skin-blotching. But the one time I cried, silently, in front of Wendy, she manfully ignored it. I know she noticed the tears, because her voice became softer as she related the planned course of treatment, but she didn't call attention to them, and she didn't tell me that Simone was going to be okay, because we both knew there was insufficient evidence for such a statement.

Reflected by her, my anxiety and skepticism, my obsessive research and desire to quantify, were recast as strengths rather than neuroses. The mental qualities that were so superfluous and unwieldy in my everyday life made me uniquely equipped for the intensive care unit. I would have thought I'd be a Hand Flapper, bringing to disaster the same *whatever shall become of me?* siren-wail of panic that I brought to ordinary Thursdays, but with a worthy adversary, the adrenaline-powered dervish of my mind ceased to be a loose cannon and became an asset. If you try to drive a wire nail into the wall with a sledgehammer, you are likely to make a mess, but sledgehammers have their place, and given the right job, can actually be quite useful.

"I just read too much," I'd said sheepishly when Wendy first asked whether I had medical training.

"Simone's lucky you do. You're a strong advocate for her, and she needs that. Don't be afraid to speak up. You know her best, because you're here every day. You're the expert."

I'd seen this myself the morning before, when Scott and I entered the room, where a neonatologist, a nurse practitioner, and a nurse had all recently examined Simone, none of them noticing what we saw immediately—that her fingers were stuck in the tape around her ventilator tube, and she was trying diligently to unstick them. I knew that Simone was easily overheated, and that morphine disagreed with her. I knew that she was sensitive to noise, and that anyone speaking above a murmur would cause her oxygen saturation to nosedive. Wendy made me feel I was part of the team, not a ceremonial motherhood figurehead after all. I unabashedly adored her, and she unabashedly adored my daughter.

"*God*, I like this baby," she'd sigh, as Simone batted irritably at her hand—and you could tell she meant it. Simone, she remarked, was tough as nails, and had *personality*, not like some other babies. "Simone knows what she likes and what she doesn't," Wendy said, as proudly as if she'd given birth to her herself, "and she's not shy about telling us, either."

This was something of an understatement. "THE ANGRIEST BABY," I'd nicknamed her, watching as she brought all her strength to bear in a cross attempt to repel the hand of a nurse with the temerity to adjust her endotracheal tube. Overpowered, Simone resorted to tiny, furious smacks, and then kicking, as determined to foil the nurses as she'd been during all those days on bedrest.

It was comforting to see this continuity of temperament. My temperament, on the other hand, was in flux. Anxiety requires you to think about the future—what might happen, what could happen, what will happen—but the future is a luxury. There isn't time to think about the future when an alarm is sounding. There *is* no future in crisis mode. There's only the present, and a sort of desperate mindfulness.

When I worked as a waitress at a diner, my favorite part of the day was the lunch rush. For some reason it rendered me placid and calm, the kind of calm said to come from meditation—though meditation, for me, has the opposite effect. Stillness is the worst possible strategy for clearing my mind of thoughts, instead driving them all into the open where they run around screaming and breaking vases, but the frantic immediacy of a busy waitressing shift silenced the yapping of my cortices. There wasn't time for much thinking, which was fine, as the tasks I was performing required little. Table seven needs coffee. The woman by the window wants more sugar substitute, and the check. Remember: a patty melt on rye and a cheeseburger, both medium-well. Two Diet Cokes, a small orange juice, and an iced tea—no lemon.

I performed actions I'd performed hundreds of times before, one after another, without even the space for a sip of water, and the busier I was, the calmer I became.

After only a week or two in the NICU—though it seemed years longer—I began to feel the same thoughtless sense of going through the motions I'd had while wearing an apron during the teeming diner hours between 11:00 and 1:00. When I arrived in the morning, I parked in the same ramp I'd used since my first trip to Labor & Delivery at 16 weeks. I took the elevators to the second floor and walked through the archway, big letters above it spelling BIRTH CENTER. I passed the triage check-in desk and the pregnant women in pajama pants, clutching pillows. I hit the switch on the wall to activate the automatic double doors, and walked by the family waiting room, filled with almost-grandparents and almost-aunts, waiting for news of new arrivals. I passed the Creepy Twin Painting, which I can only assume was a gift, because surely no hospital would have commissioned such a thing. It showed four sets of garish, dyspeptic toddler twins, arrayed on a couch—some were sitting, some climbing or scrabbling at the others. I remember a grumpy red-haired duo and a pair of sorrowful black girls in matching dresses.

Next came a wall of pictures: NICU graduates, then and now, with snippets of their stories and initial birth weights handwritten beside them. Sometimes I lingered there; I scoffed at those with weights that seemed insufficiently dire. Three-and-a-half pounds? Please. That baby could carry my baby on its back! I searched out the earliest and smallest, the ones who had been like Simone, hoping to find them entering science fairs or posing, upright and unharmed, in pumpkin patches.

At the locked door labeled Neonatal Intensive Care Unit, I pick up the phone.

151

"I'm here to see my daughter in room 36," I explained at first, though soon everyone will know me, and I'll only say "Hi, it's Simone's mom," before they buzz me in. I smile at the familiar hallway faces on the way to our room; the nurse outside stands up when she sees me. "How is she?" I ask, and while I listen I disinfect my hands with the sanitizing foam mounted on the doorframe. Inside, my eyes adjust to the dimness, and I look first at the monitor, then at the ventilator settings. I take off my coat and put my milk in the fridge and my bag on the couch. On the desk beside it is the goat figurine that watched over me on bedrest. He's facing Simone—on loan to her for his protective qualities. Finally, I wash my hands at the sink and approach the softly humming isolette, lifting the quilt to peek inside.

"Hi sweetheart," I whisper. "Hi there!"

Radiology appears after rounds—invariably in the form of a fresh-faced woman-child—rolling an X-ray that strains the definition of "portable." In a dubious attempt to introduce whimsy to pediatric illness, the machine is ocean blue and decorated with tropical fish. You see this a lot in children's hospitals: blood pressure cuffs in a bunny motif, teddy bears on EKG leads. Nurses arrange Simone upon the flat film plate that slides into her isolette, and we all step outside while the Lolita-in-Disney-scrubs dons her lead vest and presses what looks like a detonator.

For the rest of the morning, I type and pump and watch the monitor. Oxygen saturation values—sats, to those forlornly in the know—ought to be between the high eighties and mid-nineties. The amount of oxygen delivered by the ventilator can vary from 21% to 100%, with 21% being our goal. It is comforting, the quantifiable nature of these numbers, and how directly they correspond to the health of my baby. Her sats should be high, the oxygen low. Bad numbers, sick baby. Good numbers, healthy baby. Well, healthy-ish.

Scott arrives around noon, and we go downstairs to eat lunch at a sunny table by the windows looking onto the frozen courtyard. Afterwards he naps in our room on the couch, while I sit next to him with my laptop.

I type, and watch the numbers, and pump. The results of Simone's latest blood gas come in—they are better, or worse.

Every four hours, the nurse performs Simone's "cares." They're clustered this way to avoid disturbing her more than necessary, as gloved hands and alcohol wipes are not very womb-like. First comes blood pressure and temperature—sliding the thermometer under Simone's arm, which she resents deeply—and then changing her diaper to record her output. The nurse listens to Simone's lungs and suctions the ventilator tube as needed. She gives medications, measures belly circumference, and then attaches a syringe to Simone's feeding tube, drawing back to check for residuals from the last feeding. Simone never has residuals.

In the NICU, patients are assigned primary nurses, who work with the same baby every shift they're on duty. One of Simone's primaries is named Amber, and I love her fiercely. At first I was suspicious, as she was practically a neonate herself. Tall and thin, with birdlike features and stick straight hair, Amber wears no makeup and has a smile as sweet and wide as an orange slice. It seemed improper that someone so young should be caring for my sick baby, but I got over this quickly when Amber asked whether I'd like to take Simone's temperature and change her diaper. From then on these duties are mine and mine alone, and every four hours the two of us care for my baby in tandem, Amber changing her bedding while I lift Simone carefully off the blankets.

Nine days after Simone was born, I got to hold her for the first time. I pulled a chair close to the isolette, and exchanged my shirt for a gown that opened in front. It was a two-nurse job to disconnect the ventilator and transfer Simone to my chest before connecting it again, and to arrange her many wires before taping them to my shoulder. I cupped her feet with one hand while the other covered her back, and Amber handed me the furry miniature blanket I'd bought, to drape over Simone as she snuggled between my breasts. I couldn't believe I was holding my own baby, her body shielded by my palm and her feet pressing against my other hand. Scott was videotaping, and in the footage I mostly stare at Simone, occasionally looking up at him, savage with delight.

It is said to soothe a baby, to be held skin to skin. It's called Kangaroo Care, and was developed in South America, when sick premature babies were returned to their mothers to hold because the hospital wasn't equipped to treat them. The skin-to-skin closeness had a miraculously salutary effect, slowing heart rates and keeping temperatures and respiration even. Baby kangaroos are all born prematurely, after only a month of interior gestation—about the equivalent of a human embryo's seven weeks. They are lima bean sized, like shiny red worms with two rudimentary arms that allow them to clamber into their mother's pouch. They stay there, attached to a nipple, for the nine remaining months of development. I envied kangaroo mothers their mobile NICUs.

While I held Simone, I watched the monitors. I was afraid—again— that she'd deteriorate quickly, proving my unfitness. The monitor didn't sound, but we did eventually notice that one of her feet had gone purple from being held so tightly against my chest. I guiltily relaxed my grip, and watched my baby's toes return to a less corpsey color. Thanks to a cascade of hormones, I was limp and sleepy, and weeping milk. I would say that I was overcome with peace, if I were the sort of person who says things like "overcome with peace." I was holding my daughter, after all that had happened. I started to sing to her, then became self-conscious, and stopped.

Simone and I had combined to create a fleshy furnace, and when our time was up and they transferred her back to the isolette, my back was slicked to the polyester gown. I felt stoned with joy, which would last until the next terrible blood gas result or discouraging chest X-ray, probably a day or less. The highs were so high, and the lows were so many.

At the end of each day we gather our things and make our way to the parking lot, where I've befriended the attendant, a dark-skinned woman of indeterminate ethnic origin, with a long thick braid. Being a Stranger Talker is a family trait I inherited from my grandfather, who once left us all in the car at a gas station while he went to pay, and had to be dragged back twenty minutes later, so intent was he on chatting with a pump attendant. This is the same grandfather who worked on the railroad during the Depression, and used to bring hobos home to dinner. I think Stranger Talking is a fine tradition, and it astounds me that Scott can exchange ticket and money with another person without so much as a smile or *have a nice day*. He mocks me for trying to make friends of everyone I meet, but I maintain that it makes life cozier to see familiar faces, and in the evening when we drive up to the window, my parking attendant grins.

"How is baby?" she asks, and I say, as always, "She's wonderful."

Nineteen

In the wee hours of February 21st, I was awake. I'd risen as usual to perform what I called my One Man Band routine: slapping one of Pumpy's cones upon each breast and holding them in place with my arm while I pumped, ate two saltines, drank a glass of milk, and checked my email, all while calling the NICU for an update. It was my custom to stumble back to bed afterward for another few hours of sleep, but this time I stayed up, crouched before my laptop. That afternoon, Simone was scheduled to have surgery to close her patent ductus arteriosius, an errantly open blood vessel between the aorta and pulmonary artery—in layman's terms, a hole. *A hole in my baby's heart.*

We knew about this hole when Simone was only a day or two old. The ductus arteriosius is a temporary canal all babies have in utero that closes after birth. Unless that birth is grievously premature, in which case it sometimes stays open, letting blood sluice in great sloppy gushes into the lungs, where it doesn't belong. I'd always pictured lungs as big empty sacs, like those rice-paper balls you can blow up and bat around, but in fact they're closer to sponges. All that blood sloshing into them not only means less for the rest of the body, but it also weighs them down, making them more difficult for, say, *a baby the size of a pigeon* to heave open.

As soon as the doctor finished explaining about the hole, she went on to tell us they weren't going to do anything about it, which seemed foolhardy, at the time. My understanding was that the heart was one of the more important pieces of the body—not a frivolous organ, like the spleen. Maybe if it had been a hole in Simone's spleen, I would have been less concerned, but when someone informs you of a hole in your baby's heart, your immediate instinct is to sew that bitch *up*. Why, I'd have done it myself—I'm no surgeon, but I did get an "A" in home ec, and hearts shouldn't have extra holes in them. That's just science.

But:

"These things often close on their own," said the neonatologist. If Simone's didn't, they'd try to treat it without resorting to surgery, with medication. This "medication" is ibuprofen, by the way, though they call it something fancier in the NICU, so that you won't be alarmed by the fact that your child is getting the same thing for her *heart-hole* that you take for *menstrual cramps*. However, before they took the drastic measure of breaking out the Basically Advil, they wanted to watch and wait, and in the meantime I nearly forgot about the hole altogether.

Only in the NICU could you forget such a thing, but I had other potential crises to worry about. Simone's head ultrasound was scheduled for Valentine's Day, when she'd be six days old—day seven of life, in NICU speak. The head ultrasound is the SAT of the neonatal set, the Big Game, with a scout in the stands. In general, bigger preemies born later do better than smaller preemies born earlier—but the real determinant of outcomes is whether there's bleeding in the brain. The vessels in the brain of a premature baby are so fragile that they can be broken by mere birth and sudden existence outside their cushion of amniotic swill. The earlier a baby, the more fragile the vessels, but compare a 27-weeker with a good-sized brain bleed to a 24-weeker with none, and even with 3 fewer weeks under his belt, the latter has a better chance of emerging with faculties intact.

You can't study for a head ultrasound, so I just worried, thoroughly, and didn't remember the hole in Simone's heart until I heard she'd be getting an echocardiogram the same day they looked at her head. Valentine's

Day was as good a time to examine a heart as any, I supposed, I just hoped the radiologist wouldn't let reading the echocardiogram delay news of my baby's brain. I spent the afternoon startling at every approach of footsteps, and finally Tara, the fellow, appeared to report: Simone had only a tiny grade I bleed, meaning it was contained in the ventricle, away from the serious grey matter.

"There is no difference in outcomes between babies with grade I bleeds and babies—"

"With no bleed at all!" I finished for her, jubilant. I'd read that study myself!

My jubilation was tempered by news of Simone's still open ductus. The echo had shown it large and defiant, and they started Simone on a course of Basically Advil. Thanks to the hole, Simone's blood gases had worsened and her blood pressure was unstable. Our honeymoon period had ended just as my postpartum crash was hitting its stride, and I was weepy and overwhelmed. I longed for those last days in the hospital, when all I'd had to do was wake in the morning and wait for my breakfast sausage, the details of my day delegated to others, my daughter just down the hall. Little things, the inconveniences of insurance forms and parking tickets, were beyond me. Procuring meals seemed especially herculean, because it involved choices. I was too tired for choosing; when I couldn't decide what I felt like eating, I ate nothing at all. I might have gone on this way for some time if not for my mother, her masterful puppet strings stretched across the ocean, orchestrating a rotating crop of friends and family to appear with takeout in the evenings. Each time I was astounded to find that they'd brought just what I hadn't known I'd wanted, and having people for whom to put on a brave face dragged me from the depths, as I began to find my sea legs and settle in for good.

When I look back at that first month in the NICU, it seems to stretch on and on with a plastic quality that defies quantification. I try to quantify it, mind you: *Did it feel like a year? Six months?* But the answer eludes me, because truthfully it felt as if time had stopped altogether, or at least as if the NICU were located somewhere outside its purview.

The first round of Basically Advil was unsuccessful, and so a second three-day course began. Simone's feedings were stopped during these courses, and I reverted back to near-uselessness, watching helplessly as Simone's alarm rang again and again as she struggled to take in oxygen. A day into the second course, it was decided that surgery couldn't wait, and would be scheduled for the next day—but when the next day came Simone was better, and surgery was off again. This was dizzying, but typical: in the NICU you are yanked repeatedly between the abyss and safety above it, in a continuous emotional bungee jump. Simone was allowed to finish her second course of ibuprofen/heart-hole-mender, and that Wednesday they performed a final echocardiogram to see whether the ductus had surrendered.

It had not. In fact it was larger, which hardly seemed fair. Surgery was scheduled for the next afternoon.

And that is how I came to be awake at five in the morning on February 21st, reading up on the procedure on the day it was scheduled to be performed. There were two options for closing the vessel: some surgeons sewed it shut, while others preferred to use a tiny clamp. I wondered how they made a clamp that small, like a staple you'd find in the office of a dollhouse. And what would happen to this clamp? Would it stay the same size, as the vessel grew? Could that be right?

Either way, the procedure involved making a small incision in the side/backish area (technical term) of my daughter, lifting up my daughter's lung to gain access to my daughter's heart, and either clamping or sewing the open ductus shut. My former eagerness to do away with the hole had evaporated—in fact seemed rash, in retrospect. Someone would be *lifting the lung of my daughter.* I'd been assured this was routine, but I wondered if the surgeon had SEEN my daughter. They say one's heart is the size of one's fist, and Simone's fist was the size of a very small peanut M&M. In fact, she was really not much bigger than the bulbous nosed man on the Operation game board. I'd played that game often in my youth, and I remembered it as exceedingly difficult, even when extracting something as large and easy to grasp as The Bread Basket, and I had been an uncommonly careful and dexterous child. The most common complications of the surgery were damaged nerves or paralyzed vocal cords, from nicking something unintended. Not hard to do, in such a small space, where even a tremor would travel outside the margin of error. I imagined the loud buzzing sound an Operation board makes when such a thing occurs, and Simone's wee nose lighting up like a bulb.

As I pored over a diagram of the heart and its vessels, Scott was asleep. He didn't want to know the details; he found it easier that way. He did not live or die by Simone's every blood gas, because he didn't know what a blood gas was. Not that he couldn't have—it was just that were my husband kidnapped by pirates and made to walk the plank, he would likely welcome the blindfold, whereas I'd want to see exactly how many inches of wood remained before I plunged to my doom.

I was trying to respect our different coping mechanisms. Scott was a font of practical support, tending to the laundry and bills and anything else that by virtue of falling beyond the sphere of the hospital had been rendered invisible to me. Within that sphere, I was the one grounded in the practical: Scott was as absent from the emotional reality of our situation as I was from its material counterpart. He was engulfed by Ames' death and held Simone at a distance—metaphorically, I mean, as he hadn't actually held her yet, and had touched her only a handful of times. Emotionally, we were in some variant of the myth of Orpheus, with Scott as Eurydice: in our version it was Eurydice who looked back and remained in the underworld, while Orpheus stared obstinately forward and kept walking.

I hadn't written much on my website in the past weeks, because I'd no sooner formulated an entry about how well Simone was doing, than she wasn't, and vice versa. But it was late—or early—and I needed comfort, someone to exclaim with me over the absurdity and terror of surgery on such a small scale, while remaining full of the hope I was too superstitious to risk myself. My readers, I knew, would understand, and wouldn't find my board game comparisons flippant or inappropriate. When I wondered whether the surgeon would humor me by playing an exhibition game of Operation before they began, when I asserted that I would be happy to sign the consent forms once I had seen him remove both the pencil and the awkwardly shaped sparerib, my readers would know that I was joking only in the most serious way possible. I had to laugh at being made to watch videos about Shaken Baby Syndrome when I couldn't hold my baby, and at the preposterous difficulty of sewing up a vessel that was itself the diameter of a needle. It was the only way I could talk about my fear and sorrow without compounding it, or resorting to clichés that seemed through their ubiquity to have become incapable of holding any meaning at all. The sun was coming up as I finished typing my entry, and I returned to bed, feeling lighter.

We were roused later a few hours later by a call from the NICU. There had been a cancellation, and they were moving Simone's surgery up on the schedule. To when? Well, how soon could we get to the hospital?

We arrived just in time to meet the surgical team, who were clad in identical blue scrubs. The surgeon himself looked uncannily like a young George Clooney, which may not have had any medical relevance, but seemed to help, somehow. He became less attractive when he moved from empathetic small talk to warnings that the structure of the ductus is unstable, and that occasionally it will bleed riotously during surgery and kill its host baby. I reminded myself that he was required to disclose all risks, and that death was far less likely a complication than, say, a paralyzed vocal cord. *Though,* I thought to myself, *as Simone can't produce any sound around the ventilator tube wedged in her throat, we might not know about THAT for months!*

This line of reassurance seemed to be crumbling, and so I tried another, reminding myself that the surgery was routine. One of my medically-knowledgeable readers had likened it to a beat cop writing a parking ticket, a task one performs so often that it demands almost no thought at all. Not that I liked the idea of a scalpel being wielded *thoughtlessly* over my 1lb, 15 oz daughter. Hmmm. Was there such a thing as a surgery that was *too* routine?

I decided to stop reminding myself of things. I asked about the vessel clamp and what would become of it, and was relieved when the surgeon said he preferred a stitch. I read the consents carefully before signing them, like the lawyer's daughter I am, though it was only a formality. Simone needed the surgery, and I couldn't do it myself, home ec honor roll or not. The surgeon looked calm and tan, and I noticed his very expensive watch, thinking that surely such a watch spoke of many successful procedures, and few mothers left to wail at diminutive gravesites.

The anesthesiology contingent was chipper, even jovial. They bantered and smiled at us in their paper hats as they disconnected the ventilator. A nurse anesthetist (So cheery! Were they dipping into the Fentanyl?) attached one of those hand-held bellows contraptions to Simone, squeezing the bag at rhythmic intervals. She'd act as a human ventilator on the way to the operating room, and I hoped she didn't trip or lose the beat. I leaned in to whisper goodbye.

"We'll have her back to you in less than an hour," the nurse said, still squeezing, with a sympathetic smile. Then they rolled Simone's isolette, IVs, and an oxygen tank away from us. I trailed helplessly out the door and down a few feet of hallway after them, and then I stood still and watched as they turned the corner with my girl in her Plexiglas bubble. A nurse walking by saw me, and stopped.

"Can I help you?" she asked, and I shook my head, pointing in explanation at the sight of the last blue scrub cap disappearing around the bend, then turning away as tears began to slink down my cheeks.

While Simone was in surgery, we packed her things and took down the decorations. The hallway we'd been in had too few babies, and they were consolidating us to a more populated area. Our new room was on a busier, brighter thoroughfare, closer to the entrance of the unit. But it was room eleven, and as eleven was my favorite number, this seemed like an auspicious sign, or would have, if I believed in signs, which I would have assured you I did not.

Neither did I believe in good luck charms, but the first thing I did in the new room was place my goat on the desk facing a new isolette, which we made up with Simone's best blankets. She was due for a fresh isolette anyway, as they needed to be sent away for cleaning or a tune up every few weeks. When she emerged from surgery, Simone would not only have a hole-free heart, but a whole new world to live in.

I sat and waited; I watched the clock. I tried to imagine what might be going on right that very minute, and then tried NOT to imagine it. It had been ten minutes less than an hour when I heard wheels and leapt from my perch on the outermost inch of a couch cushion.

The operation had gone beautifully. That was enough for me at the time, although later I would read the Operative Report, my favorite part of which was the sweeping away of a laryngeal nerve "using blunt dissection with a Q-tip"—proving that neonatal surgery was just as adorable as its patients. Simone was on her side, and I could see an inch-long patch of Steri-Strips covering the incision on her back, extending under her armpit. I remember thinking that when she was older, the scar would scarcely be noticeable. But it turns out that scars grow with the body like the rest of the skin, which I suppose makes sense, and at two it still stretches from under her arm onto her back, the scar now several inches long.

The neonatologist had warned us that while some babies show an immediate improvement, others are slower to recover from surgery, and it could be days before the good wrought by the stitch became evident. Simone, however, seemed better already. Her alarms were silent, and she was sleeping peacefully—or passed out, blitzed on morphine and Fentanyl. Her hair stuck up in the back, and her hand was curled around her beloved ventilator tube. During diaper changes she usually waggled her legs in irritation, but that day she let them flop to the mattress the moment I released her ankles. Scott and I giggled at this and everything, postsurgery, our relief oozing out as laughter

I felt like knitting, or performing some other peacefully maternal task, but instead I went to my two-week postpartum appointment down the hall. Dr. McGleamy checked my incision, and when I complained of back pain, gently pointed out that I was sitting with my shoulders hunched dramatically forward. I hadn't noticed, but the way they resisted straightening told me I'd been holding them like that for some time.

"What you need to do," the doctor ordered, "is pour yourself a glass of wine and take a long, hot bath."

Before he entered, the nurse had given me a questionnaire meant to screen for depression. The questions ask you to evaluate how you've felt in the past seven days, and were plainly not constructed with a NICU parent in mind. For example:

1. *I have been able to laugh and see the funny side of things:*
   a) *As much as I always could*
   b) *Not quite so much now*
   c) *Definitely not so much now*
   d) *Not at all*

2. *I have looked forward with enjoyment to things:*
   a) *As much as I ever did*
   b) *Rather less than I used to*
   c) *Definitely less than I used to*
   d) *Hardly at all*

I can find humor in even the blackest of times, but it does *dampen* one's amusement, having a child in the hospital. As for "looking forward with enjoyment," frankly, I had little to work with. I spent all of my time in the NICU. The only thing I looked forward to with enjoyment was dinner, not because I was depressed, but because I wasn't a sociopath. Who looks forward—with enjoyment!—to their baby's chest X-ray? Similarly confounding were queries about whether I had been coping as well as ever, or been so unhappy that I had been crying, or had trouble sleeping, or felt sad.

I'd never liked these sorts of questionnaires. They purported to have been assembled scientifically, and yet there was number three: *I have blamed myself unnecessarily when things went wrong.* If you blame yourself for something, are you really the best person to ask about whether that blame is necessary? If the guilt were justified, wouldn't that be just as depressing? And if you knew it wasn't, doesn't it make sense that you might not feel so guilty after all?

What stopped me entirely were numbers four and five:

I have been anxious or worried for no good reason.

I have felt scared or panicky for no good reason.

I nearly always felt I had good reason to worry, but in this case, I knew that I did, a rare triumph. Were they more concerned with my anxiety, or its rationality?

"I *have* been anxious and worried," I told the nurse, when she returned for my worksheet, "But...you know. Simone had surgery this morning. I wouldn't say I'm worrying for no good reason. I think it's an excellent reason, actually. One of my better ones."

The nurse looked over the questionnaire and my answers, and her lips knit themselves into a little moue.

"Why don't we have you take this when you come back in a couple of weeks," she said, slipping the paper into the trash.

Back in the NICU, Eloise arrived for a visit. Simone was stretching from time to time with her arms behind her head, like a pin-up. We cooed over her and took blurry pictures in the dim light, through the walls of the isolette. After Simone's 4:00 cares, we turned her onto her belly, a cheek on the washcloth I'd slept with the night before. The ear she'd been resting upon was crumpled into a ball, and as the nurse smoothed it we joked about pinching both ears into elfin shapes for the camera sometime, before they developed cartilage and spoiled our fun. Simone slept on, and Scott and I were certain that if it weren't for the ventilator, we'd have heard her snoring indelicately. We gazed at her with amused affection. I updated my website, ending the entry on an uncharacteristically mushy note:

"I am so lucky to have this strange new creature to care for," I wrote. "I cannot wait for tomorrow."

CHAPTER

····································

Twenty

I 've never been a soldier, but I would imagine that even when you're treading carefully, aware of the possibility of landmines, the actual explosion is shocking. Back me up here, veterans: stepping on a landmine is always a surprise, otherwise you'd have avoided putting your foot down in that particular spot. In the NICU, you tread carefully, though most days are fairly routine—the baby is a little better, or a little worse. You try to keep your guard up, but the same fear that is meant to soften the impact of catastrophe amplifies your relief at success. Then you take another step forward and are blown swiftly into irreparable fragments.

At 4:30 the morning after the surgery, I dialed the NICU for a status report after my usual pumping and snacking. I don't remember who our nurse was that night, in fact the only part of the call I remember with any clarity was the shock of the noise in the background when the phone was answered from Simone's room—a rattling, shuddering noise, like a roughly idling engine.

That sound, the nurse explained, was THE OSCILLATOR. Simone had maxed out the settings on her ventilator, and they'd had to bring in a different, stronger machine. Her condition was critical—or, if you want to get technical about it, more critical than usual. Meta-critical.

My face flushed hot while the rest of me went cold with shock.

"Why didn't someone *call* us?" I asked, "You could have *called!* Why didn't anyone *call*?"

Sometime after we'd left, flush with victory, Simone's respiratory function began to deteriorate. (Nobody called us.) She needed more oxygen, and then more again still. (They didn't call us then, either.) When she was up to 100% they began increasing the ventilator's pressure settings, until an X-ray showed Simone's chest expanding as her diaphragm dropped, pushed down by the volume of her lungs. (Still! No call.) Any more pressure might have caused her lungs to develop tears, resulting in permanent damage, but her blood gas showed she was still not breathing well enough to rid her body of carbon dioxide. (Operator? Operator?)

Enter THE OSCILLATOR. A conventional ventilator works by fully inflating the lungs. It makes sense—after all, that's the way WE do things. We take a breath in, filling our lungs with air, and then we whoosh it back out again. But that filling of the lungs exerts pressure upon them, and lungs can only withstand so much, especially when they're a shriveled, underdeveloped pair belonging to a premature baby. THE OSCILLATOR is a different sort of ventilator, simultaneously gentler and more powerful, that works by vibrating oxygen in and carbon dioxide out via hundreds of tiny, scarcely inflating breaths per minute. It's the difference between the powerful *Flap! Flap!* of a crow's wings and the delicately manic buzz of a hummingbird's.

THE OSCILLATOR is the size of a sturdily-built sixth grader and sounds like a propeller plane trapped inside a metal filing cabinet. No style guide would say the name of THE OSCILLATOR requires capitalization, but the way the nurses and doctors spoke of it, and the nature of the machine itself, seem to demand more aggressive type. Simone had always been connected to machines, but this was different. The others may have beeped or whirred or made a rhythmic, breath-like hiss, but sometimes it was easy to forget they were mechanical at all. But THE OSCILLATOR's noise was so loud and flagrantly industrial it seemed to belong in an auto repair shop or a factory—certainly not at the bedside of a baby. It was incongruous and horrifying, as if I'd entered to find doctors stringing jumper cables between Simone's heart and a car battery.

When we arrived at the hospital we could hear it as soon as we entered the unit and started down the hallway, an ominous staccato roar. The machine took up most of the room, and we had to squeeze past it to see the isolette. Babies on THE OSCILLATOR are kept sedated, but even unconscious, Simone was not still.

"We need to see her chest wall bounce to know it's working," a nurse explained. Simone's whole body quivered and shook with the force of the ventilator's vibration. She could have been used as a neck massager or marital aid, perhaps laid across my shoulders to relieve the tension that terror had driven into my muscles.

Much of that day is blurred, and it is only from reading my email I know that even with THE OSCILLATOR, Simone was requiring a lot of oxygen, though the doctors were hopeful she'd begin to wean down soon. Despite its indelicate appearance, THE OSCILLATOR was a sophisticated piece of equipment that had saved many, including the premature baboons upon which it was first used.

I'd sent my mother an email with the news, but when she called we could barely hear each other over the noise, and I wandered out into the NICU family lounge, where it was quieter. I hadn't spent much time there—it seemed mostly filled with the young siblings of NICU residents, watching cartoons while their parents used the computers or talked to relatives. There was a kitchenette, with a refrigerator and a perpetual pot of coffee. Sometimes I'd see a woman in a hospital gown, still bloated and disoriented-looking, and week before I'd heard one such woman talking on the phone. She was discussing her newly-born twin boys and I'd felt a rush of envy at the mention of twins, magnified by the fact that she had at least one other, older child rummaging through the communal toy box. Her conversation continued and she began to cry, telling the person on the other end of the line that one of her sons wasn't expected to live much longer, and I felt suitably ashamed of myself.

Now THE OSCILLATOR had driven me from the room where my daughter was struggling to breathe, and *I* was the one in the lounge on my cell phone, trying unsuccessfully to hide my tears as I talked to my mother, my voice wobbly and strained. Conversations with relatives were mostly the same, in these situations. *What happened?* they all asked. *How did it happen, and what will happen next?* And I repeated my least favorite reply: *I don't know, I don't know, I don't know.*

"How is baby?" the parking attendant asked that evening as I drove up to her window.

"Ohhh..." I could not quite muster a smile, and settled for suppressing the sob that had risen in my throat. "Not so well, today." I tried for optimistic disappointment. My voice cracked.

The woman's eyebrows knit in concern.

"*Sick?*" she asked.

"Yeah," I admitted with a quaver, as I handed her my pass.

The woman tilted her head and exhaled, shaking her head, in the International Sign for Sympathy.

"I hope she get better soon."

I nodded and smiled, and wished her good night. At home, I turned on the television and sank onto the couch. I pulled Pumpy into my lap, connecting the cones and screwing on the collection cups.

Oh no! Oh no! Oh no! Oh no! she wheezed, as I stared blindly at the screen.

The next morning, Wendy was there when we arrived, and we all packed into the room alongside THE OSCILLATOR. I looked at the monitors, at Simone's perilously low blood pressure, and then at my daughter herself. She was almost unrecognizable. Her chin and cheeks were bloated and her fused eyelids fattened, as if she'd been in a fight and lost. Her formerly wrinkly-skinned legs had plumped to shiny sausages, the skin stretched to capacity. She didn't move except for the frantic quivering of her chest. There was something familiar about her new, pillowy face, and I realized with a shock that she looked eerily like Lou Dobbs. We still watched CNN most nights as the Democratic primaries grew bloodier, and while I'd never liked Lou to begin with, after this I'd be unable to stand the sight of him.

"Simone's white-count shows an increase in immature cells," Wendy said, gently. "Do you know what that means?"

"It means her body's making new ones," I said, slowly, "and releasing them before they're mature...to keep up with demand." My mind turned. "An infection," I said, dully.

"We're not sure yet, but we've started the cultures."

It was the second septic workup of Simone's life, and she was only two weeks old.

"But whatever the reason," Wendy continued, in her brisk, soft drawl, "The fact is our girl's having a real hard time."

Scott's parents called then, and while he talked to them, Wendy led me outside to the computer to look at a chest film. In it, Simone's lungs were so densely hazy I couldn't make out the contour of her heart. I felt sick, seeing the X-ray skeleton of my daughter on the screen, but it wasn't until Wendy pulled up a blood gas from the night before that my hand flew to cover my mouth. Simone's pH had been 7.13, and her CO_2 64.

[I have the sense, somehow, that you are not hearing the same ominous organ chords that I was, reading those numbers, so let me give you some context: the lowest end of the reference range for pH is 7.35, and CO_2 should no more than 45. In mammals, a pH of less than 6.8 is generally an indication that you are, well, no longer among us. Simone had never had numbers so dire—numbers just as dramatic as, say, drawing the DEATH card at a Tarot reading: a skeleton grinning up at you, holding a scythe. Do you hear the organs now?]

"They told us some babies have a rough few days after surgery," I said to Wendy. This was a prompt. Her line was "*Yes! That is exactly what this is! And soon it will be over, and we'll all have champagne! Or we would, if this weren't so routine and utterly unremarkable. This will hardly merit apple juice.*"

That was her line. But instead she said, with a worried and conciliatory wince of the mouth:

"Sometimes they do. But not like this, usually. Not this... Well. Not usually like this."

I will tell you right now, though we wouldn't know for another day or so: Simone did not have an infection. My best understanding is that the whole thing was an overreaction, her body working itself into a lather over imagined disaster, thus creating an actual disaster of its own. God knows I can relate, though a mental panic attack is rather more benign than a panic attack of the mechanisms responsible for physical homeostasis.

Surgery is traumatic. The body doesn't split hairs when it comes to the difference between a lion's claw and a scalpel. Simone's body sensed injury and began the inflammatory process, loosening the vessel walls to allow fixing sorts of cells (medical term) to pass through to the site of trauma. It also allowed fluid to weep out, reducing the amount within the vessels and causing low blood pressure, so low that Simone's heart was beating over 200 times a minute in a futile effort to compensate by slinging her blood faster and harder.

In its eagerness to ensure enough for the heart and other vital organs, Simone's brain decided to reduce blood flow to luxuries, like kidneys. After all, who needs a kidney when you've been attacked by a lion?

The kidneys became startled. "*Good heavens!*" they said, ruffling their nephrons, "*Our body's been cut open! Lean times are upon us, and we ought to conserve what fluid we have!*" The fluid weeping from vessels into the sur-rounding tissue ballooned Simone's weight to over two and a half pounds—practically the size of a puppy, rather than the kitten we'd come to know. It waterlogged her tiny lungs. But the kidneys obstinately retained it.

You know, I've never been a fan of kidneys. More bother than they're worth, I say, what with their stone-making and delicate sensibilities. Kidneys are the hothouse flowers of the organs—flying to pieces over blood pres-sure too high or too low, picky about which medications they will tolerate, calling for their salts at the first sign of trouble. The liver's not particularly stalwart either, but at least it has the decency to regenerate.

The point is—Simone was in a sort of shock. As her respiratory abili-ties dwindled, the lack of oxygen in her cells made matters worse in a vicious cycle I am not quite smart enough to understand, and then there is something called the renin-angiotensin system, and here is where I throw up my hands, because it is all too complicated for someone who never finished (or started) medical school, even more so when it's your OWN baby with the face of Lou Dobbs, lying in an isolette. What I did know was that Simone was in the awkward position of needing simultaneously more and less fluid: more in the vessels, and less...not. The solution seemed obvious—the brain ought to admit it overreacted and instruct the fluid back where it belonged, raising the blood pressure and appeasing the kidneys and restoring my baby to health.

But it didn't. And so my daughter received her six millionth blood transfusion, along with platelets, Lasix, Dobutamine, dopamine, morphine, and hydrocortisone—not to mention her usual Ativan and caffeine, her nutrition and lipids, and whatever else they shot into her PICC line and peripheral IV after I lost track. Lasix was a diuretic, intended to strong-arm her kidneys into peeing the fluid out, and each time I changed a tiny diaper and set it upon the scale, my heart rattled around my ribcage, hoping. But it was never enough, and by 2:00 in the afternoon, Simone had stopped peeing altogether.

In the midst of this, according to my email, I managed to correspond with my cousin Amy, who was on dinner duty that night and had offered to take us out. We decided on Vietnamese, and I expressed excitement at the prospect of my first drink in months, eager, as my other cousin had put it, to "test my fresh, pink liver." I told her we needed a break from the hospital, and that I looked forward to more tales of the doomed and one-sided love affair between her horse, Junior, and Tony the pony. Amy lived an hour west, on a spread of land she shared with her husband and a small menagerie. Stories of Junior's desperate pursuit of nearness in the face of Tony's stolid indifference were one of the few things guaranteed to make me laugh. Tony was short and rotund, but Junior was a towering, majestic-looking equine specimen. When his pony was detained indoors, out of his reach, Junior reacted strongly—running back and forth outside, along the wall of the building, his horsey scream of dismay becoming softer in the distance, then louder again as he doubled back. For days after Amy told me this story I replayed the scene in my head, giggling every time. In retrospect, it was unkind of me to laugh at poor Junior, but I took what amusement I could find.

Also according to my email, while Simone was not peeing and THE OSCILLATOR shuddered, I played online Scrabble. I chatted with Jenni about the kitten from the *"Hang In There!"* posters, an icon of perseverance for our generation. I wished I had one of those posters for our NICU room. ("Oh Simone, BE THE KITTEN!" Jenni replied, when I told her how bad things were.) If the electronic record is to be believed, I did a lot of things that day, and once reminded, I even remember some of them. I know we did go out for dinner that night, and I think I recall having a glass of wine. What I can't seem to place is the part where Wendy told me my baby might die.

In the post I wrote the next evening on my website, I placed that particular revelation in a phone call, but I don't think that's how it happened. Maybe I purposely conflated the phone call late that night with an earlier conversation, too exhausted to write the details of both. More likely, I conflated the two because the full weight of the conversation didn't hit me until later, during the phone call. Maybe my memory is just unreliable, though it seems unfair that it should fail me so consistently on the things I most want to remember, the most important and difficult pieces of this story. Though perhaps that's not an accident—stress erodes the brain's ability to form memories in the first place. Maybe the ones I'm looking for simply don't exist. My memory used to be freakishly sharp, or I guess not so much sharp as sticky: even when I didn't mean them to, things clung to it. I recalled any phone number I'd dialed more than once, what people wore on Mondays years in the past, and long strings of text I'd read as a child. I remembered that mosquitoes were more likely to bite you if you'd eaten a banana, because of the potassium, and I even remembered reading that fact for the first time—in the library of my elementary school, in a book about mosquitoes, and I could take you now to the spot where it was shelved, and point to where I sat, crosslegged, in front of it. Alas, my memory isn't what it used to be, my recall complete in some areas (for instance, the "useless mosquito knowledge" division), and in others possessing startling gaps.

What I do remember is standing in Simone's room, with Wendy next to me. It had to have been after Simone stopped peeing at 2:00, and after her chest X-ray came back at 3:00, the results of which are what ended my Scrabble game and spurred Jenni to entreat Simone to BE THE KITTEN. The X-ray showed her lungs almost completely collapsed. It's called "atelectasis"—a word I liked at first because of its similarity to my name, but which I quickly grew to hate.

There had been a demoralizing conference of Simone's medical team. The nurse bustled around with suction catheters and alcohol wipes while the respiratory therapist adjusted the ventilator and typed on the laptop atop his rolling stand. Wendy and the neonatologist frowned into the incubator. I'd squeezed in to look at my swollen, motionless baby, and Scott hovered behind me. There had been a summary of the day's dosages and settings and test results, and no one looked happy.

"She needs to pee," said Wendy, grimly. This was the consensus. If only my daughter would pee, the dominos would begin to fall in the other direction, the direction away from THE OSCILLATOR and frowning, solemn-faced neonatologists. It was so simple, but the drugs weren't working, and so everyone stood around with terrible looks on their faces, restating the obvious.

"She just needs to *pee*," Wendy repeated, sounding frustrated.

"Has anyone thought of putting her hand in a bowl of warm water?" I quipped. I'd tried to smile as I said it, but it came out sounding desperate, revealing that I wasn't really joking at all. Honestly—had anybody tried that? Sure, I'd been kidding, trying to break the tension for a moment, but hadn't that method—the hydrodigital method, we could call it—been successful at slumber parties and frat houses for years? Maybe it wasn't such a crazy suggestion: the neonatologist would look startled for a moment, but then she'd order the nurse to fill a specimen cup with warm water. We'd all watch as Wendy gingerly submerged Simone's hand, and we'd watch my baby's tiny diaper swell with fluid. The monitors would reflect an immediate improvement, and a shout of glee would go up all around, the respiratory therapist turning from his laptop to applaud. Afterwards, Wendy would hug me and the doctor would shake my hand, commending me upon my cool-headed yet creative problem solving.

"Sometimes we get so wrapped up in 'medicine' and 'science' that we forget about simple common sense," she'd muse, and I'd give a self-effacing shrug, just happy I could help in some small way.

But that's not how it went. Instead I got a laugh from Wendy and polite smiles from everyone else—except Scott, who leaned into me and muttered, *"I can't believe you just said that."*

The crowd dispersed into the hallway, and Scott lay on the couch to take a nap. He curled in a fetal position, the hood of his sweatshirt pulled protectively over his face. I was amazed that anyone could sleep with THE OSCILLATOR chugging along beside him, but my husband's ability to achieve and maintain unconsciousness had always been precocious, with sadness in particular having a soporific effect.

I could see Wendy outside, talking to the doctor, and afterward she slid the door open and came inside again to stand next to me, pulling the curtain behind her to keep out the light, the way Simone liked. My arms were folded across my chest, holding each other—my default posture of late—and I stood by the sink just inside the doorway, listening to THE OSCILLATOR. We regarded Simone in her isolette.

"This will start to resolve eventually, right?" I said, finally.

"I hope so," said Wendy.

"I mean, things are bad *now*, but she'll get *better*. We'll still get to take her *home* with us, at some point. She'll still come *home*." I turned to face Wendy and laughed at myself, wiping an escaped tear from my face. "Basically, these are all the same question, me trying to avoid asking what I really want to know, which is whether my baby's going to die." The word "die" sounded raw and vulgar, hanging in the air, and I laughed again, embarrassed, feeling like a peeled egg. "I know you can't tell me that, obviously, that she'll come home." More desperate laughter from Alexa.

"I'm concerned," Wendy said at last, after a long pause, "I'm concerned about how much oxygen Simone's needing. This is not what we were expecting after surgery, for her to be so sick, and right now, I'm worried about our girl. Even with all the help we're giving her, she's working awfully hard, and unless she turns a corner soon...I'm concerned that she can't sustain this course much longer."

Somehow, this was both shocking and exactly what I'd feared she'd say.

"What do you mean, 'sustain this course?'" I asked, to be sure, "Do you mean she can't get any worse? Can she stay the same?"

"No. She needs to start getting better. Not all at once, but we need to see some improvement."

I didn't know how to force the next question out of my mouth, and so for a minute I didn't say anything.

"So, how much longer *can* she...*sustain this course?*" I asked, at last.

Wendy gazed over at Simone and then turned back again, her eyes level at mine.

"Maybe a day or two."

Oh, my memory. My useless, patchy memory. I remember the conversation, and the sickening jolt, like being elbowed in the stomach. I remember the sudden sense of urgency, as if I should be running somewhere, maybe to defuse a bomb. I remember that 48 hours seemed like no time at all, and I remember asking Wendy what else we could do—because certainly there had to be *something*—and being told:

"We just have to wait."

But I still don't remember *when* it happened, and it seems important, now that I have email to confirm that we went out for Vietnamese that night. Did I leave, after hearing that my daughter might have as little as two days to live, to eat wontons and listen to equestrian anecdotes? Did we return to the hospital *after* dinner, the conversation with Wendy happening *then*? I remember being upset after talking to Wendy; I remember laughing at dinner. Thus, dinner must have been first. The two events don't even belong in the same day, and my brain would never have put them there if not for the irrefutable electronic evidence, ruining my memory's narrative integrity.

We must have gone back. Still, Simone wasn't in immediate danger of dying. She was even somewhat stable, if by "stable" you mean "consistently critical." There wasn't anything *we* could do. She couldn't be held, or fed, or even touched much, and THE OSCILLATOR made lullabies inaudible. We were, as Wendy had instructed, waiting. For Simone to get better and live, or get worse and die, or stay the same and *then* get worse and die. I suppose she could also have gotten *better* before getting worse and dying, but thankfully this option did not occur to me.

This was my first run-in with what I would come to know as the Zen of Neonatology. In fact, "Zen and the Art of Neonatology" could have been the title of this book. Medicine in the NICU is about balance, acceptance of the unknown, and patience. While those may be lovely qualities, they have never been my strong suits, and I found them terrifying in the context of medical treatment. At birth, for babies born on the precipice of viability, the neonatologist will often step back to see if the baby "declares itself"—by crying, or making an attempt to breathe. It is all waiting and receptiveness and *maybe*, in the NICU. A lot of "We don't know" and "No one is certain why" and "What is Buddha? Three micrograms of dopamine." Compared to the German level of control and precision involved in IVF's attempt to force the reproductive system into a homogenous predictability, Neonatology is the sound of one sterile-gloved hand, clapping.

It was 2:00 AM when I jolted out of what had been a complete and welcome lapse in consciousness. It was quiet, except for the noise of a fan and Scott's regular breathing. I felt like a ragged edge, simultaneously exhausted and painfully alert. A streetlamp in the alley cast a dim glow beyond the window, but inside it was dark, and I groped alongside my bed. I'd taken to sleeping with both phones next to me, in case the NICU should call. I sat up and dialed.

You know, this is the chapter that has taken me longest to write. You wouldn't *believe* how long it has taken, how many tangents I've veered off upon, how many days I've spent writing and rewriting the same page, or deciding it was critical that I look up the inventor of THE OSCILLATOR, instead of just getting on with the story, already. And this is why. Because I knew this moment was coming, the part where, if this book were a movie, I'd have to look away.

I don't know who Simone's nurse was that night either, or whether I talked to a nurse at all. But someone answered, and broke the news: Simone had begun needing more oxygen. Her settings had been increased, and increased again. She was on THE OSCILLATOR with the oxygen at 100%, and still her saturation was dipping and dropping. I could hear her alarm, striking its warning notes over the now-familiar background rumble. My heart was beating, beating, beating.

Regardless of what you may hear from coaches or business gurus, there is no such thing as giving more than 100%. Simone's situation was a near copy of the one—had it only been two days before?—that had prompted the bringing out of the Big Guns. So what do you do, then, when they're already out? THE OSCILLATOR had been the younger, more talented understudy, the pinch hitter or relief pitcher, the interrogation method of last resort. Every metaphor was equally untenable, and reduced to the same conclusion: we'd exhausted the reserves. I felt cornered and claustrophobic, and the dark was a suffocating blanket around me.

"She still hasn't *peed*?" I cried, more of a curse than a question. Actually, said the voice, she had—not long ago, for the first time in twelve hours. It was only a milliliter or two, not enough to notice without the scale. Nonetheless, I tried to leverage this small quantity of urine into reassurance (after all, the letters in "urine" are all used to form "reassuring.")

"But she did pee," I said, with a wretched eagerness, "and that's what she needs to 'turn the corner,' or whatever. So that's *something*, right?"

But the voice was blunt. No. Not really. It made no difference at all.

I think I asked whether we should come in and was told no, that they'd call if she got any worse. I think I made them promise. Maybe I talked to someone else. Like a million other details, these are absent or indistinct. Unfortunately, I remember with a crisp, visual clarity sitting on the bed afterwards, holding the phone and realizing, thinking, knowing all at once in a dizzy, vomitous surge: *My baby might die.*

I am not a stupid person. I had known that this was possible, even likely, relatively speaking. I had been living with that knowledge for weeks—why else were my shoulders curled so insistently inward, and whither my appetite? But *this* knowing, as I sat on the bed still clutching the phone, was different; it was divorced from statistics and probability, stripped of organization, and it bypassed the brain altogether, unfurling inside me like a snake. I would bet that anyone whose child has died or come very close can tell you exactly where they were when this moment leapt upon them. *My baby might die.* Not theoretically, in the event of hypothetical circumstances, but actually, that same day or the next. *My baby might die.* Just like this. I had only held her once; it had been a week ago, just.

I could see it: I was slipping from the NICU with Simone under my coat and running away, just the two of us, to a cave somewhere. I would nurse her to health with cool compresses and tisanes made from bark and toadstools. I'd find the dry grass under the snow and build a fire, and then I'd heat rocks and wrap them in rags to keep us warm. I'd squeeze drops of milk into my baby's mouth; I'd fashion her a bed of moss. We would be far away, in a secret, craggy place. And if she died, I would stay in that cave and hold her until I died, too.

Maybe there wouldn't be any tisanes or compresses. Maybe I would just find somewhere hidden, after it was all over. Maybe it would just be me, clutching my cold, stolen baby, her hastily disconnected wires floating from beneath the hem of my coat.

Scott was awake. "It's bad. It's really bad," I choked. I was holding one of Simone's dirty blankets we'd taken home to wash. I imagined it smelled like her, and in a reversal of our washcloth routine, I craved the comfort of my baby's scent. Maybe it was only the NICU I smelled. I fumbled for a Klonopin and swallowed it dry, then sank and curled onto my side holding Simone's blanket. I pressed my face into it like an animal and breathed and sobbed and breathed and sobbed.

Twenty-One

Two days later, THE OSCILLATOR was wheeled from Simone's room, never to return. I'd called for my wee hour update, and when the nurse picked up the phone I noticed the quiet, almost as loud as THE OSCILLATOR had been itself.

I ran back through the apartment in the dark, to shake Scott awake and babble the news. I writhed with glee; I was all jazz hands and delight. "SIMONE OFF OSCILLATOR!" I wrote in a jubilant email to my mother, before I returned to bed.

"Progress in the NICU isn't linear," Wendy said to me, once.

"Simone will get better, and then she'll get worse, or have a setback. But then she'll get better again. And that will repeat, over and over, but she'll start covering more ground going uphill than she loses slipping back." She held her hand at an angle and moved it to demonstrate. "Do you see what I mean? She *will* make progress, but slowly."

This may be the central teaching of the Zen of Neonatology. At the time, I was very focused on the logistics: how many steps back, exactly, would there be? When would we start to gain momentum? Was there some sort of benchmark I could use? I expected the back and forth to end, but now it seems obvious that this shuffling, dance-like process is everywhere, even outside the NICU, though generally it occurs over longer periods of time. You stumble, recover, and hopefully, keep moving forward. Really, what more can you ask?

Five hours after the terrible phone call, we'd awoken and driven silently to the NICU, only to find that just as we'd begun to prepare for the possibility that Simone might die, she'd begun to get better. A dose of hydrocortisone raised her blood pressure, and she had soaked her diaper with fifty milliliters of sweet, sweet urine. Pee had never made me happier. When I changed her an hour later she'd done it again, and I smiled goofily, feeling the heft of the diaper in my hand.

When the morning X-ray came back, I huddled by the computer to see the results. Wendy flipped between the new image and the one from the day before.

"You'd think it was a different baby!" she said.

You really would have. Simone's arms and legs had resumed their waggling, rising up into visibility now and then as I sat beside her isolette. But the most dramatic change that morning had come when the respiratory therapist replaced Simone's breathing tube for the first time. The one she removed looked like something left for years at the bottom of a murky pond. It was covered with thick green lung secretions, and stained an unwholesome color.

"Oh my *God*," someone said.

"We should save this," said Wendy, setting it carefully on a cloth, "to show people." With the new tube in place, Simone's saturation numbers shot skyward, and her oxygen was turned down. At rounds, Wendy produced the old tube and passed it around, to exclamations of wonder and disgust.

"It must have been like breathing through a *straw*!"

Back in Simone's room, I let myself cry the terrified tears that I hadn't realized were squatting heavily in my throat. Standing by her incubator, I cupped my girl between my hands while she pressed her foot against my palm. I'd meant to scold her, for frightening us so, but found I lacked the stomach for even facetious maternal chiding.

"Such a good, brave baby," I whispered instead.

As the Zen Masters might have expected, Simone was worse again the next day. She also had a new nurse, whom I would have killed for a nickel, maybe less. Most nurses held back the latches when they closed the portholes of an isolette, so that the SNAP! as they fastened wouldn't startle the baby inside. Not this one. She slapped the doors smartly shut, with a sound like the crack of a baseball bat—a terrifying noise if ever I've heard one—and she kept on slapping, even after I asked her to stop. Perpetually effacing, I'd even framed my request as an apology, as if it were simply an eccentric peccadillo of Simone's, this being bothered by loud noises eleven weeks before her due date. Neonates—what can you do?

When I arrived that morning, Simone was on 67% oxygen on THE OSCILLATOR, up from 33% the night before, and she'd stopped peeing once again. I noticed her blood pressure had fallen—over the weekend we'd found there was a magic pressure number below which Simone wouldn't release a drop of fluid, and I asked the nurse if the doctor was going to increase Simone's Dopamine to help her reach it.

"She won't pee with her blood pressure that low," I confided.

"They seem to think it's satisfactory," she said blithely, referring to the doctor and the new nurse practitioner. Wendy was off for the week.

"I know, it's higher than most babies need," I said, with a wave of my hand (*Neonates!—what can you do?*), "but Simone is picky that way."

"Well, like I said, they seem to think her blood pressure's fine."

I missed Amber, and the rest of Simone's primary nurses. They knew her as well as I did, and I didn't realize until they weren't there how much I relied on them for my well-being. It was easy to relax during the day knowing they were in charge, easier to leave Simone at night when I knew that Carrie, the night primary, would be there to notice if Simone was "not herself," which in preemies is often the first sign of infection, and sometimes the only one you get before things go seriously awry. Simone's primaries were the ones who would teach me how to take care of her—small things at first, like how to swab her mouth with a Q-tip dipped in breast milk to moisten her dry lips while activating her budding tastebuds and sucking reflex. They helped me grow comfortable positioning Simone in her incubator all on my own, encouraged me to hold her when I was secretly afraid to do so, and eventually gave me the confidence to be her mother, even without a nursing staff to back me up.

Wendy was working at a different hospital on the day of the porthole-slamming, but she'd promised to stop by on the way to or from her shift. I'd told her, with as much sincerity as I could muster, that this wasn't necessary, but she kindly ignored me, and when she arrived I rushed at her like she was the shore and I'd been recently shipwrecked. While I babbled about pee and oxygen she took charge and within an hour dopamine had been ordered and the need to "be aggressive" about Simone's blood pressure had been officially charted and duly noted by those on call. By the time Wendy left, Simone had peed and was on the mend again. I could have peed myself, out of sheer relief, but instead I took my husband out for our first post-baby dinner date, and had my first post-baby cocktail and a plate of pasta with lobster cream. We sat at a table next to the fireplace and made a toast. We felt celebratory, the fire cracking and popping like applause and champagne corks. That night, or early the next morning, I called the NICU, and like I said: the first thing I noticed was the quiet.

Two days later, on a Wednesday morning, the first thing I noticed was a pinprick-sized opening in the corner of Simone's eye. You could see it when she raised her eyebrows, which she did often and violently, obviously convinced that they were the mechanism responsible for eye-opening. She'd waggled and waggled in vain, and finally, a corner was coming unfused.

That afternoon, I was holding Simone aloft inside the isolette, one of my hands through each of the two portholes on my side. Across from me a nurse plucked out the bedding Simone had drooled upon, and smoothed a fresh piece of flannel in its place.

I was shifting my weight from one hip to the other when a tiny eye slid open and *stared straight at me.*

I almost dropped my only living child.

"Her EYE opened!" I cried. Scott was upright and next to me in one motion, but the eye had already closed again, definitively. If the first time you opened an eye it was to find yourself being held in midair by a giant who proceeded to scream at you, you might not be in a hurry to repeat the process, either.

The next day Simone was a little sicker, and the day after that she was worse again still, in the increasingly predictable tango of unpredictability. That evening, however, she was much improved, and lay on her stomach chomping with surprising vigor on a tiny pacifier, as I dotingly held it in her mouth and Scott beamed benevolently beside me. This was "very mature" behavior, they'd told us, this strong sucking instinct. I didn't mention that it was closer to chewing than sucking—surely irrelevant. In fact, chewing was probably more sophisticated still.

There was a great deal of eyebrow movement. And then, like a heavy blind being drawn up, the eye Simone wasn't lying upon opened, and looked around. My own practiced eyelids flew open.

"Hi! *Hi* sweetie! *Hiiii!*" I burbled. We watched her watch us, but after a few seconds...

...the eyelid drooped back down.

But then!

She struggled again to raise it, and peered at us, slightly out of focus. I felt my face assuming a dopey, liquid expression. Scott smiled—he'd become less tentative, lately, and more present. We watched our baby gnaw industriously upon her pacifier.

A pacifier is such a nice, normal baby item. Only babies use them, not like ventilators. You wouldn't find a fetus with a pacifier, either.

Saturday morning I held her for the first time since before her operation, one day shy of two weeks after the only other time I'd held her at all.

The picture we have from that day is the first one taken of us together, unless you count the Polaroid of our fingers touching through a porthole the day she was born. In this one we are chest to chest, her mouth open in sleep, a bit of my breast visible. It is an extraordinarily unflattering shot, partially because of the crazed grin on my face, and partially because of the perspective. I was sitting when Scott took the picture from above, and because of Simone's diminutive size the eye doesn't know what to make of the scale. I look unnaturally lengthened, unnaturally large—exactly, I said, like a delighted giant who's just found a HUMAN BABY abandoned on the forest floor.

You can't see it in the picture, but Simone is making a honking noise with every breath, the sound of air moving around a ventilator tube that had become too small for her growing throat. She was almost two and a half pounds, after all, and it was no longer all water weight. The small tube allowed air to leak out, skewing her settings, and I'd started calling her "my little gosling," because the honking sounded exactly like a flock of geese, headed south. I suppose they might have sounded the same way headed in other directions, but I wouldn't really know. It didn't matter, because on Monday they were going to replace the tube with a larger one, and the honking would be gone.

When the subject came up at rounds, it prompted a suggestion:

"If we're going to have the tube out anyway, why not give her a trial of extubation before we put the new one in?" someone asked.

A trial of extubation! A chance to breathe without a tube down her throat, the next step toward the ultimate goal of breathing with no tubes anywhere at all. They'd remove the too-small ventilator tube, and give Simone a chance to breathe on it—pronounced See Pap, and standing for "continuous positive airway pressure." On rated CPAP, air is delivered in pressurized puffs through large accordion tubes leading to prongs in the nose. If Simone couldn't handle CPAP, well, no matter: she'd needed her tube replaced anyway. It was brilliant. I wished I'd thought of it myself.

Simone was doing so well, much better than she *ever* had before the surgery, proving once and for all that hearts really oughtn't to have holes in them. She was eating again, which meant I'd finally regained my place among a bevy of medical professionals, electronic devices, and plastic products as one of my daughter's most vital caretakers, and they'd removed her last umbilical catheter. The night before the big day, I slept through my usual call to the NICU, and on the ride in to the hospital the next morning, I treated Scott to my Ramones-esque rendition of "I Wanna Be Extubated."

"Twenty twenty twenty-four hours to go-oo-oo," I sang, drumming on my thighs, and bouncing a little in my seat.

We burst into Simone's room to find it crowded with people, all clustered around her isolette. They looked up when we entered—the nurse, Wendy, the neonatologist, and the new neonatology fellow. We froze there, in the doorway, the smile removed from my face with what felt like a slap. Wendy stepped forward to explain what we'd have already known, if I'd called for my customary update.

Sometime after midnight, Simone bled into her diaper. Not a pinkish stain, but a dramatic splash of crimson. Her creatinine level was high, which meant there had been damage to her kidneys. There was a spray of bruising above her groin, and one leg was slightly dusky with a weak pulse, most likely meaning it wasn't getting enough blood. We'd come all the way back around to that first night, the one with Simone's twilight-colored fingers and the threat of amputation. An ultrasound had been ordered; radiology would arrive any minute.

"Progress in the NICU isn't linear," Wendy said to me, once. *Om.*

CHAPTER

Twenty-Two

There was a blood clot in Simone's aorta. Of course there was. Of COURSE there was. I couldn't decide whether I wanted to roll my eyes or bludgeon someone with a satisfyingly heavy object, maybe a marble bust of the founder of neonatology. Perhaps I'd prefer to lie down on the linoleum right where I was, and go to sleep. I was so tired. Oh, I was tired of it all.

In my mind, there had been a long, halcyon period of wellness between the disappearance of THE OSCILLATOR and the appearance of blood in my baby's diaper, but a glance at Simone's wall calendar revealed that only a week had separated the two. One week! That wasn't "non-linear progress," it was Charlie Brown, Lucy, and a football. My camel's back had finally crumpled, the camel himself taken out back and shot. Fuck you, NICU, and the mechanically-ventilated horse you rode in on.

If I were to go all Kübler-Ross on you, I might say that the period immediately after Simone's birth, during which I was too delirious with joy to notice her peril, was Denial. The weeks after, when I carefully monitored her every vital sign in the hopes of gaining a modicum of control, were obviously Bargaining. But by the time the ultrasound results were back, revealing a large clot in my tiny daughter's aorta, and reduced blood flow to both of her kidneys—which, by the way, were failing—I had moved on from both of these. To Anger.

Scott's parents were in town, and they appeared at the door of Simone's room just as the doctors left. I felt instantly testy and territorial. Partly, this was camouflaged shame at my failure to be present when the crisis occurred. I hadn't been there, and look what I'd let happen!

Scott broke the news, and as the designated keeper of information, I was barraged with questions, to which I gave terse, impatient answers— when I had answers to give.

"I don't know," I snapped finally, weary of their tears and supplication. I never seemed to get *my* turn to be baroque. I wanted someone else to take charge, to be strong and tearless and comfort *me*. I resented having to remain unemotional and know what all the numbers mean. A farfetched resentment, as no one had suggested I do so in the first place. My lust for information and squeamishness around displays of emotion made me suited to the position. Some are born neurotic, and others have neurosis thrust upon them: I was definitely the former. In fact, She Who Remains Unemotional and Knows What All the Numbers Mean was practically my Indian name.

But that day I had no time for logic. I was too busy tending the fire of my petty, formless fury, which attached itself to anyone unlucky enough to cross my path. The ultrasound tech appeared with her machine, and everyone left except Scott's father, who, to my great annoyance, insisted upon remaining.

"They won't *tell* us anything," I said, crossly, "They can't. They're *not allowed,* until the doctor looks at the images. There's no point in staying here."

He might well have remarked that this didn't seem to be stopping *ME,* but he was too quiet and polite for that. I stood by Simone's isolette with my arms folded, staring vigilantly at the screen, though I could decipher little of what I saw. My vigilance wasn't the type to be dampened by lack of understanding.

The one thing even I couldn't miss was the object squatting in the middle of a busy vascular thoroughfare. The technician clicked and typed A-O-R-T-

A next to a picture of the vessel, and I blanched.

In an hour, Wendy would explain that the umbilical catheter they'd removed a few days before—on account of how *well* Simone was doing, HA HA HA HA!—had formed a long clot around itself. When they pulled the catheter free of my baby, the clot remained.

"We aren't as concerned with the clot remaining in the aorta, because it doesn't seem to be obstructing blood flow. Unfortunately, we think pulling the umbilical line also sent a shower of smaller clots into the bloodstream, and these damaged the kidneys. Simone may have lost perfusion to her leg for a while. We'd like to see the kidneys start recovering, and that leg pink up."

To solve the Mystery of the Failing Kidneys, Simone's team planned to enlist the help of nephrology, a specialty I always confused with phrenology, though I hoped to God I could avoid doing so in the presence of my daughter's nephrologist, as something told me it might be offensive to imply that she spent her time not studying kidneys but rather telling fortunes based upon the contours of the skull. Simone would likely be started on a blood thinner to dissolve the aortic clot, because while it wasn't a problem as it was, pieces could break off, galloping along my baby's internal superhighways.

"Those pieces could be very dangerous," Wendy said.

"They could go to the lungs or the heart, you mean."

"They could, yes."

To sum up: Simone got better. So much better that she no longer needed her umbilical catheter, which had allowed for frequent blood draws but carried a risk of infection. The happy occasion of the catheter's removal set in motion a chain of events that made Simone much worse, complete with failing kidneys and a risk of one-leggedness, stroke, pulmonary embolism, or death.

Let's put it another way: say you have that disease of which televised medical dramas make such frequent use, the one where you cannot be exposed to sunlight. You while away the hours behind blackout curtains, writing overwrought poetry and dreaming of Acapulco. One day there is a cure, and upon receiving it you emerge into the sun, blinking. You take a celebratory lap around the block, pallid arms held high in triumph.

Then you die of melanoma.

Get it?

It would have been funny, except that it wasn't. Worse, having removed the umbilical catheter meant that in order to draw blood for the labs necessitated by her newest crisis, they had to stick Simone anew, this time using a vein in her head. I watched as they put a rubber band around her skull to act as a tourniquet, as they used a needle to painstakingly collect the amount of blood required for the test—a tiny quantity that was nonetheless difficult to obtain from a baby whose entire blood volume could have been easily absorbed by one roll of paper towels. The first sample clotted off, rendering it unusable, and so they went back to do it again, forgetting as they replaced the rubber band that the last puncture hadn't yet healed.

"Oh my God!" I heard one of the lab technicians say, and I looked up just in time to see blood spurt alarmingly from my baby's cranium.

The next morning, I did not miss calling for my update. And when I called, the nurse reported that Simone's leg was fine, there was no blood in her urine, and that though she'd heard there was bruising, she didn't see anything like that, herself.

Oh for heavens's sake! I thought blearily, *She's got the wrong baby!*

But she didn't: when I arrived, the previous day's angry bruising was almost invisible, and Simone's left leg was a pleasant pink. Her creatinine was still high, but at rounds the neonatologist proposed a familiar plan, if you can call it that: "WAIT AND SEE."

The one bright spot was that waiting and seeing about the clot and kidney situations put "learn to breathe" back at the top of Simone's to-do list, and three days after it was first cancelled, the trial of extubation was back on.

Dear Simone,

Saturday you were one month old. You nestled against me, one arm thrown companionably over my right breast, your feet pressing into my hand. When I spoke, your irises rolled toward the top of your head, looking for the source of my voice. Though I wish you were still safe inside me instead of running with the NICU's fast crowd—digesting milk and developing a fondness for benzodiazepines while your contemporaries bob lazily in their amniotic cocktail—part of me feels lucky to have these extra months with you. I would willingly give them up to ensure your health, but as that has not been presented to me as an option, I might as well enjoy this stolen time with my daughter of the softly furred shoulders.

On Thursday, my little gosling, the honking of your air leak had grown impossible to ignore, and your too-small breathing tube was removed. It was determined that as long as it was out, you ought to be given a chance to breathe without the ventilator, via CPAP. A hat was pulled onto your head and its straps used to secure a piece of tubing covering most of your face, a pair of prongs pressed into your nostrils.

You were horrified. First we take a TUBE out of your THROAT, and then we strap some contraption into your NOSE? No. NO. Absolutely, a thousand times, NO.

You raised your hands and used them to push violently at the tubing, all the while screwing your face into an expression of fury. More importantly, you clamped down with your chest, refusing to breathe and fighting every artificial breath the machine attempted to give. Your oxygen saturation dropped, and then dropped lower still. Your nurse called for the practitioner and there was much sighing and headshaking by the respiratory therapist. You weren't doing well, she said—snottily, I thought, as I fought both my tears and an urge to force tubes up her nose to see how she liked it. "Not doing well" was a phrase I had heard applied to you before, but this time it meant not that you were ill, but that you were failing, and I took exception.

It has been a long month for the both of us. I am nearly thirty years old, and there are nights when the unfairness of it all makes me want to lie on the floor and scream; at only thirty weeks, I thought you could be forgiven a fit of pique. While the nurses prepared for reintubation, I moved to the other side of the isolette and put my hands through the portholes to cup your head and feet. You were calming down, now, and taking a few breaths. I told you what a good job you were doing, in the same soothing voice I plan to use someday when helping you through things more complicated than breathing, things like bicycle riding and unrequited love. You began to breathe, breathe, breathe, and stop....and then breathe, breathe, breathe, and stop.

"You have to keep doing it," I said, rubbing your feet to remind you.

Breathe, breathe, breathe, and stop...I massaged your toes, and could feel you thinking "What, the lungs-in-and-out thing? I just DID that."

How exhausting it must seem: in and out, in and out, FOREVER.

By then you were keeping your oxygen saturation in the low 80s, but it wasn't enough, and the nurse practitioner disconnected the CPAP and pulled you from the isolette. She tipped your head back and swiftly slid a tube down your throat, larger this time to correct the air leak. Back on the ventilator and doped up on Ativan and paralytics, your eyes drifted open.

My good, sweet baby.

I promise you, it will get easier. All of this will get easier. It seems impossible, but someday your breath will be effortless and unnoticed. Someday we'll both take it for granted. Until then, though, I will be right here, applauding your efforts and wishing I could do this for you. I suspect this is only the first in a long line of similar wishes.

I love you more each day, and happily you are too young to recognize that as a hackneyed sentiment. It is true, after all.

Love,

Your Mama

I wrote the letter above a few days after the fact, and while I think it captures most of the experience well, what it leaves out is the force of my fury after the trial was over. "Failed extubation," they called what had happened, everyone shaking their heads afterwards while tears of indignation seared the backs of my eyes. They hadn't given Simone a chance, springing the CPAP apparatus on her that way. None of her primaries had been working, and though I tried to warn the unfamiliar nurses and respiratory therapists that my baby was particular—that she was not going to care for the idea of someone strapping things onto what was, legally, HER head—either they weren't listening or they didn't take my daughter's determination seriously. They hadn't been present at the ultrasounds for which she refused to show her face, or the hospital monitoring she eluded again and again, but *I* had been, and I knew. They'd already decided to reintubate before Simone had attempted her first breath, and whenever the "failed extubation" was mentioned at rounds over the next days, I piped up testily.

"She was focused on getting the tubes off," I told them. "She didn't even start trying until after it was too late." Everyone knows it doesn't count as failing if you didn't really *try*. Any of my former schoolteachers will tell you I failed to live up to my potential, but it was my obvious lack of effort that cleverly kept that perceived potential intact.

When Amber returned, she wasn't surprised in the least by Simone's performance.

"We'll do it when I'm here, next time," she said. Next time, they would afflict Simone with hats and straps first, and let the ensuing tantrum blow itself out before removing the ventilator tube and adding insult to injury by asking her to breathe on her own.

Breathing is hard work, if you don't know how. Even if you do, it's not necessarily a cakewalk. Doctors were always telling me I was doing it wrong—Too shallowly! Too fast!—and I'd been practicing for years. Focusing upon it makes matters worse—which is why yoga inevitably left me gasping—and Simone had no choice but to focus upon it, as the part of her brain that controls the drive to breathe was still under construction. But the mental effort was the least of it. Physically, breathing was strenuous—her lungs wouldn't finish developing for more than another month, at 35 weeks, and it required a huge muscular effort simply to lift her chest wall against gravity to inflate them. It was an effort no baby so tiny should be asked to make, and we had asked her to make it again and again, a miniaturized myth of Sisyphus playing itself out inside her ribcage.

Watching her breathe and stop and breathe again, I'd felt her exhaustion acutely. My situation was not so different, forced repeatedly to face something that felt unfaceable. I staggered forward bearing the knowledge that My Baby Might Die, relieved of it for a moment only to find myself brought low again, bowed under its weight. Seeing my two-pound daughter pushing indignantly against hands so much larger than herself had only magnified my own indignation at the too-much-ness of it all, and I felt tightly coiled with resentment.

CHAPTER

Twenty-Three

Not long before, I'd attended a breastfeeding class for NICU mothers, held in the family lounge's conference room. I'd seen the flyer shortly after Simone was admitted, and though it said otherwise, assumed it was meant for women whose babies were, you know, *breastfeedable*. After all, what would I do—bring Pumpy, so we could work on our latch?

One of the NICU lactation consultants who'd had a preemie of her own thirty years before, often popped into Simone's room to answer pumping questions and praise my bountiful supply. Every time she visited, she urged me to come to class. It was only an hour, on Wednesday! None of the others in class were breastfeeding yet, either! Most temptingly of all, after diagnosing my raw nipples as a case of chafing, she promised a free pair of pumping cones in a larger size. And so I finally relented, thinking it might be nice to meet some of my new NICU kin.

It might have been, but as far as I was concerned, the women I met in class weren't them. At twenty-eight, I was the first of my friends to procreate, yet there I was the oldest mother in the room. But this wasn't what set my classmates and me on opposite sides of an impassable chasm. No, that was the fact that my baby was by far the earliest and the sickest, despite having been in the NICU longer than all of theirs, save one who'd been born at 28 weeks and was nearing discharge, his last remaining task to master feeds by bottle. Standing outside the hospital nursery, I'd expected to feel out of place. Now it appeared that even in the rarefied environment of the neonatal intensive care unit, I was an anomaly.

Across from the bottle-feeder sat a childlike Asian girl who'd just delivered twins, each of her two babies bigger and healthier than my one. She spoke only a sliver of English, when she spoke at all, and looked understandably overwhelmed, leaving me torn between envy and pity. Next to her sat a woman about whom I remember nothing but what I saw as her relative luck, and then there was me, alone at the end of the table: dry-eyed, white-faced, and wrapped in the wooly bulk of a maternity cardigan. Simone's nurse had promised to send someone to retrieve me at the first sign of trouble, and I tensed at the sound of footsteps.

"It doesn't have to be an emergency," I'd cautioned, firmly. I wondered how long it would take to make it down the hall to where I was.

The last member of the class sat at my other side, wearing flannel pajama pants and a robe over her hospital gown. She was chubby, with a guileless face and limp red hair, and a smile that was watery but genuine. Her son had just arrived at 33-weeks, and she dissolved into tears at the slightest provocation. In fact, she cried through the whole class, when she wasn't asking endless, witless questions in a wobbling voice.

"I'm sorry," she said, with a pitiful attempt at laughter that was more like a smile with a hiccup, "I'm just having a hard time."

One could hardly blame her—it must be terrifying to have your baby arrive seven weeks early, skating the edge between three and four pounds, and the extra two months gestation she'd had over me wouldn't make it less wrenching to leave her child in the hospital. She didn't belong in the cheerful nursery hallway full of untethered babies any more than I did, and comparing one's pain to the pain of others is a fruitless exercise.

But it didn't matter. I hated her anyway.

Every time she removed her glasses to wipe the tears from her eyes, every time she released a sob, I wanted to slap her, hard, with the full flat force of my hand. I wanted to push her over backwards in her chair, or shake her shoulders until her head rattled. *I'll show you something to cry about*, I'd say, marching her in to see my daughter. When she asked about my baby I expelled Simone's statistics like bullets, looking into her shocked face with stony nonchalance.

I was shocked myself, by my own venom. I'd never had much patience for those who expected applause for continuing to exist despite misfortune, wrapping themselves in the ragged stole of victimhood. And yet if anyone were guilty of these things, it wasn't the frightened new mother apologizing for her tears—it was me. To my credit, I greeted her apology with a wave of my hand and warm assurances that hormones and fear had gotten the best of us all at one time or another.

"No need to apologize," I'd said, pressing down the ugly part of myself that sneered: *You big baby.*

At the time I'd thought my uncharitable bitterness toward my classmates was an isolated incident, brought on by stress or maybe skipping lunch. Alas, after the kidney debacle and failed extubation, it quickly became clear that this was not the case. As I passed NICU rooms with open-air cribs, I scowled at their pudgy newborn occupants. I snapped Simone's door shut at the sound of a crying baby, or a laughing nurse. Some babies, I thought, couldn't cry around the tubes in their throats; some people didn't FEEL like laughing. I was unfit for the public sphere, and on one of the rare occasions I ventured into it, was driven weepily out again when a pregnant woman—past her due date and straining the bounds of physics—had the gall to complain of discomfort.

I did not recognize the mean, covetous person I had become, with her miserly accountings of relative suffering. If I tended toward any extreme on the spectrum between self-pity and gratitude, it was usually as a result of my precocious ability to elevate thankfulness to pathology. In my role as World's Most Superstitious Atheist, mourning one's lot seemed an invitation to further disaster, and I secretly felt that mourning Ames would mean looking deep into the maw of the gift horse from which I'd snatched my daughter. I knew how pointless this exhausting relativism was, and usually I kept myself in check, recognizing that complaining is one of life's great pleasures and a basic human right. Knowing that someone, somewhere is starving or being dispatched via garroting makes it no less frustrating when you, personally, lock your keys in the car mid-thunderstorm, or shake up a perfect martini only to find you lack both olives and clean glasses, forcing you to quaff your gin from a ramekin. I was merely careful not to take that gin for granted, reminding myself that It—whatever "It" was—Could Always Be Worse.

Besides being utterly useless, self-pity breeds a bitterness that implies entitlement, as if you have been cheated out of something promised to you. This unreasonably affronted new me had subdued my humbler nature and locked her away in a trunk—where of course she remained, too polite to make a scene, insisting she found the lack of oxygen bracing. From time to time I could hear her discreet tapping, but it was muffled by the sounds of Simone's monitors and the laughing birth-center families I passed on the way to the NICU.

Our cultural mythology tells us that tragedy and adversity change people. A few are transformed into cautionary personifications of grief—Loss-Mess Monsters, I call them—the barren madwoman rocking a tattered doll in the asylum's corner, Heidi's fierce hermetic grandfather, alone on the Alp.

But more commonly, we see survivors take up yoga, giving up meat and gaining perspective. They leave high-powered but ultimately soulless careers, learn to smile at children who kick the backs of airplane seats, buy magnets endorsing the ever-controversial Laughter, Hope, and Living. They begin to take pleasure in small things, like collecting sea glass, or smelling the air after it rains, while lesser people mourn their ruined suede. They learn to pronounce Quinoa. They smile serenely, without showing their teeth. They staff soup kitchens and take in ancient, diseased shelter dogs so that the animals may die with dignity. I, myself, was going to become a Card Person.

But what if the crucible of tribulation revealed something else entirely? Something that lacked even the grand and sympathetic cast of a Madwoman or Hermit, a damning flaw of character that had till now been obscured by good fortune and politeness? Someone relayed to me a news story about a woman who gave birth prematurely on a train in India, her baby falling through the toilet to the tracks below and rescued, miraculously alive, days later. My response was to ask how far along the baby was, and when I heard 30 weeks, I *rolled my eyes,* as if his survival were nothing special, as if at *his* advanced gestation he ought to have been able to use his still attached umbilicus as a lasso to hop aboard the train's caboose.

What if, instead of a Tour de France win or passion for volunteering, I emerged from my trial with only deepened forehead wrinkles and the ability to resent the health of babies? What if all I gained was fear and exhaustion? What if I *was* changed—into someone I didn't particularly like?

One of the primary targets of my uncontrollable ire was the petite hospital chaplain who came around from time to time, her eyes limpid with sympathy. She had short, graying dark hair and wire-rimmed glasses, and wore a wee leather backpack that I found inexplicably infuriating. Why bother with a backpack that small? What could she possibly carry in there, besides maybe a lipstick and a few communion wafers? Even the way she walked—with a childish eagerness—irked me, and just the sight of her in the hallway made me swell with rage: *She'd better not come in here,* I'd think, narrowing my eyes from behind the door.

I wasn't sure what my problem was. The first time the chaplain visited— before the advent of my HULK SMASH! period—I wasn't angry at all, just impatient. She sat next to me and made small talk while my eyes leapt back and forth from the monitors. I tried to maintain the illusion of mannerly attention, but it was difficult once the exchange of pleasantries ended and I realized that what she really wanted to talk about was me. Back then, I struck myself as irrelevant; I answered questions about my wellbeing with information about Simone's medical condition. The chaplain, however, was insistent. "Journeys" and "paths" were mentioned, all of them mine. She steered a discussion of looming PDA surgery right back in my direction. Surgery on my baby! That must be hard, for me. How was I, anyway?

It was exasperating: *I* was peachy, it was my daughter who might not survive the week—couldn't she see that, based upon which of us was on the ventilator?

I became polite but suppressive, ready to get back to my monitor monitoring, and she left shortly after, having taken the hint. I bore her no ill will. I just didn't have time for anything as useless as self-reflection. My daughter's oxygen saturation wasn't going to watch itself!

The next time she came around, though, it was different, and I was curled on the couch like a cobra, ready to strike. I DARED her to mention "God's Plan," or "Finding Meaning"—in my head, at least. In reality I merely answered her questions with clipped monosyllables, constitutionally unable to be any ruder. If she wondered what had happened to the courteous if distracted girl she'd met a few weeks earlier, she didn't let on, though she also didn't linger. As I watched her leave, my nostrils flared. *Just try and come back, with your useless backpack and nods of understanding,* I thought. She understood nothing! Maybe she could bring the grief counselor with her next time—go ahead, lady, make my day. They thought they'd seen cold shoulders, but oh ho ho! I could ask after their children with all the warmth of a just-shaken martini.

My God, but I was unpleasant. That poor woman. What was it that made me want to run down the hall after her, shouting "Hey! Come see what I found in this foxhole?" I'd never had a problem with religious people before, but now the sight of a cross made my lip curl, like a guard dog, or Elvis. Maybe it was because so many of the websites I found by other preemie parents were awash with talk of miracles, and statements like "we weren't expecting Hortense until April, but God had other plans!" It felt like an affront, that anyone might believe that this conflagration of biological misfortune and terrible luck had been scheduled, and I was frustrated by the certainty these parents seemed to have that in the end, everything would work out for the best.

I was a mild sort of atheist, normally. I didn't have a *dis*belief so much as a lack of one. I'd seen no evidence to support the existence of a God, but it was plausible that knowledge of the transcendent might only be possible via transcendence—maybe in a vision, or a sudden deep certainty visited upon you in the produce section (*He is all around us!* you cry as you fall to your knees, clutching an avocado). I couldn't rule it out, though personally I viewed the question of God as irrelevant. Surely it was a waste of energy to worry about something wholly outside the world we had, which was worrisome enough as it was. Squabbling between religions struck me as about as useful as arguing about what color unicorns might be. Why not focus upon being kind to our corporeal, *earthly* companions and call it a day? I've heard the argument that only the threat of hell keeps us from anarchy, but I find that a little insulting, the idea that it isn't so much that kindness is *good* as that *it's the rule.* I don't trouble myself about commandments, and I have yet to kill a man just to watch him die. There are social contracts, and sensible evolutionary reasons for cooperation, but even leaving self-interest aside, can't we collectively agree not to be douchebags without pinning all of our good behavior on a higher power. It wasn't the belief in a higher power that bothered me, though. I believed in one, too: whatever combination of natural law and chance gave rise to things like the annoyances of menstruation and traffic jams. *Contingency* seems as good a word as any, the point being that we are acted upon by forces and events we cannot control. But contingency wasn't conscious. There was no plan, and no absolute good or necessity was implied simply by virtue of an event's occurrence.

What bothered me, especially after Ames died and Simone was born sick, was that some omnipotent paternalistic figure (whom I always pictured as played by Peter Lorre, cackling over the blueprints of a hapless human existence) had a reason for it all, that whether Simone lived or died, the outcome was essentially the same: *His Will Be Done.* Some babies were spared and others were not; some were miracles and others were "angels," and however painful we found the result of the divine calculator, we might as well make lemonade out of the lemons we'd been given for babies.

Because I am nothing if not contrary, however, it soothed me beyond measure when people prayed for Simone. Thanks to my website and a network of friends and family, my daughter was in the thoughts of people all over the world. What was there not to love about that? I didn't care who they were praying to; just the knowledge that her name was being spoken by a fierce and widespread contingent of supporters gave my comfort. I even prayed myself once, the day of the kidney incident. I said the Mi Sheberakh, a Jewish prayer for the ill that someone had sent me, and the part I liked best was at the end: *"The One will send her, speedily, a complete healing—healing of the soul and healing of the body—along with all the ill, among the people of Israel and all humankind, soon, speedily, without delay."* It was a pushy sort of prayer, a stern instruction, and it suited my mood. The one WILL send her! A *complete* healing! Soon, speedily, without delay! Enough was enough, already.

Twenty-Four

A second trial of CPAP was scheduled for a week after the first one. When I returned from getting a cup of tea that morning, Amber rushed to my side, grinning.

"Do you have a camera?" she asked, pulling me toward the isolette, where she stopped and pointed. "I found her like that."

I peered inside. Simone was asleep on her stomach, her arm bent and a hand by her face. The fingers on that hand were all curled into a fist, except for one. This particular finger was extended, in a gesture I hadn't figured I'd see from my daughter for at least a decade.

"I guess she heard about the extubation," I whispered.

It's true, Simone wasn't any more thrilled with the CPAP apparatus the second time around. She struggled, mightily, but eventually surrendered, and only after she'd become accustomed to the indignity of the hat was her ventilator tube removed. And when it was, she took one breath, and then another. She kept on breathing, while pressurized air whooshed up her nose to help keep her lungs inflated.

In order to prevent the air that was whooshing in from whooshing right back out again, her mouth hole had to be shut, either via a chin strap (which, unsurprisingly, she hated) or by plugging it up with a pacifier. My daughter may have failed to keep the prongs from being forced upon her, but if she was wounded by the ingloriousness of defeat, the pacifier quickly made up for it. It was still big for her mouth, but she masticated it voraciously, almost unhinging her tiny jaw, like a snake. Between the apparatus and the pacifier, almost none of her head was visible at all, but still I stole peeks at her all afternoon, marveling at the fact that she was breathing of her own volition. I sat typing jubilant updates to family, happier than I had been in a week, unbothered even by the faint sound of a baby crying down the hall.

Or... Wait a minute. I stopped typing and listened closely. It almost sounded like it was coming from—

I leapt up, and snatched the blanket from the isolette. It was! It was MY baby, crying! Her cry was hoarse from the irritation of the ventilator tube, but it was definitely Simone—I could see her mouth open in indignation, her arm groping toward the pacifier that had rolled to the edge of her bed. I reached in and obligingly replaced it, grinning like a simpleton. They say a mother abhors her baby's cry, and probably that is so, if she isn't hearing it for the first time after six long weeks of silence, but as it was I spent the waning daylight beaming whenever I heard that small, angry sound, popping up to pacify my baby at intervals that might have been annoyingly brief, under other circumstances. It was one of my better afternoons.

By the next morning, Simone had only forgotten to breathe once. One solitary apnea episode in more than 18 hours was precocious, and even the neonatologist seemed impressed.

"It's the mark of a mature central nervous system," he said, and I blushed prettily, feeling smug. That would teach some people to say things about certain babies "not doing well" and "failing extubation."

Not that Simone wouldn't be back on the ventilator by the end of the day. Her blood gases were uninspiring, and the CPAP pressure settings remained at the maximum. Sophisticated as she was, my daughter was still small and unathletic, and though she remembered both to inhale and exhale, she could do neither with sufficient gusto to clear carbon dioxide and keep her diminutive air sacs inflated.

Discussing this at rounds, I was encouraged not to be discouraged, which was highly unnecessary. Secretly, as they'd reintubated Simone after her first abortive attempt at respiration, I had wondered whether she would ever learn to breathe on her own. It seemed like she'd been on the ventilator for eons. What if she just never got the hang of it?

Now she obviously had, and so as far as I was concerned, the extubation had been a roaring success. She'd lasted only twenty minutes that first attempt, and this time she'd gone on nearly a day, and might have continued indefinitely had she possessed a few grams more of meat on her ribs. No one would fault an armless girl for failing the rope-climbing unit, and I felt the same principle applied to Simone's second CPAP trial. She'd taken every breath save one, and if her chest muscles were lacking the sinew to make them count, she remained blameless.

As a high school sophomore, my horror of team sports prompted me to choose weight lifting as my mandatory gym elective (no amount of grumbling would convince the administration of the oxymoronic nature of such a thing). I'd figured weightlifting would be less fraught with opportunities for humiliation, less fraught with chances to anger overly serious teammates, less...well less fraught all around. And it was, too. The class was made up of myself—all 95 pounds of me—and the wrestling team, and as there were few pieces of equipment I was burly enough to utilize, I kept to myself, spending my hour hoisting a small hand weight and doing dozens of crunches. By the end of the semester I had a truly formidable set of abdominal muscles and the ability, after much practice, to bench press the unadorned metal bar that others hung with weights. I also had my one and only satisfactory grade in gym class, because I could hardly be penalized for the inability to perform tasks for which I was physically unequipped.

I had a hair appointment scheduled that day, made weeks before. I'd planned to cancel if Simone was doing poorly, but under the circumstances I thought a celebratory outing was just the thing. It would be my first midday excursion from the NICU, and it was a lovely day for it. March in Minnesota isn't exactly balmy, but it is one of my favorite months nonetheless, and to me has an essential springness about it that is undiminished by its tendency to produce startling quantities of snow. By March, the old snow is melting and rushing noisily in the gutters, and when new snow comes, it doesn't overstay its welcome. The living things that sensibly abandoned us once our climate reached its uninhabitable nadir are returning again, robins hopping everywhere like living, breathing, red-breasted metaphors. The sun is shining longer and brighter, and as a population who has grown accustomed to blackness by 5:00, we become positively unhinged at its brilliance. Our winters are so cold they can quite literally kill you, and visiting Minnesota on a 45 degree day in March, you will see people in flip-flops, joyously discombobulated by the advent of temperance. For me, the start of spring that year was full of pathetic fallacy, and as I walked into the salon I felt like the cruel, dark season of death and hospitals was finally waving its snow-white flag of surrender.

In the waiting area I sipped tea and stared at the fire, energized and paralyzed at once. It was thrilling to be out in the world, amongst people speaking in regular voices, but I also fought the sort of sudden exhaustion you get when you stop to rest after a great effort. I thought, for the first time in a long while, of Ames. Seeing Simone's distinctly *distinct* personality made me wonder what his might have been like. Would he have been quiet? Cheerful? He'd been such an agreeable fetus.

My stylist emerged and led me back. She asked how I was, and whether my mother—also a client—was enjoying Switzerland. With a shock, I realized that the last time we'd been to see her was October, when my mother was visiting and I was still in the early, secret stages of a twin pregnancy.

"Well..." I began, reluctantly, "My mother got hit by a car in November, while she was crossing the street."

"Oh my God! Is she okay?"

"Um. Well, both of her legs were broken," (The stylist's mouth dropped in an expression of horror) "and she was in the hospital for about a month." (More horror!) "But she's recovering nicely, now," I assured her. "Your poor mom! Did you go over there, then?"

Oh dear.

"Well...no. I couldn't, because I was pregnant with twins." (Expression of joy!) "But the boy died at 22 weeks..." (Horror again!) "...and my little girl, Simone, was born about a month later, at the beginning of February, so she's still in the hospital." Watching it play out on the poor woman's face, I felt bad for subjecting her to our operatic tale of woe. I laughed. "It's been an eventful winter for our whole family, I guess."

Simone was being reintubated when I returned, I could tell because she was out of her isolette on a flat surface, surrounded by nurse, nurse practitioner, and respiratory therapist, all of whom looked up at me when I entered.

"You might want to step outside," someone said. I ignored them and put my coat away in the closet. Why were they always saying that? Hadn't they gotten the idea, by now, that I wasn't going anywhere? Especially for an intubation I'd known was coming, a procedure I'd seen twice already. It was too bad she hadn't managed to last two hours longer, to make an even 24 hours, I mused, and then I began to notice that something was wrong.

All of it, from my walking into the door to the end, must have taken only a few minutes, but time seemed to click by as slow and deliberate as a camera shutter in low light, each second stretched and held. The nurse was bagging my daughter at an unusually rapid rate, and the nurse practitioner had a look on her face that for a long moment I didn't recognize. With a jolt I realized it was fear, and at once saw Simone more clearly. She had a pale, bluish cast—floppy, like a rubber baby doll. My gaze flew to the monitor, and I could hear the blood pumping behind my ears and on through my temples. Oxygen saturation: 34. Was that even possible? Her heartrate was a 49, a flat, scrolling line replacing the series of peaks that would have represented breaths, had she been taking any. I heard the quick *whoosh whoosh whoosh* of the bellows under the nurse's hand, but still: 34. 36. 34.

"You should step outside," someone said again. Panic unfurled in me like one of those capsule sponges that bloom in water into shapes or animals. It filled my chest, a dinosaur, a moose of panic. *What the hell is going on here?* I wanted to demand, but I couldn't speak.

The nurse practitioner explained that her first try at intubation had failed, but because the paralytic drug they use in the process had already been given, Simone's chest was rigid, and the puffing of the bellows met with too much resistance to be effective. *I should run into the hall,* I thought. *Help!* I would scream, *Somebody help!* People would come running, except that I hadn't moved, and was only watching Simone's arm, the pretty color of a hydrangea, wobble as they worked over her.

So this is how it will happen, I thought. *This is it, right now, the moment my baby dies.* I felt the vertiginous rush that means I am going to faint, but I didn't faint. I started to cry. The nurse shook her head, her mouth thin.

"Should I call someone?" she asked.

"I just need to get that tube in," snapped the practitioner, and she began her second attempt, pulling Simone's head back roughly. 35, 34, silence, and that flat line, that dramatic crutch of television death scenes. The nurse is putting pressure on my baby's throat, and then the tube is in, and they connect the bellows and puff, puff, puff, puff.

"Her heart rate's coming up," the nurse said. It leapt to 78 beats a minute, and then up went her oxygen saturation, and in seconds, it was over, and the world slipped briskly back into focus. The respiratory therapist gathered supplies back into the red intubation box, the nurse cleared the used syringes and reconnected the ventilator, slipping my baby back into her hutch.

I kept my voice calm, and pretended there were no tears dripping onto my neck as I asked the practitioner sensible questions about oxygen deprivation and brain damage.

"Oh no," she assured me. The whole event had lasted less than ten minutes, according to the traitorous clock, its blank unconcerned face counting minutes with an incredible regularity. Everyone filed out, and I stood and held Simone's cold hand while she slept. Another nurse practitioner came in, and laid a hand on my arm, promising that nothing out of the ordinary had occurred. I knew this to be true. I reminded myself about fiberoptic scopes and tracheotomies. I'd seen these last performed with pens so often in fictional settings that I felt I could have done as much myself, with one of the assortment in my handbag.

When I was alone I leaned forward at the edge of the sink, thinking that this was when a glass of something potent ought to be pressed into my hand, for the shock. Brandy or scotch, which I would throw back with a gulp. There ought to be dogs roaming the NICU with casks around their necks, trotting into the room at moments like these. In Switzerland, there probably were such dogs.

My freshly pampered hair shone in the light above the mirror, and I wanted to vomit at the sight of it. It wreathed my head with culpability; the headlines flooded my brain unbidden—"*Foiled Again!: Baby's Death High Price to Pay for Subtle Highlights.*" I noticed then that my anger was absent. I couldn't remember when I'd last seen it, but I missed it once it was gone.

Twenty-Five

After all that waiting and seeing, Simone had another episode of kidney failure. Before the NICU I hadn't known such things happened in episodes—failure has such a *final* sound about it, you know—but nephrology appeared again, in the form of a woman who laughed when Simone objected to her examination and offered the opinion that my daughter would be trouble in her teen years. A hematologist came to call, and then the neonatology fellow arrived to sit next to me on the couch.

"We're going to start Simone on intravenous heparin," he told me. "Once we get to therapeutic levels, we'll switch to a form that can be given in shots, but until then, we will need to monitor her heparin levels several times a day."

It was all too obvious where *this* conversation was headed.

"You need to put in a central line," I sighed. Of course they could have used the *umbilical* line if it hadn't been pulled, but then if it hadn't, Simone wouldn't need the heparin in the first place.

As it happened, some nurse practitioner upstairs on the PICU was a genius with pediatric intrajugular lines, and this legendary venous seamstress came down and stitched a central line right into my baby's jugular. It had multiple ports and was secured with what looked alarmingly like plain black thread. It troubled me, given Simone's proclivity for toying with her various tubes and wires, and sure enough, her hand was drawn to it immediately. She slept holding the plastic tube curled in her fist, the other end *sewn into her goddamn jugular*. The jugular is not a vein to be trifled with, this much I knew. "Going for the jugular" is a fairly straightforward idiom, and I had no reason to doubt its medical accuracy.

"What if she tears it out?" I asked the nurse, eyes narrowed at my daughter as she moved a little in her sleep.

"It's stitched in there pretty good," came the blithe response. I wasn't sure if this was reassuring or not. "If she *does* pull it hard enough, it'll probably just slide right out."

"Of her *jugular*," I confirmed, with emphasis.

"Yup."

I mentally threw up my hands. It seemed clear my fury was gone for good, because otherwise I would have been fighting the urge to strangle someone with a length of endotracheal tubing. Instead, I just felt spent.

The next day, my mother arrived, cleared to fly at last, home for almost a month. The last time she'd seen me I was 11 weeks pregnant and beginning to show, both babies alive and on the inside. The last time I'd seen *her*, she could walk. Now she was on the sort of crutches one associates with the disabled, the kind with handles to hold and cuffs that wrap in a half-moon around your wrists. In Europe these are the standard, but as they watched my mother make her hobbling way down the NICU hallway, nurses and doctors gave her the encouraging smile afforded only the brave and retarded.

"People think you're a cripple," I said after I'd launched myself at her for a hug.

She brandished one of her supports. "I can't imagine what gave them THAT idea."

"No, I mean because of the wonky crutches."

My mother looked at a nearby nurse, who smiled warmly at her.

"They probably think I had polio."

"You should make the most of this," I said, wisely.

It was hard for my mother to make her way across the room, even with her crutches. It was hard for me to see how hard it was. She arrived beside Simone and I whipped off the isolette cover, proudly.

"She's so tiny!"

"Not really," I said, with the air of one not easily impressed. "She's pretty big, now, compared to how she *was*."

"*Hellooo!*" my mother cooed, not at me. I hadn't been sure how my mother would feel about being a grandmother, being young yet, and far more vibrant and social than I had ever been, myself. From the time Simone was born, however, my mother had all but appropriated her as her own baby. And now I might have been a lamp or curtain for all the chance I had of drawing her attention from my daughter.

"I'm your *Nani,*" she whispered, close to a porthole. She began to sing to Simone through the Plexiglas. Simone, for her part, was fast asleep.

"She likes me," my mother said with confidence, stepping back and looking satisfied. "I can tell."

That night, we attended a Pink Martini concert with friends. Pink Martini's music is a collage of kitsch and sweeping orchestral arrangement, the voice of their confidently swaying chanteuse accompanied by a confounding variety of instruments, one of which appeared to be a large dried squash. They have a song called "Hang on Little Tomato," which I sang to Simone often when she was tiny and I wanted her to do just that.

Pink Martini ended the set with their customary send-off, "Brazil," and an impromptu conga line sprang up, snaking around the theater to the syncopated maracas, horns bright and golden in the background. My mother and I kept our seats—she because crutches tend to curtail one's congadancing, and I because of a congenitally high level of inhibition. But with the singer's voice soaring and the samba samba-ing, with my mother home and Simone still alive, with even middle-aged wearers of khaki dancing in the aisles while holding the hips of strangers, I felt caught up and overcome. I smiled with damp eyes and clapped along, my heart beating a joyous, Latin percussion.

Of all the things people said to me while Simone was in the hospital, the one I hated the most was *I could never.* "I don't know *how* you do it," they'd say, "I could *never!*"

"I think I'd die," some asserted in a wondering tone, as if they'd just discovered this in a rummage through their innermost souls. "I think I would *die* if I had to see my baby like that, in a hospital. We took him to the *emergency room,* once, with awful croup, and *that* just about killed me."

"You are handling this so well," another said, "I could *never.* I wouldn't be able to *function!*"

People who say *I could never* think they are commenting upon your strength and bravery, but are in fact doing just the opposite. "Better you than me," they are saying. *I could never* is an alchemy that transforms your situation into a commentary on the depth of the *speaker's* feelings—as contrasted with the shallowness of your own. Right? Because when someone says *I could never stand to see my baby in the NICU,* the unspoken corollary is *because I love him so much.* Not like *you,* a woman untroubled by such intense maternal affection. *I could never* is *If you really cared, like I do, you couldn't go on.* Perhaps asserting its unmanageability helps create the illusion of distance from whatever terrible thing you—such foresight, to have a heart constructed cleverly of steel!—are enduring so enduringly. What do they think would happen, if such tragedy were visited upon a living, bleeding mortal, like them? Maybe that they'd roam the town in their pajamas, counting backwards by sevens. Maybe that they'd simply be extinguished, in a puff of sorrowful smoke.

When I was at my angriest, *I could never* inspired a snappish reply.

"Well," I'd say, with a tight smile, "I didn't really have a choice." I would have liked to scream it at them. I wasn't trying to win admiration for my feats of derring do. The days kept coming, and my heart kept beating. Was there an alternative of which I hadn't been made aware?

The worst part of *I could never* is that it's a lie. Even two years later I still hear it, when I talk about Simone's early days, and now my response is always the same blunt statement of fact. *You could so,* I say. Yes. And you would.

215

Through the long month of March, amid kidney crises and CPAP trials and blind unreasonable fury, I woke in the mornings and drove to the hospital. When I was able, I held Simone against my skin, and sang round after round of "Hush-a-bye, There's a Fly." I told stories featuring Mitten, the goat who stood sentry near her incubator. In another life Mitten lived high on a Swiss Alp with Mother Goat, venturing forth for a series of adventures. There was *Mitten Goes to School!* and *Mitten at Sea!* and *Ooh La La: Mitten in Paris!* Simone rolled her eyes upward in search of my voice, and I tried to explain that she couldn't see through the top of her skull, and there was no point in trying.

"Eyes don't work that way," I told her. "You can only use them to look out through those holes in front." I stroked the down that still grew upon her shoulders. Occasionally, while I held my baby as if she were an embryonic kangaroo, Scott sat next to us reading *Corduroy* aloud. Sometimes I read it to Simone alone, sitting next to her isolette with the portholes open.

My website was receiving visitors from an unfamiliar address, and one morning I followed them back to a message board where strangers were discussing my baby, comparing her to a severed dog's head once kept alive by Russian scientists. It was child abuse, they said; I had bucked nature in my zeal to reproduce, and as a result had visited unimaginable suffering upon a baby who would either soon die or wish she had. I almost envied them their certainty regarding my daughter's medical condition, however misinformed: according to them, Simone was on a "blood circulator," kept alive by doctors only because of my mad insistence upon offspring, as lighting seared the air behind the hospital's tower and I tapped my fingers in insane glee. Laughable as their vitriol ought to have been, I wasn't laughing. I sat in front of the computer for over an hour, unable to look away, crushed. I was enervated with sorrow and shame for all the cruelty now and to come in the future, heaped upon my lovely, blameless daughter. Someday she'd be teased, she'd have her heart broken, she'd lose a beloved pet—all the *awful* firsts, far less frequently anthologized than first word or first step or first day of school. I hated knowing they were out there, waiting for her.

Later, at the hospital, I sat, composing a response to Simone's detractors with a biting, languid flippancy I did not feel. In her incubator, Simone rose into view, doing a full push-up on her spindly arms, bearing her own weight with a strength that, technically, she should not have possessed. This was common among preemies, this slightly unsettling brawn. Simone could do a push-up while on a ventilator while I wasn't sure I could manage one even on my knees. *Take note,* I told myself, watching her.

The next week, when they removed Simone's ventilator tube for her third trial of extubation, it stayed out.

"I think she's going to make it this time," said Simone's night nurse, Carrie, on the second full day of NO VENTILATOR.

"Really?" I'd asked, guarded.

"Really."

I didn't dare believe her, and when I called that night and heard Simone had left even CPAP behind, I was as shocked as if this hadn't been the plan all along. Respiratory therapy appeared to retrieve the ventilator from its precautionary station in the corner out of her room, and we were shedding equipment by the day. Simone's feeding tube was moved to her nose to leave her mouth unobstructed, and after that, all of her medications were administered through that tube, via syringe. Thus the last IV pump was silenced with the end of the heparin drip, the day after Simone was extubated. Each time a nurse stopped by to reappropriate one of the unused pumps for a newer, needier baby, I remembered the full beeping wall we'd had running on admission.

Simone's face was clear now except for the slender feeding tube taped toward her cheek and the oxygen cannula snaking under her nose and around the sides, secured at her cheekbones by something like round Band-Aids with sticky flaps to hold the tubing in place. The tubing was transparent, and with such a discreet—almost dainty!—oxygen conduit, Simone was no more conspicuous than any elderly woman with emphysema. She looked around curiously and stuck out her tongue; she sucked on a pacifier and yawned. Her movements were losing some of the jerkiness of earlier weeks, when she'd been able to initiate action but not control it, sending limbs flying precipitously skyward. Now she raised a deliberate arm to tangle her fingers in the monitor wires, worrying at her remaining tethers like the edge of a favorite blanket. She was a three-pound kewpie doll, all impish sideways glances and giant, wide-roaming eyes. There was a mischievous dimpling of her rounding face. All at once she was more baby than fetus, an ordinary human baby who just happened to reside in a small Plexiglas box.

CHAPTER

Twenty-Six

Here is where the carousel of time lurches back to life, with an escalating musical wheeze. Having been stretched to its limit, my perception of time's passage snaps smartly back again, contracting upon itself in reflex. A rather overwrought way of stating the obvious: that time flies when you're having fun—or whatever facsimile is available in the NICU—and when you're not, it doesn't.

I would have testified under oath that Simone spent three-quarters of our hospital time on the ventilator, in a plodding, fearful darkness. I remember it that way, and the remaining portion as a brief and giddy whirl. Alas my calendar, which has no reason to lie, informs me that Simone was on the ventilator for seven weeks, only a few days more than half her total NICU stay. I suppose my misremembering stems from the contrast between the two periods, not just in mood but environment: could the story have occurred along a prettier literary timeline? My pregnancy swanned along at an imperceptible downward slope until the darkest days of winter, when panic and tragedy beset me until after Simone was born, her relapsing gradual improvement mirroring the weather's relapsing gradual thaw. My daughter shed the heavy apparel of winter—ventilators and bulky CPAP headpieces—for something lighter, and a few days after her move to the cannula it was April, and spring had enthusiastically sprung. Less than two weeks into our new era, Simone would be transferred to an unusually spacious and airy room at the end of the hallway, providing further dramatic definition. This room, you see, had *windows*. They looked out upon a sidewalk behind the hospital, where nurses clustered for cigarettes alongside trucks and Dumpsters, but I didn't care. Now that Simone was getting older she no longer required continuous twilight, and the shades were opened for hours at a time, letting in swaths of cheerful sunshine.

Scott and I were moving too: the naked wrestlers had been evicted, and we were ascending to the top floor to take their place. When our landlord first offered the apartment—eager, probably, to avoid future noise complaints should he inadvertently rent the spot to nocturnal amateur bowling-ball jugglers—I declined. The wrestlers had lived in our building's last unremodeled unit, and I couldn't relinquish my clawfoot tub and granite countertops for mysteriously-stained red and white tile. Instead our landlord, who'd had a daughter in the NICU himself, offered to gut and refinish the offending rooms in time for Simone's anticipated homecoming. It seemed fitting to have a fresh start, and I heard the hopeful sounds of construction starting up as I dressed in the mornings—which I was beginning to do with less apathy. My mother and I had undertaken post-tragedy makeovers that entailed an extraordinary amount of shopping. My favorite purchase was a pair of orange patent flats, embellished with nautical rope that knotted in front. The loose ends of the knot were capped with gold tips, which made a satisfying clacking as they flapped against my toes. These shoes belonged dangling over bow or stern or aft, atop some sailing craft of the mid-1960s, on feet attached to a Tippy or Babs. Stepping down the hall on their nubbly rubber soles, it was impossible not to feel jaunty, even in a hospital—this was the footwear of an optimist. My mother was home and walking better all the time, and in the evenings we went out for long dinners with multiple courses and wine pairings, or met my brother for drinks at the St. Paul Hotel, near the hospital, where I drank sidecars and ate lobster dip and composed limericks on napkins. Ask anyone who has been depressed, or who has worked as a miner. Ask anyone who has endured a northern winter or a fall down a well, and they will tell you: the light is never brighter than after a sustained period of darkness.

"You might want to start bringing in some of Simone's clothes," a nurse mentioned a few days after the final extubation.

"Sure!" I said. "I'll do that!"

When she'd gone, I turned back to my laptop and typed a quick email to my mother. It looked like we had some more shopping to do, seeing as Simone didn't technically *have* any clothes.

Off the ventilator, babies could begin the transition to an open crib, and without the isolette's tropical climate control they'd need to rely upon more conventional methods of keeping warm—like pants. Well, not pants, specifically: they didn't make any that could be induced to fit such a small baby, but at almost three-and-a-half pounds, Simone was big enough for gowns, and teensy unitards with the sleeves rolled up. A preemie-sized onesie would swim on her like a caftan, but it was serviceable, and if baby socks came up to her knees, well, they'd keep her calves from getting chilly.

The nurses had looked at me askance when I denied any immediate plans to set up a nursery, and they all seemed to assume that I had stockpiles of dresses and sleepers and hats. I'm not sure when they thought I might have acquired these things: I hadn't stayed pregnant long enough for a baby shower, and with Simone's tenuous condition the last thing I'd needed was a bunch of miniaturized sweaters that I might have to return after her funeral, sobbing in front of some teenager at the customer service counter. But with the go-ahead from a medical professional, I dove with zeal into the task of outfitting my baby in polka dots and embroidered whales and garments with snaps to allow for the passage of monitor wires. My mother and I cut a wide swath through various baby stores, combing them for the smallest sizes. Most of what we bought bore tags reading "under seven pounds," which certainly applied to Simone, and would continue to apply to her until she doubled in size. I washed the lot with baby detergent and brought it in, filling a drawer with brightly hued baby clothes, exciting the nurses. They were more excited than I was, managing to give the impression that this is why they'd taken up the profession in the first place. I suppose dressing babies in cunning outfits is understandably preferable to sticking them with needles or watching them die.

Four days into April, my maternity leave ended. I'd sort of forgotten I was still employed, until the week before, when my friend Becky forwarded the email she'd received about my expected return: "Welcome Back Alexa!" read the subject line. There was no doubt that once Simone came home I would be staying there with her—prematurity left her lungs too vulnerable for daycare—but opaque benefit policies demanded I return for two weeks post-leave. The idea of walking past my coworkers and sitting at a desk amongst those who knew what had happened, or had at least heard the gist via office gossip, made me lightheaded and queasy. I was granted clemency the day before my scheduled return, but my relief was overshadowed by my mother's departure for Switzerland. I didn't want her to leave, but I grudgingly abetted her, administering her pre-flight heparin shot, meant to keep clots from developing around the pins in her legs.

"That was almost painless!" she marveled, when I was finished, "You're an excellent nurse."

"It's just practice," I said modestly, recapping the syringe. She rode next to me on the way to the airport with tears in her eyes, while I kept up a reassuring banter, feeling helpless and clumsy. Emotional displays were not really our family's bag, and I tried, awkwardly, to offer comfort as I dropped her at the terminal with her luggage. Then I drove away, having a little emotional display of my own.

When I arrived at the NICU the next morning, Simone was dressed for the first time in a striped pink gown and matching socks. We were still in our windowless room, and its dimness made most photos blurry, but I took dozens that day. I couldn't get over the sight of her. She looked bigger, and not just because the clothes were ill-fitting—I think it was the mere fact of clothes that did it. She didn't look sick, suddenly. She looked like a real baby.

Simone turned two months old the day of her first eye exam, which was the most disturbing procedure I'd witnessed in the unit thus far. They usually did it early in the morning when parents weren't around, for just that reason. Even the nurses admitted they could barely stand to watch, and suggested this might be one thing I ought to sit out. Of course I refused, so I was there when the pediatric ophthalmologist came around, a kind, soft-spoken woman who proceeded to prop my daughter's eyelids open with what looked like spiders made from bent paperclips. Simone was swaddled and restrained, her eyes widened by the metal prongs, looking like something thought up by the Marquis de Sade's less conventional cousin, the one the Marquis never invited to Christmas Dinner because he was into some truly sick shit. The ophthalmologist's assistant handed her a headset with an eyepiece, through which she peered while prodding Simone's naked eyeball with a Q-tip. Each time the ophthalmologist touched her eye, Simone let out a sound like a threatened cat, an other-worldly squalling that had me digging my nails into my crossed arms.

The rest of Simone's two-month festivities involved her first immunizations and testing positive for MRSA. MRSA is the infection you always hear about on the news, when some hapless youth gets scraped up on the football field and dies of sepsis three days later. It's our punishment, as a species, for gulping antibiotics at the faintest suggestion of discomfort, with no thought for natural selection, or what our symptoms are trying to accomplish. Fever isn't an agent of spite, for instance—it has a purpose, and is quite useful, within reason. I would think the body's natural defense systems must get fed up, after a time, of being interfered with via cold medicine. I wouldn't blame them for staging a strike: *Fine, hotshot,* they'd say the next time illness struck, *YOU deal with it.*

Simone wasn't actually infected with MRSA, merely "colonized," which meant a MRSA collective was squatting in her mucous membranes: they'd diagnosed her with a Q-tip to the nostril. Harboring a MRSA colony isn't dangerous unless you have a sore or cut by which it can enter your bloodstream, but infection kills in the NICU, and knowing that deadly bacteria were casing the joint—the joint being *my baby*—unsettled me. Because of the colonization, there was an isolation cart outside her room, and all medical personnel had to don protective gowns and masks before entering. It made sense, but was a little insulting, especially considering she'd gotten the MRSA from the hospital in the first place. Glass houses, and Let He Who Is Without Sin, and all that.

The following day, I learned that Simone's eye exam had shown the early stages of Retinopathy of Prematurity, a side effect of the supplemental oxygen that saved her life. Like the MRSA, it was nothing to worry about, *unless,* and she'd be monitored to make sure it resolved on its own instead of worsening. But these two unknowns conspired to exhaust me.

"When will I feel less like every moment with Simone could be my last?" I wrote, *"Will I ever be able to take her, just a little tiny bit, in the happiest possible way, for granted?"*

I asked this question of her nurse, Maura. Well, what I actually asked was whether we could, at last, count on taking our baby home alive. It seemed a safe bet at that point, but I needed to hear it from a medical professional. Simone was no longer in critical condition, she was off the ventilator, off CPAP, off her IVs. Aside from learning to take feedings by mouth, she had no other major hurdles to clear—the rest was a matter of degrees. Less oxygen, more weight, fewer medications.

Maura sighed.

"We had a little boy not long ago who was all ready for discharge. He was healthy—he wasn't even born all that early, compared to a lot of babies, here." She shook her head, shutting a drawer of Simone's supply cart. "And then the day before he was scheduled to go home, he got an infection. And died."

I gaped at her. I'd always valued honesty, but in this case, a simple "no" would have sufficed.

Happily, Simone seemed undeterred by the capricious nature of fate, and a few days later she was transferred to a crib, and on down the hall to her new room—out in the air at last, like the fat hallway baby we'd seen so long before. Her transition was unusually rapid, as her isolette had been set at the lowest temperature for some time. My daughter's natural thermostat consistently hovered between "Bahamian paradise" and "Lava, molten," and I hold her responsible for my lack of ability to feel cold while she was in the womb. The first day I came in and found her in a crib—open at the top, as cribs are—was surreal. She was swaddled into a bundle of blanket, licking her lips and looking around expectantly, as it was nearly time for a meal. I could simply reach out my hand and touch her, which I did—after disinfecting, of course—half expecting to run up against an invisible wall, something only discernible by mimes. It was weeks before I stopped startling every time I walked into the room and saw her lying there, awake and unguarded. She looked so vulnerable! Was it...*wise* to leave a baby exposed like that, alone in a room with dangerous equipment? What if she managed to flop over the edge and hang herself by the oxygen cord? What about thieves? Had they thought about thieves?

She was wearing a hat, that first day, but we would soon learn that her natural furnace was so fierce that it must be allowed to vent through the top of her head, or she would develop a fever. She once got a septic workup because an unfamiliar nurse, who didn't know any better, put her in a hat—it is hospital policy to keep all crib-dwelling babies hatted, particularly preemies, who are bundled within an inch of their lives to compensate for their lack of body fat. By the time I arrived that morning, blood had already been sent for culture, and I removed the offending headpiece and cooled my flushed, listless baby with washcloths soaked in cold water, explaining that there was nothing wrong with Simone that bareheadedness wouldn't cure. The nurse thought this was highly unnatural.

Simone's first bath, the day after she was moved to a crib, was conducted in a square bucket the size of a sheet of paper. It would have held a rotisserie chicken snugly, yet for my daughter the tub was luxuriously large, big enough for a duo of preemies in a romantic mood. We filled the bucket with warm water and baby wash, and—after plucking off her monitor leads—slid Simone into the bubbles. Carrie held her upright in one hand while I washed her slippery little limbs with a washcloth. Simone seemed delighted by the experience—after more than two months of a life spent bath-less, it must have felt good to be clean—but I doubt she enjoyed it half as much as I did. After she was dried with heated towels and dressed, I brushed her thin tuft of hair with a doll's comb, laughing aloud with uncontainable merriment.

"I don't think I've had this much fun in...well, *ever*," I admitted to Carrie. We returned Simone to her crib, and I sat on the couch watching her, getting up every minute or two to pet her arm or scratch her fat belly, just because I could. *My god!* I thought, electrified with amazement, *I have a BABY!*

Scott was peeved at having missed Simone's first bath, and made me promise we would schedule the next one for a day he didn't work. He'd held her for the first time the week before, while she was bundled securely in a hospital blanket. Holding her was simpler with no ventilator to disconnect, and now that Simone had made her way from death's door to its driveway, his fear of accidentally enacting one of *Of Mice and Men*'s less savory chapters seemed to have abated.

The next week at bath time he gamely took Carrie's place holding Simone in the water.

"She's too slippery!" he said after a minute or two, a note of panic in his voice. I took over and he assumed the role of Washer in my stead. I laughed at him as we switched, but stopped pretty much as soon as I had my daughter's eely back in my hand. Scott was right: she *was* too slippery, like a bar of soap coated in oil, a bar of soap that was moving. But we managed not to drown her, and afterwards Scott talked to Simone while I grinned in the background. We had given our baby a bath. We felt like a family.

One morning as I rounded the corner to our hallway I heard an unmistakeable chugging, and tasted metal on my tongue. It was THE OSCILLATOR, and even though I knew it wasn't in Simone's room I hurried to her, my heart making sickening leaps. As I passed the room with THE OSCILLATOR I looked inside. A woman was crying, while the neonatologist made explaining motions with one hand, holding a chart in the other. Outside the room was a man with black brimmed hat and long side curls, talking on the phone. Was it her husband? Her rabbi? I felt ill the rest of the day, the sound of THE OSCILLATOR snaking down the hall to where I sat with Simone.

I saw the crying woman a few more times, in the hallway or talking to doctors, the somber figure of her rabbi/husband often present as well. I even caught a glimpse of her baby, who was bigger than I had expected. A few days later, THE OSCILLATOR was gone, and so were they. I didn't ask what had happened. I didn't want to know.

Twenty-Seven

"What's that?" I asked, looking at Simone's chest X-ray. It was mid April, and by then her chest X-rays were rarely a cause for concern. Mostly they just showed whether she needed more of the diuretic that helped relieve the fluid burden on her lungs. But this time I pointed to a thin white line across part of her chest. It looked like a tube—had she been lying on one when the X-ray was taken?

"Those are rib fractures," Amber said, blithely.

"Excuse me?" I asked, aghast, "Just when did she break her *ribs*?" Was there a NICU Fight Club of which I was unaware? Had she been in a rumble? Probably it was the gigantic baby down the hall. My mother and I had first noticed him the day she left, and we both startled at the sight of him, hulking in a bassinet with a shock of obscenely thick black hair. He looked about fifteen years old, that baby, and mean. He looked like a bully. He wasn't even on oxygen, and so could have easily leapt from his bed and crawled down the hall, after hours.

"The fractures are because of her Osteopenia," Amber explained, pointing to a photocopied fact sheet taped to the cupboard. I hadn't paid much attention to the sheet, which outlined the exercises performed twice a week by Simone's physical therapist, a boundlessly cheerful, compactly-built woman with two first names. The sheet mentioned that Simone's therapy was due to "Osteopenia of Prematurity," a demineralizing of the bones due to lack of vitamins and minerals and such which I'd known was common to babies born at her gestation. But I hadn't known that it resulted in honest-to-god *fractures*. I'd never had a broken bone, myself—thanks to years of avoiding physical activity and proximity to sports-related projectiles—yet my daughter, who wasn't even due to be born yet, already had two.

It was another reminder that, while she might eventually look like an ordinary baby on the outside, on the inside she would be forever marked by her unorthodox venue of development. Maybe this is why I took such comfort in the fact that in at least one area, Simone was undeniably precocious.

As soon as she'd made her way to a cannula, I'd been encouraged to "put her to breast." No one expected her to do any actual *feeding;* rather, she'd get the lay of the land, so to speak, and maybe begin to develop gustatory interest in my nipples. Actually, she'd done this almost from the start, wiggling her head little by little in their direction during our kangaroo time. I'd been instructed to keep her from getting too fresh with me—she could choke; she wasn't ready—but my baby was like a truffle pig. If there was food nearby, she was damn well going to find it. I bought one of those semicircular breastfeeding pillows, and the first time I propped Simone atop it and held her head near my bosom, she lurched forward and latched on, sucking away. The nurse gasped and pulled her away, getting herself slapped in the process. Simone was opening and closing her mouth, determined. She'd *known* I had food hidden in there!

There was a hurried conference between the nurse and a lactation consultant, and it was determined that I could let Simone drink a bit, as long as she didn't seem to be choking. I was given a floppy silicone sombrero for my nipple to wear, which made it easier for Simone to get the whole thing in her mouth. The Milk Hat, as we called it, also slowed the flow via four small holes in its tip. I popped it on and let Simone at it, and she drank with gusto for ten minutes before falling into a deep sleep.

Eating and digestion are often a trial for preemies, but for Simone, nothing came more naturally. When they pulled back on her feeding tube before a meal to check for residual undigested food, there never was any. *Waste not, want not,* was her motto. Her feeds were stopped from time to time because of medication interactions, but never because she stopped tolerating them. In fact, she greeted every increase in volume with gusto. The angriest I have ever seen my daughter, *to this day,* is when she was weaned from a feeding every two hours to one every three. She gave us a 20-minute grace period, and when it became clear that food was not forthcoming, she flew into as much of a rage as a 2.5 pound baby in an isolette can muster. She nearly extubated herself, becoming so agitated that she had to be given a dose of Ativan. I understood, because of The Sausage Incident, and could hardly blame her for being indignant. You only have so much to look forward to in the hospital, and meals loom large in your day. It took her a week to adjust to the new order of things, and even then, WOE BETIDE the nurse who was late with a feeding.

Within a week of her first lunch at my bosom, Simone was taking full feedings there. She'd become a sort of NICU legend, nurses and lactation consultants stopping by to marvel at the Little Preemie Who Could (Breastfeed). I used the "football hold," (which came naturally to me despite having never held an actual football), palming Simone's head with her legs at my elbow. She gulped and suckled, smacking at my breast to speed up supply. I particularly liked when she took my nipple in her mouth and shook it fiercely, as if to break its neck. I laughed then, and again when she fell back drunkenly against the cushion with her eyes glazed, milk dribbling from her chin. I'd hold her against my shoulder and rub her back firmly until she burped, and then I'd watch her sleep for a while before returning her to the crib and lowering the windowshade. It's work, breastfeeding—for the baby I mean—and after taking one meal that way she'd sleep through her next one entirely as the syringe pump delivered it through her feeding tube.

The one problem that cropped up was reflux, severe enough to cause her to stop breathing, or to choke toward the end of a feeding, turning blue and limp while a nurse rushed in to sit her upright and rub her roughly. Like everything else about her, Simone's esophageal sphincter—or food anus—was immature, lacking the muscle tone to keep what went down from coming back up. We didn't see the effects of this immaturity until Simone started getting full feeds of milk at volumes large enough to stretch her tiny stomach. It started back in the old room, when I'd hold her while her tube feeding was delivered, and noticed that toward the end she'd writhe and arch while her oxygen saturation dropped, having deep spells of apnea during which her heart rate fell like an anvil. When your baby has only finally learned to breathe, it is nerve-racking to see her refrain from utilizing that hard-won knowledge, and suddenly the ventilator's absence seemed foolhardy, like engaging in respiratory trapeze without a net. Once we'd started breastfeeding Simone would do her stunt on my lap, alarms sounding as her lips turned a gothic purple. I tipped her up and a nurse strode in, lifting Simone's chin while I spoke to her sharply.

"Take a breath!" I instructed, smacking at her back. She looked at me as the nurse pinched her legs, and at what seemed the last possible moment, she breathed again. Each time I felt certain that years were being shaved from my life, and thought it was a shame that the time I was losing would be subtracted from the end—a peaceful time, probably, with no floppy, choking babies to resuscitate. But I was told that this particular kind of not-breathing was purposeful—in fact a sign of cleverness. When milk rose mutinously in her throat, Simone was taking action to prevent the liquid from being aspirated into her lungs.

"She's protecting her airway," the nurses assured me. While I applauded my daughter for being proactive, "protecting her airway" also meant "shutting it down," and the end result was a baby the color of the Atlantic on a rainy day.

Pacifiers after meals helped keep the gorge from rising, and when she began crying twenty minutes before each feeding she was started on Prevacid, which kept acid from her empty stomach from burning her throat. Her crib mattress was raised at one end, and she slept at a near 45-degree angle, swaddled and strapped into a teddy-bear printed papoose that tied to the crib slats. The papoose was called a "Danny Sling," and I imagined its namesake as a tragic figure who had choked to death on his own emesis, an infantile Jimi Hendrix. We'd have to use a Danny Sling at home until Simone outgrew her reflux.

Reflux aside, I was growing more confident by the day. I fetched her pacifier and changed her cannula, and as always I changed diapers and took temperatures. I silenced the occasional alarm for oxygen dips and reflux spells when the nurses couldn't get to it in time, and my startle reflex was slowly returning to my previous level of sensitivity: somewhere above mugging victim, but below Vietnam vet. With Simone tethered only by her oxygen cannula and the monitor wires, I could even extract her from the crib myself, though at first I was reluctant to do so. It seems a simple affair, but it is easy to get tangled up and find yourself holding a baby with not enough leash to make it to the couch. Soon, however, I was juggling tubes and leads like a pro, swaddling and unswaddling, plucking Simone from her crib when she cried or even when she didn't, just so I could hold her on my shoulder and gaze at her sleepy face. Unfamiliar nurses seemed startled by this, and remarked upon how comfortable I was "handling" her. I'd lean over her while she slept and stroke her forehead free of the worried lines there. When she was on her stomach or side I'd stand next to her face and listen to the sound she made—a perfect imitation of a slowly opening door in an old, creaky house. I could probably have recorded the noise and sold it for use on an album of haunted house effects, but instead I videotaped it. We took a lot of grainy videos, then, and in the best of them Simone is asleep on my shoulder, the camera focused on her face and open, softly snoring mouth. She wakes up little by little, eyes open a bit then closed again, and I say something— "Hi there, sweetie!"—and she smiles for the very first time, eyes still closed, at the sound of my voice. I must have watched that 15 second clip 1500 times. I watch it still.

Simone's nurses urged us to buy a car seat, if we hadn't already (go on, guess). Buying a car seat is significant in the NICU, because the Car Seat Test is one of the final steps before discharge. The position a baby assumes in a car seat—folded at the waist, legs slanted up—is notorious for causing apnea. Even in term babies, it smooshes the contents of the stomach unwholesomely throatward, and allows floppy infant heads to tip forward onto their chests, compressing their airways. Before the NICU sends a baby off, they strap her into a car seat in a laboratory, monitoring her for an hour or so, until they are satisfied that she isn't likely to expire on the ride from hospital to home. Wouldn't *that* be something, after all.

So I ordered a car seat, searching out a brand safe for babies as small as five pounds; though Simone was still a pound shy, I felt certain she'd fatten up by discharge. I was beginning to be able to say the word "Discharge" without attaching air quotes with my tone. One of Simone's nurse practitioners, getting ready to leave on a three-week vacation, called me at home: she wanted to say goodbye, because chances were we'd be gone by the time she returned. Simone's eye problems were resolving, and after treatment, her MRSA tests were negative. She made it from high-flow nasal cannula to standard, the sort we could deliver at home, and her oxygen was turned slowly down, until it rested on the lowest setting.

The morning after it got there, I went in late, after running an errand I no longer remember. Having apparently failed to absorb any wisdom from past experience, I had forgone my check-in call the night before, and arrived to find that all hell had once again broken loose. A nurse and a nursing student—both about fifteen years old—greeted me with the news that Simone had netted a septic workup after a night featuring seven spells of apnea, one so severe that she'd had to be manually bagged. I felt lightheaded and short of breath, and wondered whether I might need to be manually bagged as well. Simone almost never forgot to breathe, she knew better, and she'd never needed such drastic measures to bring her out of a spell. Seven in a night was unprecedented, and she'd been switched back to the high-flow nasal cannula. I heard the nurse, who'd moved back outside to make a phone call, say "She's here now," and realized she was talking about *me*, the lazy mother who'd rolled in with the morning half gone.

She'd been talking to Simone's nurse practitioner, one I'd never met before, who arrived a few minutes later. She was tall and brusque, with bold glasses and a large nubbly sweater over her scrubs. She was a little show-offy, seeming to take pleasure in her use of jargon. My usual stoicism had fled. Instead I stood gaping as she opined that Simone could have an infection, OR the spells could be a sign that she had tired from her two days off high-flow, and had failed her trial of the regular cannula. Was everything a *trial* with these people?

"You should be prepared to hear about the possibility of a tracheostomy if we can't get her off the high-flow. We talked about this at rounds and I said 'When I talk to Simone's mom, I'm going to use the T-word,' and Dr. G said 'If you don't, I will,' so I'm just telling you outright, so that you can be prepared."

I sputtered something. I think it came out *I don't understand.* A tracheostomy meant a hole in my daughter's throat, which would be attached to a portable ventilator. There is only a slender window of time during which babies can acquire the ability to coordinate the suck-swallow-breathe dance needed to eat. I knew if a baby was still on a ventilator at that time, they'd be given a trach so that their mouth was free to learn those important developmental skills. But I'd forgotten to worry about this: Simone had been off the ventilator for two weeks. I knew she had to be on regular nasal cannula to be sent home (there is no home version of CPAP or high-flow), but this seemed extreme. The day before, she'd been almost off oxygen entirely. Who WAS this woman?

Whoever she was, she was still talking.

"Her lungs don't look that bad on X-ray, so I'm thinking it may be a floppy airway." She made a flapping, windshield-wiper motion with her hands. "I'm thinking we should schedule a bronchoscopy for next week, to get a look in there. Tracheomalacia—that's a floppy airway—happens a lot in preemies." She flipped through Simone's chart. "Another thing I noticed is that her weight seems to have plateaued. Here, let me show you."

I followed her dumbly outside to the computer, where she pulled up the graph plotting Simone's weight against that of other preemies. She'd been consistently following the curve of the 3rd percentile, and now she had dropped just below it. I nodded as the practitioner pointed to the black dots representing the daily weight of my baby in grams, the way the last few dots were nearly horizontal. Back inside, she flipped some more pages and continued: "This is another indication that she's just working too hard to breathe, and expending too many calories." She smiled, this time patronizing my baby. "She's telling us this is too much for her. A tracheostomy would relieve that burden. Another option might be a G-tube—it's just a small procedure, a port inserted right in the abdomen so you could administer her feedings through a tube. That way she could get the nutrition she needs without expending the energy of eating. Of course, we have a good four to six weeks before we need to decide any of this."

By now I was crying, flattened and bewildered. I didn't know where to begin. Tracheostomy? G-tube? Four to six weeks? I'd thought Simone would be home within three. I'd been duped. I'd thought she was doing so well.

The prepubescent nurse returned, accompanied by her even younger nursing student. and gave me a sympathetic smile. She didn't know me, and probably thought I was always like this. I could count on one hand the number of times I'd cried in front of medical professionals in the NICU, and all of those had been a matter of scattered silent tears that escaped and were extinguished promptly. This time, I couldn't seem to stop. I called Scott at work and stammered out a few words—"Simone," "sick," and "tracheostomy" among them. He said he was on his way.

The student kept touching Simone, cooing at her, holding her pacifier and generally hovering around like Simone was *her* baby. Off the phone I stepped up to the crib and took her place next to my daughter.

"I've got this," I snapped. I felt like growling at her. What was she doing in here, anyway, bothering my baby? There was nothing nursely that needed to be done, and she didn't get to fondle her charges as a job perk. Simone HAD a mother, and it was me, or I was her, or she, or whatever. I stood next Simone's crib and tried not to cry anymore.

Scott arrived just as I returned from getting a cup of tea. I explained the situation in furious whispers. Scott looked concerned—not for Simone, but for me: I was still crying, my face patchy and swollen. He'd never seen me like this in the NICU, and suddenly he was talking in a soothing voice, like I was a horse that might spook easily.

The nurse practitioner returned with another student, this one studying to be an NP. They needed a spinal tap, and the student of nurse practitionery was going to perform it, if that was all right with me. I assured her it was. After all, this was a teaching hospital! How else would she learn?

"I'll be right here," said the practitioner, "and I've done a *million* of these."

Oh shut up, I thought.

Simone had never had a spinal tap before. The student looked nervous, and all I could think of was the phrase "champagne tap." If a medical student gets a clear sample—you know, one with *no blood in it*—on the occasion of their first lumbar puncture, the teaching doctor is supposed to buy them a bottle of champagne. I thought that if this student *didn't* get a clear sample, she ought to buy ME a bottle. It was only fair.

"You don't have to stay for this," the practitioner said.

"No, I want to."

Scott grasped one of my folded arms. "There is no reason you have to see this," he murmured, "Let's just go."

"No. You can go if you want, but I'm staying."

"Well, if you're staying you'll have to gown up," said the nurse practitioner, "This is a sterile procedure."

They gave Simone a dose of morphine, and the nurse held her curled tightly into a comma, exposing her back. The patient didn't care for this,, and the nurse was instructed to apply more pressure. The student NP applied a drape and swabbed my baby's back with Betadine, while I stood with my back against the sink, tears dripping silently into my mask. Simone's oxygen saturation was going down, hovering in the low 80s. Morphine never agreed with her.

"Get me a dose of Narcan," said the NP, reaching over to turn Simone's high-flow from two liters to three. The hissing filled the room; I'd forgotten how loud it was.

"She'll be agitated when she comes out of it. Hold her tight," the NP instructed, and the nurse bent Simone further comma-ward.

Simone's oxygen saturation wasn't coming up. In fact, it was faltering, in the 70s now, then the 50s. There was conference with a passing nurse about Narcan and another dose was fetched from down the hall and administered. Simone was grey and mottled. I knew from watching ER that Narcan undoes the effects of opiates, but it didn't seem to be helping. Something was wrong. The NP student looked terrified, and Simone's oxygen dipped to 25 before the nurse began to bag her. They got her oxygen saturation to climb again, but it would only go into the high 70s. Something was *wrong*. I stared at my poor limp baby, my eyes swollen and my lashes stuck together in gooey mascara spikes. After almost half an hour, bagging was keeping Simone just over the cusp of the 80s, and then the nurse decided to check the connections.

"Is this supposed to be attached somewhere?" she asked, holding up a stray nozzle. The hissing sound that had filled the room after the NP turned up the high flow dial had been coming from *the oxygen cable she had disconnected*. All this time, Simone had been receiving no oxygen at all. I wanted to smother the NP with a pillow. I wanted to kick the world in the shins.

Simone was redraped, reprepped, and finally tapped, after a few excruciating-to-watch false starts, false starts involving a needle in my baby's uncomfortably curled spine. It was no champagne tap, and there was only enough spinal fluid for two of the three tests they'd planned to run. They tried to get urine via a bag taped to my daughter's labia, which failed, and then via a needle directly through her stomach into her bladder. As soon as it was inserted, Simone peed, and the syringe came up empty. You had to admire her sense of timing. The urine sample was finally obtained with a catheter, though there wasn't enough for a full urinalysis. After her bloodwork indicated a likely infection, an IV of antibiotics was started in her scalp. The first one blew, and the nurse had to find another vein, securing the second IV so that it was nearly upright, supported by tape and a block of cotton batting. I left that evening, silent and depleted.

The next day Wendy was back. My eyes were still red and burning as I babbled about tracheostomies and G-tubes, but she was reassuringly dismissive. If Simone had been tired and failing the cannula, she pointed out, her oxygen needs would have been going up before the Night of Seven

Spells, not progressively down as they had been. Wendy suspected a bladder infection had been the culprit. There was no reason to think Simone wouldn't be back off the high-flow in a few days. We couldn't rule out a tracheostomy, but Simone's occasional airway shutdowns were far more likely to be the result of her well-documented reflux than any "floppiness," and her weight gain hadn't plateaued—she'd just spent the past two weeks getting off the ventilator and transitioning to a crib, which understandably required a bit of extra effort. Her weight would pick up again when she was acclimated.

The crisis vanished as quickly as it had descended, and my relief didn't allow for a grudge. But it hit harder than the crises before, maybe because I'd thought the danger was past and wasn't braced for the blow, or because it had finally sunk in that there was never an "out of the woods," only bits that were more heavily forested than others. We were never safe, ever, even if we made it out of this place. There was SIDS, and the insidious respiratory viruses that kill so many preemies in the first two years. Even should we make it past those, who was to say Simone wouldn't pull one of our groaning bookcases upon herself, or be struck by a bus, running into the street after a ball or a puppy? There were gut-sucking pool-drains, and oh god, pools! Pools with their gates left unlocked by negligent neighbors. Once you start thinking of possible deadly mishaps, it's hard to stop, and they spooled out like something thought up by a malevolent Dr. Suess. *Wells to fall into and quicksand for sinking! Rivers for drowning, and poison for drinking! Snake bites and killer bees, feral raccoons! Snatched by kidnappers while watching cartoons!*

Or, she might be killed by a drunk driver on prom night. You just never know. I felt bone-weary at the realization, like my marrow was wrinkling within me.

Some people think of tragedy like a vaccine—surely once you've had a small amount, you develop a karmic antibody that keeps it from returning. But I knew this wasn't true, just from reading the online writing of others: a woman who had suffered multiple stillbirths, a woman whose 24-

weeker was diagnosed with an unrelated cancer at 18 months. Tragedy wasn't an inoculation, but it did linger in the blood like one; you became a carrier, or maybe it was one of those conditions that is managed but never cured. After your child has been sick, how can you ever feel safe again? How will you live a normal life, knowing that you are only ever a step from a terrible familiar place that others can only imagine? It felt unbearable, the exposure to risk far too high, a burden I was suddenly uncertain I wanted to carry. I'd always hated the saying that having children is like having your heart walking around outside your body. It painted such a clear image, the organ hopping wetly down the road, leaving damp bloody patches in its wake, bounding out of the house with a backpack slung over its pulmonary artery as you wave from the doorway. Whatever you think of the eye-rolling cheesiness, though, you can't deny there is something to it. Having a child, especially a child whose mortality has been slammed in your face again and again, leaves a part of you exposed that oughtn't to be, a place where the protective enamel has worn away and everything—hot, cold, wind—is felt with painful intensity.

The night I got my first cat, I had a terrible panic attack. Here was this sweet, wonderful kitten, and I was responsible for keeping him alive. I loved him already, and he could die, and it would hurt. I sobbed on the phone to my mother from my small apartment that I couldn't do it, that I had to take him back. *It's too much*, I told her.

The next morning I was better, and I kept the kitten and named him Claude. He waited for me to come home and ran to greet me; he rode on my shoulder like a parrot. He was my closest friend in the whole world, and he died before he was a year old, of a heart arrhythmia. "Claude," it turns out, means "lame." He'd gotten into my face powder the day before, and left tiny powder footprints around my bedroom. I slept on the couch for more than a month, because I couldn't bear to enter and see them there. I was right, you know: it was too much, but then it always is.

The high-flow was gone again; the antibiotic course was winding down. We'd had to tape socks onto Simone's hands to keep her from pulling at her IV. This annoyed her very much, but otherwise she was in excellent spirits, looking around, googly-eyed and mischievous, smacking her lips. She was wearing a fresh gown with horizontal stripes (babies can get away with that sort of thing), and the pile of cotton batting securing the IV atop her head looked like a cunning Parisian hat. I giggled, and took pictures to look at later, to remember my baby in her amusing hospital millinery. Now the very existence of those pictures seems like a comment on something, though I don't know exactly what. The kind of mother it takes to look at a scalp IV and see Paris? The strange hospital world that had conspired to produce me?

I'd struck up a conversation, once, with a woman in the elevator to the parking garage. Her baby was asleep in her stroller, her hands curled around the harness strap, and I smiled.

"My daughter sleeps the same way," I said. The child's mother smiled back at me.

"How old?"

"30 weeks," I said. I explained about the NICU, and mentioned Simone's tendency to use her ventilator tube as a security blanket. Babies! Always holding onto things!

Instead of the laugh I'd been aiming for, I got an expression of horror, and I began to giggle nervously, making myself look even worse: *I laugh at my child's misfortune!* I seemed to say. *I am cruel, or possibly crazy!*

Amber was organizing a team of NICU nurses to walk in the annual walk benefitting the March of Dimes, and she invited me to join them. I'd become almost an honorary nurse, I liked to think: I was there constantly, sometimes the only parent around, and I thought of them as my friends. They understood. They laughed at Simone's IV hat, and her clutching of ventilator tubes. I kind of loved them all, and there were times when the idea of leaving them for good made me anxious and bereft. I liked my routine, my people.

On the day of the walk, I drove into the park and felt a swell at the sight of the first March for Babies sign. The walk wasn't meant for Simone specifically, but it felt as though it might have been. The March of Dimes was responsible for the surfactant that saved her life, that made her life worth considering saving at such an early age, and seeing all these people walking in support of that could not help but feel personal. I'd posted a fundraising link on my website that had raised thousands of dollars from near strangers in twenty-some US states and a handful of foreign lands from Norway to Brazil. At the walk, the NICU team was clad in blue shirts with footprints upon them, and other groups wore shirts bearing the names of babies who hadn't made it. Some walkers were pushing their former preemies in strollers or calling them to stay on the path. These were all my people too.

Two of my favorite nurses were standing in the parking lot to greet people, and I joined them, shivering and smiling. In a revision of the "April Showers" motif, it was snowing three days before May began, but my mood remained festive. Next year, I thought, watching a nurse greet the mother of a former primary patient, I will bring Simone. My friend Jen appeared, the one who had referred me to my perinatologist and thus our NICU. I tortured myself sometimes, wondering what might be different if she hadn't recommended the switch from Dr. Schrödinger. Jen and I first met in a mind/body class for infertility patients. Some three years before we'd sat in my living room drinking sangria together, cracking bitter jokes and wondering whether we'd ever have children at all. Her one-year-old triplets, hale and hearty now, were home with their father because of the cold. We walked beside each other, marveling at where we'd ended up, and I pelted her with questions about what to expect once Simone came home. The walk was around a lake, flat and grey and cold. As we approached the finish line we were quiet, and my steps felt purposeful and proud.

Later I took a balloon to tie to Simone's crib, and ate a bag of scalding mini-doughnuts on the way to the hospital. It was quiet in the unit, most of the nurses right where I'd left them in the park, and Simone was lying awake in her crib. I'd left the balloon in the car, but I draped her in the team T-shirt I'd bought in the smallest available size (six months). It was still big enough to use as a blanket. I sat awhile and talked to her, whispering in the quiet, then I lifted her out and held her against me, swaying a little. I wondered what she had been thinking, lying there awake before I came in. One of my blog readers once remarked that she preferred the term incubator to isolette.

"Isolette is such a lonely noun," she'd said, and I'd agreed: it was, however appropriate. But Simone's crib seemed lonelier still, now that she was old enough to be awake and alert. When I entered she'd been looking around as if eager for excitement, while her nurse talked to another nurse halfway down the hall. Her alertness was painful to witness when I found her alone like that, looking like a happy little puppy, left all by herself. I'd always wondered what she thought when I was gone in the night, but now it was far more excruciating to picture. I knew it could take time for nurses to respond to a baby's cries, if they heard them at all. Sometimes, as long as no alarm was sounding, they didn't see the need, especially if a more critical baby required their attention. Simone might cry alone at night, awake in the quiet. *Where is that nice lady, the one with the milk in her,* she might wonder.

There was a newly released CD I listened to daily that April, a cheery one I'd sing lustily along with as I curled my car up the ramps of the parking lot in the morning sunshine. That second half of Simone's hospital stay lives in my memory as such a bright and hopeful and happy time, but a few months later I found that CD in the side pocket of my car door and slipped it in, and to my surprise I was in tears within a block. The familiar, jaunty songs flooded me with the same disoriented nausea you have upon awaking from a particularly vivid dream.

Part III

MOTHERLAND

Twenty-Eight

When the end comes, it comes fast. Well, that's a little mislead-ing—first, with their talk of car seats, the nurses and neonatologists whip you into a frenzy, as you allow yourself to imagine discharge for the first time, and feel ashamed at the sliver of dread you have at the idea of leaving your nurses and what has been your life for the past few months behind. And then nothing happens, or there is another crisis, and it becomes clear that whatever date three weeks hence you'd been holding in your mind is going to pass still in the NICU, and you sort of stop thinking about it altogether, until an unspecified date when you feel you could not be *more* ready, and that's when you're abruptly told to bring the car around, and put your baby in it.

Five days after the Night of Seven Spells, Simone's nurse practitioner for the day—the very one who'd had visions of tracheostomies dancing in her head less than a week before—swept into the room.

"I just want to prepare you—" she began, and my chest clenched in something between fear and annoyance, "—for the fact that things will move quickly now that Simone is back on the regular cannula. She can be discharged on this oxygen setting, and once she's taking all of her feedings by mouth we'll be sending her home."

I goggled at her, just as I had mere days before, at the mention of g-tubes and portable ventilators.

The next morning I was minding my own business when a woman appeared with a vast three-ring binder. At first I thought she might be some sort of nurse manager, as I'd seen her wandering about the hallways with clipboards from time to time.

"I'm Doreen, from Discharge Planning," she said, "Do you have time to talk?"

"It looks like Simone is coming home," I typed online, after Doreen had gone, leaving me gleeful and terrified, *"Maybe not today, maybe not tomorrow, but soon, and for the rest of her life (we may have to negotiate that last part when she reaches college age, but never mind that now).*

So, uh, I have a lot of questions. About babies. Because of how I have one. Who will be coming to live with me, at my apartment, where the nurse-to-neonate ratio is suboptimal (0-1). Currently, my knowledge of infants is more or less limited to the following:

1. Generally diminutive in size

2. Fond of milk

3. Exhibit poor impulse control

4. To clean, wipe with damp cloth

5. Should never be thrown out with bathwater.

Oh, sure, I was being facetious—kind of. I'd researched conception and pregnancy and neonatology, but I'd sort of forgotten to cover babies, aside from the things that might kill them. I didn't have a single book on the subject of their care and feeding. I hadn't studied their development, or diaper rashes, or sleep training. When I was young I'd gone through a series of animal obsessions, usually culminating in the acquisition of a new pet. There were hamsters, fish, and lizards, and a parakeet and a rabbit (all of whom, it should be noted, died rather untimely deaths), and before I so much as browsed amongst the newts I read about their feeding and housing and temperament, poring through every source in my elementary school's library. This single-mindedness went on to serve me well in researching IVF protocols, and while my information regarding pregnancy and the medical problems of preemies hadn't given me the power to change the events that unfolded, at least, prisoner of circumstance though I was, I'd understood what the guards were saying. How had I left such a large, baby-shaped hole in my research?

A few weeks before, as my mother and I procured Simone's first baby clothes, I'd made a few secret additional purchases of my own. I shoved the bags in the closet, which soon began to look like the storeroom for an infant infirmary. There were over-the-counter children's medications—Tylenol and Advil and gas-relief drops, and something called "gripe-water" meant to prevent, not induce, griping. There were packages of glass baby bottles, guaranteed to be free from the hormone-disrupting chemicals present in plastics. There were several large dispensers of hand-sanitizer, a baby first aid kit, and bath products that shrilled "SENSITIVE!" across their labels. I'd ordered two obscenely pricey air purifiers—one small, one twice the size of our dishwasher—to remove baby-harming particulates from the air.

After the meeting with Doreen, I decided it was time to branch out beyond infant death-preventatives. On the advice of the nurses, I bought a bouncing seat that held Simone upright to help with reflux, and assembled it on the floor in the NICU. On the advice of my readers, I stocked up on packages of cloth diapers to use as rags, and bought special blankets designed like straitjackets. I bought extra nipple shields and furry sleeping sacks, and a book about babies—regular, healthy ones, though I did choose the volume compiled by the American Academy of Pediatrics. I returned the baby powder and baby oil I'd already purchased, after discovering that, despite the "baby" in their names, they were full of potential danger.

I was beginning make preparations for my new charge, at least materially, and I tried, hard, to imagine myself using these things in the future. We even had a crib, a gift from my mother she'd insisted upon ordering back in March, suspicious of ambiguous shipping timelines. I'd insisted she have it sent to her house across town, where my brother now lived and the crib remained in boxes, which I did not intend to open until I was certain there would be an occupant for what occupied them.

Once the word got out that discharge had been mentioned, the nurses began a concentrated campaign to ready me for Simone's homecoming. It was a campaign, I must say, of terror. When Simone had an episode of apnea during a feeding, I watched the monitor even as I patted her back, feeling relief only when the oxygen saturation numbers began climbing at last. Now, though, they began *turning the monitors away from me.* I'd been watching these monitors for months. They told me whether things were good or bad. They were the only way I knew anything at all.

"Look at your *baby,*" the nurses said, as I craned my neck while alarms sounded, "There won't be a monitor at home."

What I wanted to know was this: Why the hell *not*? Why *couldn't* there be monitors at home? I went online and researched a bit, wondering if we could afford some sort of hospital-like setup. I'd been told that Simone might be on a monitor at night so that we wouldn't have to worry about sleeping through an apnea episode, but that monitor wasn't meant to be used during feedings. Apnea during feedings wasn't particularly dangerous, we were told, "Because you'll be right there, to correct it."

This was the scariest part of all. In the hospital, when Simone wasn't coming out of it fast enough, a nurse was right there to rush in and assist me. We'd have no such luxury at home, hence *Look at your baby.*

"Look at the skin around her mouth," a nurse said, "See how it's bluish? Watch right there, and that's where you'll be able to see it pink up again when the spell is over." I DID NOT WANT TO EVALUATE THE SKIN AROUND MY BABY'S MOUTH FOR RELATIVE BLUENESS. But I didn't seem to have much choice.

With the monitor turned away I'd panic and look around wildly, patting Simone and holding her under the chin with the V between my thumb and index finger as I'd been shown, lifting her airway clear of obstruction.

"You have to get rough with her," a nurse would say when Simone was slow to recover, and I shook at my baby a little like they'd told me to, thinking NEVER NEVER NEVER SHAKE A BABY, and wondering what in the hell I would do the first time this happened on our couch, with no call button in sight.

Doreen's visit was scarcely behind us when our landlord called to tell us that the work upstairs was finished, and that weekend, April's last, we moved. Saturday I carried armfuls of frozen breastmilk up the back stairs (there was no room in our freezer for anything else, by then), and the next afternoon when I returned from the March of Dimes walk I climbed an extra flight of stairs to our new home, freshly painted and chaotic with unpacked boxes.

Then it was May, and though it had been ten days since the warning that things would "move quickly," it was clear that they weren't, yet. Simone had been transferred to the team for "feeders and growers," babies who need only to fatten up and learn to eat before discharge. This meant a tearful goodbye to Wendy—there was a separate nurse practitioner assigned to us feeders, cautious but unfailingly optimistic, the latter quality likely born of the relative health of her patients. She was tall and loud and kept up a steady stream of compliments and reassurance, working to buoy my maternal confidence.

"I am just amazed at how well this baby breastfeeds!" she'd say, while I tried to look as modest as toplessness allowed. For a week, my favorite neonatologist rotated through our service as well, the same sharp-witted doctor who'd explained the role of weight in breathing after our second failed extubation, and clarified the clinical evidence on steroids before we used a brief course to push Simone off the vent. She was full of compliments as well—mostly for my shoes—and between her sartorial ego boost and the NP's practical one, I was just able to avoid sinking into despair when Simone's progress seemed to stall.

Before discharge, Simone had to be able to drink from a bottle, because in order to maintain her weight gain at least some of her feedings at home would have to be fortified with additional calories. Unfortunately, whenever Simone was given a nipple other than my own, she choked and sputtered and turned what was becoming my least favorite color, the mottled periwinkle of not-enough-oxygen.

It was virtualy unheard of for preemies to have trouble with bottles and not breastfeeding, but Simone had never been a conventional baby. Just to be contrary, Simone chose the occasion of her swallow study, in the presence of a highly paid radiologist, to prove that she could indeed suck down a bottle with perfect form, only to go back to sputtering and aspirating and coming over all periwinkle as soon as the test was over. Speech therapists had started to come by to work on her feedings—something I hadn't realized fell under the auspices of speech—and a physical therapist was teaching me massage techniques for preemies. Simone was so small that there simply wasn't room on her abdomen to do most of the strokes, which the therapist demonstrated on a doll while I sat across from her with Simone flat on a blanket. But I tried, gamely, and learned how to softly compress her joints and move her limbs, how to position her hips to make up for the lack of amniotic fluid resistance and the premature presence of gravity. It was all very educational, but discharge seemed no closer.

At the end of one long day I stopped off at my perinatologist's office, in search of Ames' autopsy report. I sat in the waiting room and opened a magazine at random to an article about fetal development, then shut it again, feeling ill. After twenty minutes I was called back only to hear that the report wasn't ready yet, and might not be for another six weeks. Four months seemed a long time to wait for an autopsy report, especially one on such a small baby, especially when we'd been billed for the testing weeks ago. What was available was the chromosome report, indicating that Ames' 46 were all in place. They gave me a copy of the karyotype, a sort of photograph of the paired chromosomes, little worms two by two except for the last, the little half-worm that represented the Y. He was perfect, aside from being dead. On the elevator up to the parking garage I was surrounded by couples: the women all pregnant, the husbands clutching pillows, obviously on their way to a birthing class. I felt conspicuous, with my chromosome report and plastic bag of NICU laundry, but no one even looked at me. I wanted to say something to burst their bubble of presumed safety, but I didn't. I exited when we reached my level, keeping my eyes to myself.

Early the next week, something called "Simply Thick" was added to Simone's bottles. It gave milk the consistency of honey, and all at once her problems with the bottle had vanished. Her feeding tube was removed at last, and Scott began learning how to bottle feed, which wasn't as straightforward as you might think—for one thing, Simone had to be held at a sharp upright angle, and for another she was terribly greedy, and if left to her own devices would suck and guzzle without stopping to breathe, ending in a spell of unfortunate blueness. We had to pace her, letting her take a few sucks and then tipping the bottle back so that no milk flowed through the nipple, forcing Simone to take a reluctant breath.

The Wednesday before Mother's Day, our new neonatologist cocked his head at rounds and said he thought we should plan on taking Simone home the next Tuesday.

I was really getting a chance to perfect my goggle.

Doreen appeared again a few hours later, with additional sheaves of paper for my discharge binder. She set up Simone's follow-up appointments: nephrology in August, pulmonology before then, a home nurse visiting us twice a week to weigh Simone and perform any necessary blood tests. We'd need to see the pediatrician a few days after discharge.

"Who *is* Simone's pediatrician?" she asked, pen hovering.

"Er..."

Doreen vanished and reappeared with a book of pediatricians affiliated with the hospital. I paged through it, looking for...I didn't know what I was looking for. Where their degrees were from? Whether they looked understanding, like the young Asian woman with the sympathetic smile? Whether they looked like they kept up with clinical studies, like the older woman with the Germanic name? Whether their interests were cooking or hiking or evaluating pediatric kidney function?

"Do you have any favorites?" I asked, and Doreen suggested I have someone from the clinic directly upstairs, on the third floor, come by and take a look at Simone.

"They see a lot of preemies up there, and whoever has time to come down and meet you can answer your questions about the practice."

Twenty minutes later an amiable man of about 45 entered and extended a long arm to shake my hand. He was thin, with the slight stoop of the very tall, and wearing a bowtie. This last detail seemed fitting, as Simone had been given her cellular start by a doctor similarly attired. He smiled at Simone and looked her over, talking easily about the many NICU graduates his practice treated, the hospital patients he covered in addition.

"Well she *looks* great!" he said, finishing his exam. He reminded me a little of Jimmy Stewart in *Harvey*, though I saw no pooka lurking behind him.

"Do you have room for another patient?" I asked. And just like that, Simone had a pediatrician.

A pulmonologist was also added to Simone's team, once it became clear that her inpatient status would soon be expiring. I'd been assured by Amber that this pulmonologist was the very best, and she urged me to give him a chance.

"He can be a little...blunt," she warned me. The pulmonology practice was called "Children's Respiratory and Critical Care Specialists," and though I disliked the way the term "critical" always found some way to hang around my baby, Amber needn't have worried, because I found Dr. Krolik enchanting. He was sixty-something, small and slender, with close-cropped white hair, and for our first meeting, he breezed into Simone's room where I was sitting next to Eloise on the sofa.

"I've read Simone's chart," he said in his sharp, reedy voice, "She's had quite a rough course, hasn't she?" I smiled, and he peered into Simone's crib and continued, matter of factly: "Frankly I'm surprised she's doing as well as she is. You're lucky to be here at all, you know. It could have just as easily gone the other way."

Eloise looked horrified, but I was instantly taken with him. His particular brand of bedside manner may not have been for everyone, but it suited me fine. Simone wasn't to be allowed indoors in public places until the following spring, and during her first two winters would be quarantined in our apartment to avoid RSV, a cold-like virus virtually all children get before age two, but which can be deadly for preemies like Simone with chronic lung disease, at least until they have time to grow new, healthy lung tissue.

"You weren't planning on daycare, were you?" he asked. Aha! Trick question!

"No, I'm going to freelance from home."

"Good. Because she can't *go* to daycare. Not for *at least* the first two years. Frankly I wouldn't put *any* infant in daycare, lung disease or not. *Swimming* with infections! In Simone's case, an infection could kill her. It's almost guaranteed she'll be rehospitalized sometime this first year, but with any luck we can keep her from ending up back on the vent." He looked around suspiciously. "You don't *smoke*, do you? Any smokers allowed in the home?"

"Oh no! No smokers! My husband's father smokes, but I've told him he can't smoke anywhere around Simone. I tend to be a little...well, I'm afraid the relatives aren't going to understand how serious this is, with the hand sanitizing and the quarantine. I can be a little anxious, from time to time, and I think they might think I'm just being overprotective."

Dr. Krolik raised his eyebrows. "Well, bring them in here. *I'll* tell them. I'll tell them about the baby I have upstairs right now, in the *PICU*, who frankly I don't think will make it. His mother smokes—she says she goes outside to do it, but I don't believe her. Tell your husband's father that even wearing the clothes he smoked in is a big no no. Babies absorb it through their skin. You might as well slap her with a nicotine patch."

He looked at his notes, and then up at me again, probingly. "It has been mentioned that you have cats."

Both Wendy and Amber had warned us that pulmonologists generally prescribed petlessness. Fish were probably allowed, but you get the idea. Dr. Krolik viewed cats and dogs as living, respiring lung irritants.

"Don't let him scare you," Amber and Wendy had advised, both pet owners themselves.

"Yes. We have cats."

"How many?"

"Three," I said meekly. His lips pursed, and I hurried to finish: "But we got this...comb thing that takes out their undercoat, and we plan to use it religiously. We also have air purifiers, giant ones, with hyper-HEPA filters. Hospital grade. But if you think we need to get rid of the cats we will."

I would miss them, but some maternal mechanism had shunted my beloved pets down the totem pole, and if it were a question of my baby's safety, I wouldn't think twice. Scott, on the other hand, had been a wreck since hearing we might have to find new homes for Willie, Lennie, and Irma, and had spoken tearfully of taking a second job in order to rent them a separate apartment—a sort of feline safe house, if you will.

"Would you be able to bathe once a week or so?"

I washed my hair most mornings, but lately once a week was about as often as the rest of me got clean, and Simone wasn't even home yet. Did he mean the baby?

"The cats," he clarified.

"Oh! Yes. No problem."

"Do you have carpet?"

"Oh *no,*" I assured him, "not even a rug!"

He nodded approvingly. "I think the cats can stay, as long as Simone seems to tolerate them."

Scott would be so relieved.

"You're lucky, because this is the best possible time of year for discharge. RSV season just ended, and Simone lungs will be stronger by the time flu season starts. But please, don't be stupid around the holidays. You wouldn't *believe* some people, attending these big family gatherings, with children running around everywhere with snotty noses. 'But Dr. Krolik,' they say, 'it's *Christmas.*' And then they're surprised when the baby's in the hospital by the New Year."

I shook my head in censure. Some people!

"I'd much rather keep Simone quarantined for her first two holidays than risk her dying before her third," I said.

"A sensible way to look at it," agreed the doctor.

Home oxygen tanks have fewer settings than the meters in the hospital, and the lowest amount they delivered was more than Simone needed. But Dr. Krolik didn't see the point of pushing Simone to come off oxygen entirely within the next week, and so it was decided she'd stay on 1/16th of a liter until her oxygen study in June. He also nipped in the bud some recent talk of sending us home with no monitor at all, *even at night.* He didn't think the pulse oximeter I would have liked was necessary, but agreed that a simple apnea monitor for sleeping couldn't hurt, given Simone's reflux.

"Besides," he said, "How will you get any rest if you're worried about finding her dead in the morning?"

We were two peas in a pod, Dr. Krolik and I. He was something of an institution, having been working in neonatology before there was such a thing, when premature babies were assigned to the cardiology service. Back then, they didn't have ventilators, and nurses would bag the babies by hand, working in shifts, squeezing the bellows in one-second increments for hours. He was a font of information, both empirical and anecdotal, and hearing him talk underscored again what a young specialty neonatology was, and not just in terms of its patients. When I asked whether Simone's diminished lung capacity would effect her far in the future, Dr. Krolik couldn't tell me, because the first large groups of preemies her size to survive weren't yet old enough for us to know all of the possible repercussions. He did assure me that humans use only a fraction of their lung capacity, and that though Simone would never have the plentiful alveoli of a baby born at term, she'd have enough. The problem came during illness, when healthy children fell back upon lung reserves that preemies simply didn't possess, especially now, while Simone's lungs were still healing from the ventilator damage and sending up fragile new shoots of growth.

Behold, the mountains of equipment we were required to master before discharge. On Thursday we were trained on the use of oxygen tanks, the apnea monitor, and a nebulizer shaped like a squat, smiling panda bear. The nebulizer, for Simone's prescription inhaled steroids, was loud, but straightforward. The apnea monitor had leads attached to two rubber squares that were held under Simone's arms, near her chest, by a felt strap secured with velcro. The leads were in turn plugged into the connector at the end of the wired that led to the monitor, a black thing the size of a box of crackers, nestled in a carrying case. The alarm could mean various things: either a lead was loose or out of place, Simone had stopped breathing for longer than 12 seconds, or that her heart beat had dropped below a certain rate. The alarm would sound until the problem was resolved, and you could tell which problem it was only by which tiny lights lit up on the front of the monitor.

When the trainer from the medical supply company made us test out the alarm, I startled so violently that both my buttocks relinquished contact with my chair. It was piercing, like something you'd hear during war. My husband and the trainer laughed at me. The next time, I knew it was coming. When I leapt just as visibly, the medical supply technician looked concerned.

"I have a very active startle reflex," I explained, adding my desire never to hear that alarm again to the reasons I hoped Simone didn't die in the night.

The most difficult of the medical equipment to master, for me, was the oxygen tanks. I winced when the trainer demonstrated how to open one by first attaching a heavy metal meter, explaining that if the meter wasn't screwed on correctly, opening the tank afterward could cause it to shoot off with violence. We took turns practicing, and as I turned the plastic key to release the gas, I braced for impact. In the NICU, Simone's oxygen came directly from a valve in the wall, a far superior setup. I was petrified of oxygen tanks. I was even afraid of the little bullets of carbon dioxide that came with my mother's soda siphon. The contents, after all, were under tremendous pressure, and if a soda cartridge might leave you short an eye or a finger, an oxygen tank could do some serious damage. What if I opened one incorrectly? What if one exploded, sending shrapnel tearing through my tender flesh, blowing off a hand or worse, my face? I'd be one of the horribly disfigured women you see on talk shows. Smiling a lipless smile, I would have to eschew whatever petty human emotions I'd had before the accident.

Maybe I'll let Scott change the tanks, I thought.

Our oxygen would be delivered six two-foot cylinders at a time, and whichever one was in use would be secured in a wheeled stand so that we could move about the apartment. We'd also have smaller tanks, the size of one of those big, cheap bottles of wine. These were for outings, and fit in a cylindrical tote with a strap that could be slung over one's shoulder.

Simone was being released on "reflux precautions," and as a result we were enrolled in the Reflux and Apnea program, consisting of nurses who would check in with us weekly and monitor the output of Simone's monitor. There was training involved in this as well, conducted by a pretty blonde nurse whom I quizzed incessantly about SIDS risk, gleaning the disturbing knowledge that apnea monitors rarely prevented true SIDS, as death was so sudden that by the time an alarm sounded it was too late, and the mechanism by which that death occurred was still largely a mystery.

"The risk goes down considerably after six months adjusted," she told me, and I marked the date in my mental calendar (November 17th). The class included infant CPR and choking protocols, and I gamely flipped the provided doll asunder and smacked it sharply between the shoulder blades with the heel of my hand. I swept her airway, I performed chest compressions with sufficient force to see her chest wall bow under the pressure, a bowing I was told would also be necessary on our human baby, to sufficiently pump her heart. I wondered whether I would be able to commit these steps to memory, and gratefully accepted a laminated poster. We received yet another overstuffed binder of information, and a log in which we were required to record any apnea episode that did not occur during feeding. We learned which positioning pitfalls worsened reflux, and how to insert a rolled receiving blanket under one side of the Danny Sling so that Simone could sleep on her side. In the NICU, she slept on her stomach, but that was *verboten* at home. A side position was safe with her bound securely in her harness, and reduced the risk of aspiration. They should make Danny Slings for rock stars and other highly-paid heroin addicts, I thought. Their staff could strap them in at night and roll them carefully to one side. And no one should be without a bulb syringe—I'd always thought these were merely used to suck the snot from tiny noses, but now I'd learned that in the event of reflux-related apnea, they could be used to suck regurgitated milk from the back of a baby's throat, clearing the airway.

"Keep one in the car," the nurse advised, reminding me of the danger of car seats. The idea of tending to a choking child in the middle of a freeway made me lightheaded, so I put it out of my mind. But I did go out that night and buy enough bulb syringes to have one in every room, and I popped two into the diaper bag.

With only five days' notice before discharge, scheduling quickly became problematic. I had to be at the hospital for the endless classes and equipment training sessions, and to practice performing basic maternal tasks. Simone had a feeding every three hours, and though the nurses wanted me to give as many of these as possible, I seldom made more than two a day.

I could feel myself slipping in their estimation from "admirably involved parent" to "negligent wastrel," but in my defense, there was an awful lot to do, and much of it required me to be elsewhere. We had yet to put together the crib, or buy sheets, a changing table, or diapers. There was also the small matter of unpacking our apartment, and I grudgingly realized that there might be something to the idea of preparing the nursery BEFORE the baby was about to come home.

I tottered through IKEA in foolishly chosen footwear, arms straining as I pushed one cart before me and pulled one behind, loaded with flat pack boxes containing a pine bookshelf, two pink chests of drawers, a blue chair and footstool, and a sunny yellow side-table. I made a trip to Babies Backwards-R Us, flying through the aisles like a contestant on Supermarket Sweep, snatching up a changing pad, a bath chair, and pacifiers. I piled high hooded towels and bright wooden rattles and tubs of wipes; I selected nipples and creams and unguents, and stuffed economy-sized boxes of preemie-sized diapers on the shelf beneath the cart. I bought a back-up monitor: a motion-detecting mat for under the crib mattress that sounded an alarm if it failed to detect the motion of breath. Redundancy, I believed, was essential to any effective *keep-the-baby-alive* system. The cashier who rang up my purchases looked at my belly and asked, tentatively, if I wanted a gift receipt. I laughed.

"Nope," I said, proudly. "It's all for me. My daughter's coming home."

At last, I retrieved the crib from my brother's house, and Scott assembled the pieces into their smallest incarnation, wheeling the resultant bassinet to stand next to my side of the bed, close enough that I could reach through the slats without lifting my head from the pillow.

It was Friday, and looking at the calendar I realized my original due date was in exactly one week.

"Tonight I am putting the rest of the furniture together, washing loads and loads of baby laundry, and arranging a bouquet of bulb syringes on my bedside table," I wrote, *"I think I might be nesting, which the pregnancy newsletter I still get from my former OB's office told me to expect this week, so I'm right on schedule."*

Simone was on schedule as well. She passed her carseat test, and was approved for one hour (but no more!) of automobiling. Her medications, a giant bag of them, were ordered from the pharmacy and demonstrated at length. For proof that she could maintain her oxygen saturation over a 24-hour period, she was connected to a special data-collecting monitor—for 48 hours, as the first 24 failed to record— and she passed the standard newborn screenings she'd been too new to have when she was born. She was a quiet baby, and seldom cried: concerned about vocal cord paralysis from the long-ago ductus surgery, her nurse practitioner grasped a small, pearly toe and give it a fierce squeeze. Simone looked up at us, incredulous and wounded, before bursting into lusty sobs.

"Good!" chirped the NP, and another worry was crossed from the list. Sunday was Mother's Day, and I arrived to find my first Mother's Day card propped on the windowsill, allegedly from Simone but bearing the unmis-takably neat handwriting of her night nurse, Carrie. I stayed late that evening for the nine o'clock feeding, and then we talked in the dark while Simone slept. I began emptying our drawers, and Carrie slipped me extra tape and cannula tubing. As a memento, I packed a diaper in the size Simone wore when she was first admitted. It had been too big on her then, and they'd had to fold the front nearly in half to avoid covering her belly-button. It fit easily in my palm of my hand.

Monday I stayed up nearly all night, finishing the nursery, and after-wards I stood in the doorway looking in, just as I used to do with the room of unpacked boxes we'd designated for the babies months before. One dresser was topped with a polka-dotted changing pad, and on the dresser beside it diapers were stacked neatly in soft baskets. A pink lamp cast a soft glow onto the panda bear nebulizer next to it. A quilt my aunt had made for Simone lay with a blanket crocheted by another relative, and inside the dresser drawers were hundreds of neatly folded rags, ready to absorb my baby's various fluids. In our bedroom next door, there were sheets on the bassinet, and the world's softest elephant was propped nearby.

Around noon the next day, while Scott took bags to the car, Maura and I removed the three leads stuck to Simone's abdomen and unwound the pulse oximeter from her foot. We changed her cannula and connected her to our portable oxygen tank, and I dressed her in the outfit I'd bought for the occasion, a bright dress of pink and orange and aqua, with tiny aqua pants. I added a sweater, hat and socks, and nestled her into her carseat with a pacifier, rolled blankets shoved between her legs and around her head to make a snug fit. She'd looked huge to me only a moment before—five pounds, 14 ounces!—but in the car seat she appeared dwarfed. I couldn't wait to leave, and when Scott returned we set out, with Maura pushing a cart holding the last of our belongings, the calendars and pictures we'd plucked from the walls, bags of blankets and the tub in which we'd given Simone her first bath. Through the NICU hallways we processed, beaming, saying goodbye to the people who had become our family. In the hallway outside the NICU we passed the open back door of my perinatology clinic, and through it I saw nurses I knew, particularly my favorite, the pink-cheeked white-haired woman who pulled me into an enthusiastic hug whenever she saw me.

"Wait," I said. "Can we stop for a second? These were my nurses." I stepped shyly through the door into the dark room where pregnant patients were separated by curtains, and before I had made it to the nurses' station they saw me, and poured out to exclaim over Simone and squeeze my shoulders.

Then we got moving again, and I found myself in tears as we approached the doors at the end of the hallway. We were battered heroes returned from war. We were walking into a changed world. Every step felt like a leap.

CHAPTER

Twenty-Nine

Long before I was pregnant, I became an expert on postpartum depression. I'd had a long fascination with psychiatric disorders: I read everything from books about the effect of hormones on brain chemistry to personal accounts of madness, though I became anxious reading about the mental problems of others, and after a memoir of depression I'd often require a tranquilizer and a Marx Brothers movie as an antidote. Due to its sheer statistical likelihood, postpartum depression scared me most. After all, I'd already ended up in a mental hospital without the extreme hormonal toll of the end of pregnancy, or the military-certified torture of sleep deprivation, or the constant, eroding anxiety of caring for a newborn. In my more optimistic moments, I planned to keep my psychiatrist on speed dial and figured I'd make a full recovery. In my less optimistic moments, I wondered whether I should bother having children at all, since they'd only know me as That Weepy Lady in the Big White Hospital with Chocolate-Smeared Wainscoting.

As our circumstances changed, so did my expectations. I wouldn't be recovering from a C-section, or experiencing a post-birth hormonal crash. Instead, I had a machine to monitor Simone's breathing while I slept, and in general, I knew I was in better shape than I might have been. But I was still prepared for rocky times ahead, for exhaustion and feelings of failure over breastfeeding difficulties, for the resentment and fear and guilt and tedium and terror and sleeplessness I'd read about. Mostly I was prepared for a serious uptick in my anxiety, now that I had a delicate premature baby to feed and medicate and oxygenize, without a single nurse to back me up. Imagine my surprise, then, to find that I loved every minute. Or at least 45 seconds out of every 60, which is quite impressive, considering the proportion of that time spent sponging excrement from various skin folds and mopping vomit from my sleeves. Stranger still was the confidence I displayed, something I found myself observing with shock as if from a distance. Look how easily I manhandled my baby while wheeling an oxygen tank and talking on the phone, with seemingly no gingerness at all, no fear of floppy, accidentally snapped necks, or fontanelles that really, you could easily have put a fingernail through!

"*I expected to be happy, of course,*" I wrote in my first entry after discharge, "*but I am so much happier than I hoped I might be.*"

I even managed to feel guilty about my happiness, inclined to keep it to myself so as not to make other new mothers, ones *not* greeting every day with a dreamy, happy smile, feel badly. *I'M the freak!* I wanted to reassure them. *You're doing just fine!*

Our first afternoon at home, Scott sat on the couch with Simone asleep on his chest, and we stared at each other, wondering *Now what?* Thankfully, the sheer volume of baby-related tasks and their prescribed frequency made it a rhetorical question. Simone had to be fed every two or three hours, which, if it was a breastfeeding session, could easily take 45 minutes. She had to be held upright for half an hour after feedings, and required a daunting parade of medications:

Pulmicort, a steroid treatment for her lungs, had to be delivered by nebulizer once in the morning and once at night. Also twice a day were Prevacid and Diuril, a diuretic to keep her lungs clear of fluid. Thrice daily she needed the terrifying potassium chloride, a drug I knew from *Law & Order* could be used to murder someone while making it appear they'd died of a heart attack, and every morning she got a dropper of a foul-smelling multivitamin.

Because she could only drink milk thickened to the consistency of honey, her medications couldn't simply be put in one of her mandatory calorie-fortified bottles, because the thickener would coat the sides of the bottle, making it impossible to be sure she was getting the required dose. Instead, I drew up her medications in a series of syringes, made a bottle, and then took the whole thing to the living room on a tray. I lay Simone on her breastfeeding pillow to keep her at the required upwards feeding angle. Then you had to unscrew the bottle, and hold the cap with the nipple (an X cut in the tip to allow the thickened liquid to pass through) so that Simone could suck on it while you poured a bit of thickened milk into the top and squirted a few drops of medicine into the mix. Too much medicine would thin the consistency so that she choked, and overwhelm the milk-flavor with its horrible taste, spooking the baby. But you had to pour fast enough that Simone didn't suck empty air into her stomach, while not allowing her to take in more than she could handle. It was a long, tedious process, but it gave a comforting shape to our disorienting early days, when Simone slept very little.

Scott and I had a system that seemed sensible, as he was a night person and I was at my best in the morning—I went to sleep at a reasonable hour, and Scott administered the evening medicines and all the night feedings, heading to bed at 4:30 and handing the baby to me where I nursed her, dozing, before we got up for the day. The first two days she would only sleep while being held, reacting to her bassinet as if it were lined with nettles. She particularly liked being held by me, not because I was such good company but because I was the one with milk, just there for the taking! Milk I didn't seem to be using, myself, and that shouldn't be allowed to go to waste. My new moniker, seemingly chosen by Simone herself, who smacked her lips at the sight of me, was Milk Lady. And god forbid poor Milk Lady try to take a bath, or make herself some lunch.

"Off to take a nap?" I wrote, "Not so fast, Milk Lady! Scott tried to give Simone a bottle and she pulled away, waggling her tongue at me suggestively. Bottle, schmottle! Come to me, nice Milk Lady! Come to me or I WILL RAIN HELL UPON YOU AND YOUR KIN."

I didn't mind, really. Sure, it meant I spent nearly all of my time on the couch, watching television with my top off, but there were worse ways to spend a day. Scott had a few weeks of paternity leave, so he could sleep in the mornings after holding Simone all night, and a little exhaustion-induced aphasia seemed a small price to pay for a living baby.

Two days after bringing Simone home, we had our first visit from the home nurse, who lay our naked baby on her portable scale, and took blood from her heel to check her potassium levels. Most importantly, though, she taught us a magical swaddling technique, the results of which were so dramatic that I was convinced that this was no ordinary nurse, but a gypsy, experienced at keeping human babies silent while replacing them with changelings. The Gypsy Swaddle had an instant soporific effect, and enabled us, finally, to put Simone down in her bouncy seat or bassinet. Before she'd been waking at frustratingly frequent intervals in search of more milk, demanding to be nursed to sleep even after her nighttime bottles. Her perpetual chasing of the albino dragon wasn't so bad, provided I could simply lie there and let her suckle away; however, she seemed to take the whole "Milk Lady" thing quite literally, attempting to draw sustenance from whatever part of my anatomy was closest—often my collar bone—and growing incensed when none was forthcoming. Transferred to her bassinet, she would commence a round of irritated noises that were not quite crying, but still succeeded in preventing sleep.

"Meh-ehhh," she whined, "Ehhhh. Iihhh. Eh-hiihh!"

"What? *WHAT?*" I hissed at her after a 24-hour period that contained only one continuous hour of sleep, "What do you *want* from me??" I sat there, belligerent, waiting for an answer from a creature scarcely more developed than a larva. Unsurprisingly, none was forthcoming. Or maybe it was—Simone smacked her lips at me, wiggling her eyebrows.

Many days I carried Simone downstairs and unfolded the stroller from the car. Her car seat snapped on top facing me, and I stowed the oxygen tank in the carriage's basket. We walked the neighborhood, stopping for bagels or coffee, old ladies holding doors for us and sun filtering through new green leaves. They were long, lazy walks without purpose, and I noticed everything: the graceful arch of trees overhead, the bright colors of porches and bricks and the lettering upon signs. I had to work to suppress my smile, and I did, because I was frankly a little disgusted with myself. Every potato chip, every cup of tea was the best I'd ever tasted—add a sleeping baby in a chair at my feet and Blossom Dearie in the background and I behaved like a character in a musical, bursting into tuneless song without provocation. I felt acutely happy. Really, that is the word that best describes the quality of my joy: *acute.*

My mother returned for a visit late in May, and bustled around cleaning my apartment and bringing me little afternoon glasses of champagne. She brought me liqueurs from her recent road trip to Burgundy, the peach and raspberry flavors so fresh and delicious that they caused my milk to let down right there in the kitchen. Simone couldn't go inside stores or restaurants, but our favorite Italian place was nearby and had a lovely patio, and I developed a habit of meeting my brother there for lunch. Once she was home my mother joined us, along with a rotating crop of friends. I'd push Simone the six sunny blocks, greeted with a smile by the restaurant's owner as I crossed to our table and positioned the stroller in the shade. We ate plates of airy, crisp calamari and toothsome pasta, with gelato for dessert, and an assortment of colorful libations. Simone snoozed out of sight under her canopy, and it was all so idyllic I wouldn't blame you for feeling nauseated at the mere description.

If it helps, there were all the usual difficulties—my milk supply began to dwindle, and Simone screamed and slapped me for it. Nursing my baby, just us two snuggled together, dopey with milk (her) and hormones (me) was as close to divinity as I had come. I cried as there were more bottles and fewer nursing sessions, surprised at the force of my sorrow.

There were the few times Simone's apnea alarm sounded in the middle of the night, sending me rocketing upright only to find the alarm already silent, the episode resolved on its own. And, naturally, there were the feeding-related apneas, the first of which was every bit as terrifying as I had expected, holding my baby's chin up and watching the blue recede from her lips, with a chilling nurselessness all around me. The spells did become routine, as odd as it seems, though every once in a while a particularly bad one would rattle me.

There was the fact that even as her apnea spells became less frequent, her reflux became much worse, and she was a wee Vesuvius, making me awfully glad we'd gone with a leather couch. I called her my tiny Roman, for the way regurgitation seemed only to renew her appetite, making room for another meal eaten at a lazy incline. What she did mind was the pain of the acid searing her tissues, and she was constantly outgrowing her prevacid dosage and needing it readjusted to her portlier weight. I spent hours swaying her into complacency during these times, singing endless rounds of "Fly me to the Moon," the samba-fied Astrud Gilberto version. When I tired of Astrud I sang children's songs to which I remembered the melodies but not the words, making up my own as I went along. "Oh I wish I were a little 'lectric eel" had dozens of verses, from a shark that went swimmy swimmy swimmy before tearing you limb from limb-y, to a bat that dangled dangled dangled at a terrifying angle, to an octopus who had a thing for waving at sailors on naval vessels. Scott made up songs as well: I passed through the living room late one night on my way to the kitchen to hear him crooning *"Big-Headed Baby/The villagers throw stones at you/You run away to a cave/Your only friend is the eel/He swims in the shallows/Big-Headed Baby…"* This is what happens when a new father has an MFA in poetry, I suppose.

Continuing my catalog of The Usual Difficulties, there was the one less-than-idyllic lunch date, when after 90 minutes outside on a sweltering day I became convinced that I had inadvertently baked my baby. When the thought first dawned (I believe it was after glimpsing the word "brulee" on the dessert menu) I leapt from the table and ran home, pushing the stroller ahead of me. Simone *looked* fine, but this didn't deter me from stripping her naked and sponging her with cold washcloths, then sitting with my (now VERY ANGRY) baby beside the air conditioner, pouring ice cold milk down her gullet until her hands and feet turned blue, a condition I attributed at first to oxygen deprivation, rather than, you know, being naked, wet, and drinking cold liquids next to an air conditioning vent.

There was also, always, the vague sense that I should be doing *something*, though I never managed to discern what that something might be. I was writing freelance science articles and caring for a baby, but I felt the scheduling was off, somehow. We had no bedtime routine, and our days were slap-dash and unplanned. Simone lay on her play mat, or suckled Madame Penguin, a plush bird sewn to a pacifier, and I typed or performed small tasks aimed (rather lowly) at keeping my child alive. I tried recording my schedule, once, jotting down my activities on paper as they were completed:

4:00 AM Baby wakes, nurse baby

5:00 AM Back to sleep

7:30 AM Baby wakes, feed baby, change baby, play with baby on floor

9:00 AM Pump, put baby in chair

9:20 AM Swaddle baby, put in swing, make breakfast

9:45 AM Work

11:00 AM Baby awake, change baby, give baby medicine, feed baby

11:45 AM Baby in sling, back to work

1:00 PM Put baby in swing, pump

1:15 PM Baby crying—change baby, make bottles, feed baby

2:15 PM Put baby in chair, go to bathroom, make lunch, eat lunch

3:00 PM Exercise

4:00 PM ...

I never did finish recording the day; either I got too busy or I just did-n't care enough. I did wonder, often what babies were supposed to *do* all day—probably I should be stimulating mine in some way that I wasn't, but try as I might, I couldn't get worked up enough to change my method, which wasn't one. I had never been the sort to "go with the flow"—even the expression conjured whitewater rafting or riding an inflatable some-thing over a waterfall, and I'd never understood why people found the phrase indicative of relaxation. But with the flow I did go: I'd purchased a baby book (the American Academy of Pediatrics Guide to Children and Their Many Ailments, or something) but I had yet to open it. I didn't peruse timetables, or read about my developing baby and her developmen-tal milestones.

I was all too aware of time passing, however, which turned out to be the most difficult usual difficulty of all. Every once in a while I would lie in bed staring at Simone in her bassinet next to me, and feel a pain that felt posi-tively medieval, like I was being emotionally drawn and quartered. Babies, by nature, are impermanent, and the knowledge filleted me. I didn't *want* Simone to get older. I would have liked her to remain my smiling, milk-scented newborn forever. I knew this was horrible of me, and selfish—I should have delighted in the thought of watching my daughter bloom into independence, but I didn't, at least not always. Partly, it seemed like all these different, future Simones were separate people, each cruelly killing her precedent. Sure, I'd probably love the little girl Simone, and the older-still Simone she'd become, but I also resented this stranger, deeply, because she was going to *steal my baby from me.* I wondered if, when I was very old, I would still miss my missing baby. It seemed unfair that I couldn't keep her.

One summer, on vacation from college, my mother and I lay next to one another on the rocky beach of Lake Superior. We'd been spending a July week at this same lodge for years, but this year was different: I was busy with an ill-starred romance, the dynamics of our family were shifting subtly as my brother and I became adults, and it felt keenly like the end of an era.

My mother was reading aloud from Annie Dillard, a passage about birth defects, and, in particular, bird-headed dwarfs.

"*'One bird-headed dwarf lived to be seventy-five years old, no taller than a yardstick'*" she read, looking enchanted, "*'And friendly and pleasant, but easily distracted.'* Doesn't that sound nice?"

"Mother," I said sternly, "I am *not* buying you a bird-headed dwarf."

She waved me off. "Listen to this:"

"*'If your child were a bird-headed dwarf, mentally deficient, you could carry him everywhere. The bird-headed dwarfs and all the babies in Smith's manual have souls, and they all can—and do—receive love and give love. If you gave birth to two bird-headed dwarfs, as these children's mother did—a boy and a girl—you could carry them both everywhere, all their lives, in your arms or in a basket, and they would never leave you, not even to go to college.'*"

My mother gave me a pointed look at this last, and then gazed at the lake, wistful. Bird-headed dwarfs popped up in her conversation frequently throughout the week, usually in (favorable) comparison to something said or done by me or my brother.

"I wouldn't imagine bird-headed *dwarfs* do much squabbling," she'd say while Max and I bickered over who was consigned to the back seat of the car, "What with being so easily distracted. I'd just offer them each a cookie."

Watching my sleeping baby, I at last understood what my mother had meant. Bird headed dwarfs popped into my head as well, when the idea that my present, perfect baby would disappear seemed too awful to contemplate.

I'd planned to write regular letters to Simone after birth, just as I had to both babies before, but aside from the one I penned when she turned a month old in the NICU, I only managed one other, about a month after she came home with us:

"*Dear Simone,*

I find it hard to believe, but Sunday you were four months old. Your due date, the day on which your developmental clock officially began ticking, was only three weeks ago. When strangers see you, they invariably comment upon your size: "Oh!" they exclaim, "A brand new baby!"

I am never sure how to respond. What, this old thing? We've had her for ages.

You like to dance. It's a lazy sort of dancing that doesn't involve any movement on your part; instead you curl on my chest while I bob around and sing. I recently made us a playlist (what the kids used to call a "mix tape") with a little bit of everything on it—some Petula Clark, some Stevie Wonder. Mr. Wonder was premature himself, you know. Preemies can get down just as well as anyone else. Maybe better.

You like having the bottoms of your feet rubbed. You like it when your father or I play the very sophisticated game "Crazy Arms," in which we waggle your arms about in an educational fashion. Other things you like include milk, Madame Penguin, and nudity (your own).

Before we brought you home from the hospital, I looked at swings. I had heard that babies are fond of them, but when I saw how big they were, and mentally placed one in our small apartment, I decided it was an unnecessary extravagance. Besides, I was pretty sure I would never want to put you down. Probably I would just hold you all day and evening, in my arms or in your sling. I would be like a calm, naturally maternal native woman, only with nicer shoes.

I do love to hold you, and you do love your sling, falling asleep as if it has been soaked in chloroform. But sometimes I need to use the stove, a no-no with a baby on oxygen. Sometimes I need to pick up around the house, and all that bustling and bending is hard while wheeling a tank and wearing an infant with poor head control. And sometimes I need to do something extravagant, just for Milk Lady. Like pee.

My solution was to plop you in your vibrating chair. However you were not amenable to this plan, and in the mornings while I raced around the kitchen getting your medicines and both of our breakfasts ready, you would cry accusingly at me from your purring throne. Always, always you want to be held, an understandable preference to be sure, but there are limits, baby. And so I sent your father out yesterday with stern instructions not to return without a swing, and yesterday afternoon we put you in it and turned it on.

A single ray of sun slanted though the hole that had suddenly appeared in the ceiling above us, and somewhere, I could hear the gentle strains of a harp. You adore this swing, and right now while I type you are asleep in it, swaying gently next to me. Sometimes I just stare at you, unable to believe you are really here, and really mine. When I pluck you from your crib in the morning, I feel overwhelmed by my luck, and your sweetness.

Everyone says the time goes fast with children, and while I always assumed the years would skid by, I was surprised at how damnably short the hours are as well. There is never enough space in a day for all the things I want to do with you, and mostly I just manage the basics, and tell myself that tomorrow we will do more. But I never catch up, and you are already outgrowing your first clothes.

In a way it was easier before your due date. It was bonus time! You weren't supposed tobe here, yet. But now it's official, the sand is pouring through the hourglass, and even your swing reminds me as it sways back and forth: tick, tock, tick, tock.

Every minute I spend with you is a good one, and there will never be enough of them.

Love,

Your Mama"

At the end of June, Simone was scheduled for her oxygen evaluation, the test we hoped would rid us of the cannula at last, leaving her to breathe unaided like the rest of the family. She was already on the lowest oxygen setting, and we had every reason to be optimistic. Her medications had been winnowed to Prevacid, the nebulizer, and a multivitamin. She was being discharged from the home apnea program, the services of the night-time monitor no longer required. The Simply Thick was simply passé, and she drank unthickened milk with choke-less aplomb.

The test itself was unkind to the nerves. Five hours long, it meant arriving at nine in the morning with the requested supplies (diapers, wipes, Danny Sling, two bottles, extra socks, a blanket, and an extra two-piece outfit) and transporting them, my baby, and her oxygen tank to the hospital's special diagnostics laboratory, a venue that managed to give the impression of subterranean location despite being on the third floor.

We were shown to a tiny windowless room. It was dim, and contained a crib, a creaking wooden rocking chair, and a wall mounted camera that would be observing us for the duration. Simone was festooned with a series of electrodes upon her torso, bands cinched around her chest and belly to measure their movement, a long sticky strip affixed under her nose and along her cheeks to detect airflow. There was a familiar pulse oximeter wrapped about her foot, and a special cannula strapped in place. All these wires were connected to various diagnostic devices—a stunning array—the data from which would be collected by the two technicians sitting outside the room, watching us. They were both friendly and male, one older and one younger, the older with a sharp wit and a comforting, avuncular manner.

Oxygen turned off, Simone needed to be recorded sleeping, awake, and during two separate feedings. If her oxygen saturation fell below certain parameters, the oxygen would be restarted at her current one-sixteenth of a liter, and then weaned down as far as she could tolerate.

"Go about your normal routine," they told me, and it was hard not to laugh, looking around at the closetlike room, the single rickety chair, and my baby, who had wires protruding in every possible direction. It was all very David Lynch.

"If you need anything," they said, "just wave at the camera. We'll be watching."

Alarms rang a few times during our five-hour confinement, but the oxygen remained off, and the only time we saw the technicians was when Simone spit up with an enthusiastic splatter, and one rushed in with a towel.

"I'm not supposed to say anything," said the older tech as he unhooked Simone that afternoon, "but she did really well." Not that it mattered for the moment: the report had to be interpreted and transcribed, and then reviewed by Dr. Krolik. Until then it was business, and oxygen, as usual. We stopped by the NICU on the way back to the car. We did this whenever Simone had an appointment at the hospital that summer.

"She's so big!" the nurses universally exclaimed, and we all stood around admiring our handiwork. I loved the feeling of triumphant return, the pride and glee on the faces of Wendy and Amber and everyone from the respiratory therapist to the woman who'd buzzed me in the door each morning. Everyone clustered in the entryway, remembering aloud how small and sick my baby had been, and marveling at the distance we'd traveled.

Visits weren't enough to keep my Zen from getting awfully rusty, and waiting for the results of the oxygen evaluation was excruciating, each hour stretching into days, and the days themselves—all ten or so—comprising at least half an era.

The nurse called on the Thursday of a Fourth of July weekend, while we were out at lunch.

"Simone seems to be doing well on one-sixteenth of a liter, so Dr. Krolik would like to keep her on that amount and do another study in six to twelve weeks."

"Oh, okay!" I said, with cheer so faux it verged upon parody, "That seems sensible. Thank you for calling!"

My politeness wrestled with my devastated petulance, and just before hanging up, the battle was won, and I blurted out a whiny footstomp masquerading as concern.

"I just don't *understand*. How bad was it? Is there something I should be aware of? I'm just surprised, is all, because she stayed off oxygen the *whole time.*"

"You mean *on*," the nurse corrected me, polite herself.

"No," I said, "*OFF*. OFF oxygen. As in *without* any."

"Oh dear," said the nurse, with an audible frown.

The report, you see, had neglected to mention this single, pertinent detail. Normally it would contain a sentence about the patient's oxygen being extinguished, but it hadn't, thus giving the impression that they had been unable to keep her stable without it, and performed the whole test with Simone sucking in her customary one-sixteenth of a liter.

"Oh," said the nurse, "this changes *everything.*"

Mainly what it changed was the fact that my waiting was back on. Now Dr. Krolik would have to call the special diagnostics laboratory, and they would have to speak to the technicians, and have the whole rigamarole repeated with the correct information—delayed, naturally, by the holiday weekend. I hung up near tears, returning to the patio table where my mother and Eloise waited with Simone in her stroller, oxygen tank mocking me from the undercarriage.

Five months to the day after she was first intubated down the hall from the operating room where my doctor was admiring the performance of her new staple gun, I grew impatient and called, again, hoping for news. My mother was with me in my apartment, and must have seen the shock in my face when Dr. Krolik's nurse said, breezily:

"Yup, you can go ahead and d/c the oxygen." She said it as if it were nothing, so routine that there was no need to bother with saying the whole word "discontinue."

"Really?" I squeaked, "just like that?"

She laughed a kind laugh. "Just like that."

When I hung up the phone I grabbed for Simone, tearing the cannula from her face, surprising myself with my urgency and the sob that rose behind my throat. I was scraping at the patches of tape on Simone cheeks, desperate to have them off, and my mother helped me roll the oxygen tank into the nursery. She held Simone while I rubbed the adhesive with an alcohol wipe until the stickers were removed, leaving red spots behind in my violence. I hugged my baby, fierce.

"I don't know why I'm crying," I said to my mother, laughing at the sight of Simone's face, clear for the first time since birth. I hardly recognized her. It was as if one feature had been removed and the others had rearranged themselves to take advantage of the extra space. My mother and I danced around the apartment, holding Simone high and proclaiming her freedom.

Thirty

Sometime that summer I met my friend Lizzie for a drink. She'd just returned from living in Portland after graduate school in Vermont, and though I'd talked to her on the phone from the hospital the day after Simone was born, I hadn't seen her in almost two years. Lizzie was Rick's daughter, and by virtue of our parents' friendship we'd known each other since we were young children. There is no friend I've had longer, or who has seen me through so many incarnations. She flew to New York with me to see me off to college, and she was my roommate in my first two apartments. She feels more like family than friend, and I can see her or not for great swaths of time without losing any of the ease between us.

Lizzie grew up in The Country. It was only 40 minutes from my home in the city, but to me it was another world, and the first time I spent the night at her house I lay awake, disturbed by the quiet. Twice we attended day camp together out in her neck of the literal woods. The camp was on a farm: one summer we studied French, learning the words *poulet* and *oeuf* as we gathered sticky eggs from jaded hens; the next choosing art and sculpting clay kittens with the real things for models. The camp was full of Lizzie's classmates—bold, tan children who mocked my entirely reasonable aversion to the ticks that studded the tall grass I reluctantly traversed. They laughed at my horror when these ticks were pulled from animals, gray and engorged, looking as if they ought to have "GOODYEAR" stenciled upon their sides. These same children also mocked my fear of Lyme disease, and my dislike of the river's many leeches. These hearty, apple-cheeked friends of leeches rolled their eyes when I hesitated at the door of the hayloft, looking at the pile of hay far below and wondering *what if I miss?*

Lizzie defended my wariness as a product of my residence in The City, but she knew better, and would witness thousands of subsequent anxieties over the years, arguably as familiar with my neurosis as anyone. And so it came as a genuine shock when she looked up at me across the table, where I stood, talking—bouncing my crying baby and gesturing with the cocktail in my free hand—and interrupted to say:

"You are like a completely different person."

"*Really?*" I asked, setting my drink on the table. "It's noticeable? I mean, I seem different to you?"

She nodded, vehement.

"Totally different. You're just...I don't know. You're *different*. You seem...calm."

"*I am!*" I confessed, in an excited, wondering tone. I'd noticed it in fits and starts. One afternoon, after trying (and failing) to remember my last panic attack, I realized I couldn't remember the last time I'd felt anxiety at all. I'm not talking about small, situational worries (*Did that check go through? Will I finish my article on time?*) or the frisson of nervousness I got before making certain phone calls. What was absent was the feeling of being beset by constant danger, the endless loop of *whatif!whatif!whatif!* spooling within my skull.

Within the spectrum of concern—ranging from "profoundly stoned" to "unfounded terror"—there is another, nested spectrum representing variations in temperament among mentally healthy individuals. I will never, barring lobotomy or pharmaceutical intervention, fall much below the midpoint of this narrower range, simply by virtue of my sensitive wiring: I am like an excitable tuning fork, vibrating at the mere appearance of a striking implement. Before, though, I wouldn't have placed myself within that normal span at all.

Before *when?* I wondered. I would have liked to pinpoint the start of my drift toward center, but I couldn't.

We have a tendency to view our personalities as static, as if we are reducible to trading-card versions of ourselves. We need to know who we are, if for no other purpose than to assist in the winnowing of choices from an endless abundance, and in our eagerness for coherence we often forfeit complexity.

When I was in elementary school, I passed small slips of stationery to my classmates on the playground, asking them to describe me using five adjectives of their choice. I collected the cards in a box and pored over them later at home, looking for points of agreement. Remembering this now, I don't know whether to laugh or to cry—what a strange child I was; what a backward (yet methodical!) method of self-discovery. I wish I could recall the results, but I can't. Maybe because "weird" was surely among the more common entries.

I didn't think about my identity in this conscious way once I was an adult, but unconsciously, we all smooth the differences between our actions and our conceptions of ourselves, usually deferring to the latter. Whether I admitted it or not, neurosis had become my schtick. It doesn't matter whether the reality or the idea came first—once installed they reinforced one another, living in a mutual symbiosis not unlike the one I had with my intestinal flora. If, before Simone was born, I'd been asked to make a list of adjectives that *wouldn't* be used to describe me, I would have answered thus: *Athletic, capable, strong. Brave, calm, sensible. Responsible. Unflappable. Serene.*

"*Athletic*" remains, firmly, upon that list. In the spirit of open-mindedness, I will admit that this could change; it's possible, though statistically unlikely—like true hermaphroditism, or drowning in one's bathtub. "*Responsible*" stays on the "No" list as well, along with "*serene*." But several of the other words, while not among the first I'd use to describe myself, are at least no longer among the last. "*Brave*," for instance, and even "*calm*" and "*unflappable*"—I may flap, but not so reliably as I once did.

276

The greatest upsets are "*capable,*" "*sensible,*" and "*strong.*" Approached by the younger Alexa, with her studious box of stationery and a convenient assortment of pens, it is quite possible that *capable, sensible,* and *strong* would be among the five adjectives I'd choose to describe myself, now, in the future. Maybe not, with only five—I'd need room for "*indecisive,*" "*affectionate,*" and "*easily amused*"—but you see my meaning. What I want is something deeper than a cataloguing of variable traits, something closer to a credo. Maybe a complicated, singular word like the Greeks have, or one of the compound monstrosities thought up by German philosophers to fill my college hours with torment. A word that means something like "*Persevering with reason and humor.*" I'd like to have that word, whatever it is, engraved somewhere. This is as near as I get to essentialism, the belief that—while I may lose or acquire fears, and become more or less likely to wear fashionably uncomfortable shoes or pay bills on time or chat with strangers—there is an enduring *something* that informs my perspective, culled from a gumbo of genetics and experience. *Persevering with reason and humor* is the divining rod in my breast, and there's no denying I've found it easier to follow since the Great Reproductive Disaster of Aught Eight—or, The Trail of Tubes, or The Time With All the Beeping, whatever you want to call it. I need a shorthand for referring to the period between our heartbeat-not-heard-round-the-world ultrasound and Simone's discharge from the hospital. It comes up more than you might think, and I'm reduced to vagueness: *That Whole Thing,* I say, with an ambiguous hand motion (An ASL version of the Grief Leaf? The universal sign for ventilator? It's unclear). On my website I fall back on *The Dark Time*—which is part melodrama, part caveman referring to his pre-Promethean childhood. I should just name the era once and for all: Gestation-gate, or the Wreck of the *SS Alexa*, or The Four Months During Which the Music May Not Have Died But Certainly Became Less Cheerful.

The point is, since Love in the Time of Ventilators, I've been clearer, able to trim back the fear obscuring my vision. And the view's much better from here.

Before Simone's birth, nothing caused me more anxiety than my anxiety, as phenomenally stupid as that sounds. I felt my nerves made me weak and susceptible, like a vase that's been broken and repaired multiple times, and now resides on a rickety table in the foyer of a Home For Boisterous Boys. I spent a lot of time avoiding things I was certain I could not handle, like international travel, swimming, and rejection, anticipating the anxiety caused by disaster far more keenly than any actual disaster. The phrase "nothing to fear but fear itself" enraged me—because my God, wasn't that *enough*?

Everyone loves a story of transformation. The idea of an event as a wand that waves over one person and replaces him with a wiser one is alluring, but I don't want you to get the wrong idea. A permanent lessening of anxiety is the result of accumulation—of catastrophes that fail to materialize, and unbearable things that you bear despite yourself. It's silly to think that a lightning strike to a kite or an apple-related concussion are anything more than tipping points, that we don't change, minute by minute, in undetectable increments. I discovered a flair for self-injection, held a small corpse and contemplated the possibility of another, and consistently neglected to have a nervous breakdown. Eventually, I had to admit I *had* changed, but not by exchanging the "Anxious Alexa" trading card for "Insouciant Alexa" (Collect them all!). Driving downtown, I still clutch clammily at the wheel as my heart flirts with arrhythmia, and I will ever regard those who strike balls with bats in public parks as being guilty of Reckless Endangerment (*a D felony*, she said sternly). I'm not a whole new me, just a version modified to reflect additional evidence.

Explaining this to someone recently, I compared Tropical Storm Isolette to mascara. I have a deep love for cosmetics, and could spend hours in a department store comparing this shade of pink to that, weighing the pros (laziness-friendly!) and cons (prone to creasing) of cream eyeshadow. Whenever I buy new makeup, I leave feeling giddy with the promise of metamorphosis. I ascribe transmogrifying properties to lipstick, the power to change much more than the shade of my mouth. When I fondle a heavy jar of face cream I am imagining another Alexa, one whose features are more alluringly arranged, whose skin is as poreless as glass, who possesses the will to carefully remove her makeup every night before tumbling into bed. I know I'm not alone. I have seen a wistful, contemplative look come over women holding bottles of foundation, as well as the slight sag when someone who has just applied expensive lipgloss looks in the mirror and realizes she hasn't been transfigured into Catherine Deneuve quite as convincingly as she'd hoped.

I have invisibly blonde lashes, long but thin, their irrelevance exacerbated by my gigantic, round eyes, the sort you'd find on a Muppet. My eyes are my best feature, a changeable blue, and I have always coveted for them a frame like the thick double fringe of the young Elizabeth Taylor. I wore false lashes for three years in high school, and have tried every respectably regarded mascara on the market. My favorites do an excellent job, but in the end mascara doesn't create eyelashes, it merely reveals and amplifies the ones that were there all along. Similarly, what doesn't kill you might not make you stronger so much as reveal and amplify the strength that was already there.

During my summer of morning vomiting, I was prone to panic, especially before meals—wondering whether I'd be able to force anything down and knowing that if I didn't I'd only feel worse. My mother's advice was always the same: "Pretend to be someone else," she'd say, "Pretend to be Julie Kavner." A study had shown that the act of smiling itself raised spirits, and perhaps if I *pretended* to be happy, or at least amused by my own neurosis, I'd trick myself into feeling a bit better. I suppose some would say this is unhealthy and repressive, particularly certain psychologists who are eager proponents of expressing, validating, and fondling one's every dyspeptic mood and childhood slight. I'm no psychologist, but as a tenured crazy person with years of experience dealing with the mentally ill (I've been dealing with myself for thirty years now, and friends and family to boot), I feel qualified to say that not only is this behavior extremely unappealing, but luxuriating in sadness and nursing too tenderly various grudges against history can be every bit as harmful as denying their existence. I'm pretty sure Epictetus would agree with me, given the exasperated *"I must die. Must I then die lamenting? I must be put in chains.*

Must I then also lament?" business of his. In fact, the emotional "fake it till you make it" approach advocated by my mother has an impressive pedigree: there's the Buddhist assertion that right action leads to right thought, there's scientific evidence of our craftily rewiring brains, there's even Dr. Phil's exhortation to "behave your way to success"—not a bad piece of advice, even if it does come from someone who frequently states his intention to begin "putting verbs in his sentences."

After my psych ward sojourn, I forced myself to rise every morning and take a long walk, ending at the cathedral a block from my apartment. I sprang awake at 4:30 or so, and I was usually the only one in the sanctuary aside from the tiny old man replacing the spent votives. I took deep breaths in the quiet sanctuary and stared pointedly at the painting on the ceiling labeled PERSEVERANCE, wishing I were made of stronger, braver stuff. It didn't occur to me that going through the motions might be enough to make me the person I was pretending to be. In the Nervous Hospital, I'd sewn a leather coin purse for my best friend. I felt drugged and ill from the medications, and my hands shook, but I managed to stamp it with "Greetings from The Bell Jar!" I may not have been able to see it at the time, but if that's not *"persevering with reason and humor,"* I don't know what is.

Simone's first appointment with her bow-tied pediatrician was two days after her due date, and she was undressed, and poked, and pronounced a fine, upstanding specimen.

"You're doing a great job," the pediatrician said, buttering me up for the news that Simone wasn't gaining weight fast enough. Scott and I gathered our baby and provisions and headed for home, where I felt vaguely as if something was...off. It was me, I realized. My reaction to the pediatrician's news had been a mild *I guess we'll step up the feeding schedule,* no Googling of growth charts or suspicious monitoring of diaper output. In fact, when the doctor had asked how many bottles and wet diapers Simone had each day, I had pursed my lips for a minute before giving an estimate. An *estimate!* I marveled over it online:

"This has been the biggest surprise since our homecoming, just how calm and almost lackadaisical I am as a mother. It is easily the best thing to come from Simone's varied and several brushes with death, this feeling that as long as she's breathing, the rest is gravy. I always expected that I would be the sort of parent who keeps spreadsheets detailing her kid's every feeding and bowel movement, but instead I make sure she eats every three-ish hours, and gets her medicines every 12-ish hours, and otherwise merely go about my business with my baby in the sling all day, licking the occasional dropped crumb from her head."

Simone had been home for about a month when she was stricken, forcefully, by a bout of what in my family we referred to as intestinal distress. She had a slight fever, and cried in such mournful-sounding wails that I took pity upon her and called the after-hours nurse line to see whether I could give her a whiff of Tylenol, and how much a dose might be for a baby of her stature. I almost hadn't bothered calling, and thus was a little embarrassed when the nurse directed us to proceed to the emergency room. However, I'd discover that summer that any call to the clinic's after hours line took a sharp turn for the alarmist as soon as the nurse pulled up Simone's medical history. It was all "probably a virus" until the part about the virus' host having been born 100 days early, and then it was "Why don't you come in, just in case?"

Back at the hospital for the first time, we were taken straight back to an exam room, so that Simone's fragile lungs needn't be exposed to hoi polloi. When the doctor entered with Simone's unopened chart, I explained about the feverishness and the *intestinal distress,* and cobbled together an estimated number of soiled diapers (pediatricians are obsessed with soiled diapers, I tell you).

"Does she have any health problems?" the doctor asked.

"Nope!"

He looked, pointedly, at the oxygen tank.

"Oh!" I said, "That!" I laughed. "She was born at 25 weeks, and is still on oxygen. Just one-sixteenth of a liter."

"Anything else?"

I shook my head.

"Medications?"

"Pulmicort for her lungs, and Prevacid twice daily for reflux—I guess I forgot to mention reflux, didn't I?"

I told him about it, then, and when he asked about her history in the NICU I told him about that, feeling sillier and sillier the longer I went on and the more incredulous his expression became. It was like one of those magic trick handkerchiefs that just keep coming, and by the time I'd covered both episodes of renal failure and the intrajugular heparin drip, I would have happily vanished in a puff of smoke.

We were sent home shortly—it was probably just a virus, after all—but I kept replaying the beginning of the conversation in my head, and blushing. *Does she have any health problems? Oh no! Unless you count the oxygen tank!*

There is a weariness common to parents of micropreemies, after a month or so in the NICU. I don't mean physical exhaustion, though there is that too: you shall know them by their urgent, distracted shuffle, by their inability to count exact change, by the simultaneously wild and dead-looking eyes, eyes that ought to belong to a character out of Oregon Trail—family dispatched by cholera, no buffalo in sight, and battling a brutal case of dysentery. But what I mean is the emotional leadenness that comes of learning to live with the uncertainty of having a baby who may or may not survive, in a particularly hellish combination of circumstances. A month-old baby of 30 weeks is often in critical, changeable condition, but for an extended period of time. It's like having a baby who has been in an accident or developed an acute and life-threatening infection AND having a baby suffering from a chronic disease, like cancer, with an uncertain prognosis. It's the emotional equivalent of combining a sprint and a marathon. Your baby could be diagnosed with a fatally advanced case of NEC tomorrow, or could be discharged from the NICU on his due date, alive. In twenty years, your 26-weeker might be the one with no apparent lingering consequences of prematurity, or the one with cerebral palsy, or the one who seemed fine until elementary school, and was then diagnosed with learning disabilities or severe asthma.

At some point the weariness becomes less a product of immediate dangers than of the fear that you will never be able to look at your child without seeing all the ways they could have been taken away from you. This might be more draining, even, because it makes the siege seem endless, and it's not an unjustified fear. A significant percentage of parents develop post-traumatic stress disorder once the NICU is behind them. Some never shake the constant, pressing knowledge of how precarious life is, and how capricious the application of luck. They bathe their toddlers in antibacterial soap, and wipe their counters daily with bleach, and buy special pillowcases designed to rendition allergens and dust mites to remote, tortuous locales. They insist upon helmets for tricycles and skateboarding and newly licensed drivers. They move to a new neighborhood, because the old one had too many drowning basins—oh, I mean *swimming pools.*

A little extra protectiveness and anxiety would be understandable in anyone bringing home a preemie, even the most formerly even-tempered and unconcerned. I was neither of these, and would have thought I'd be investing in home autoclaves along with my new sisters in paranoia. Long before the NICU, I'd assumed I'd choose a pediatrician based upon how unlikely she seemed to be annoyed by my nightly phone calls. The first thing I'd put on the registry I'd barely started for the twins was an electronic device meant to time the intervals between feedings and diaper changes, allowing you to set yourself alarms and record and download all the pertinent data, and even slide a tab to the left or right to indicate which breast you'd last offered.

When the time came, though, I never bothered with anything like that. I didn't even have one of those bathtub spout covers that measure the temperature and keeps you from boiling the baby or crushing her skull on the metal faucet. Not that she was even bathed all that often, to tell you the truth. A few times, I forgot her multivitamin, and when I introduced solid foods, although I started in the recommended, cautious fashion—rice cereal first, single ingredients, two days between each new offering—I quickly forgot, offering a spoonful of this, a spoonful of that, a dollop of our curry, a french fry. When five-month-old Simone enthusiastically licked the cat, I stopped to laugh before removing the hair that coated her tongue.

A large part of motherhood is about relinquishing control. Generally you have eighteen years for this project, and it happens with a series of steps: the first day of kindergarten, a driver's license, college. Gradually you accept—or try to—the fact that you cannot keep your baby from harm, not always. Being a mother in the NICU is a painful crash course in this concept, like learning to swim by being dropped into the ocean by a helicopter. In the aftermath of being dumped, flailing, into the Pacific, it wouldn't be unreasonable to experience an increase in anxiety, even to develop a fear of water altogether.

On the other hand, if you were an aquaphobe to begin with, the plunge might do you some good. It's hard to be afraid of a bathtub after that.

In the emergency room, when the doctor asked me whether Simone had any health problems, it truly didn't occur to me to answer any differently. Proximity to actual tragedy had inoculated me against smaller upsets, and I had a hard time relating to other first time mothers, with their concern over organic food and televison. Not because I didn't care about those things, but because I didn't care as much. I had more in common with mothers who were older, with more years or more children under their belts, and a similar style of battlefield triage. Respiratory illnesses, even the smallest, will always scare me more than most, because of Simone's lungs. But that's triage for you. Baby not breathing? *Important.* Baby consuming half a desiccated bagel she found beneath the couch? *Not important.* Baby crying? *Well, that means she's breathing!*

Sometimes I suspect that my anxiety going into the NICU is at least partially responsible for my lack of it coming out. It turned out that the obsessive information-gathering I'd viewed as a facet of neurosis was actually useful, even calming. At home, the first time Simone fell hard on her head I Googled the *shit* out of concussions and epidural and subdural hematomas, and signs of increased intracranial pressure in children. But as a result of all that, I know that the real danger is striking the temporal bone over the middle meningeal artery, which can bleed and kill you in twenty minutes, while a hematoma in other areas gives you more time and warning. I know that the skulls of babies are specially designed to be thicker in the front and back, and I've got those aforementioned signs of increased ICP down pat. Now when Simone hits her head, I make sure the point of contact is nowhere near the middle meningeal, I check to make sure her pupils are equal and reactive, and I keep an eye out for signs of altered mental status while dusting her off, kissing where it hurts, and sending her back to her regularly scheduled mayhem with an easy mind.

Anxiety is different from preparedness. It isn't helpful, just a desperate scramble to anticipate what awful thing will happen next. Research gave me facts: it told me what to expect when Simone had surgery, and that a baby's fever doesn't cause brain damage until 108 degrees. My fretting, on the other hand, was nothing more than superstition, a doomed attempt to predict the future by worrying about it. All my anxiety did nothing to prepare me for Ames' death, or lessen the blow. Hiding those twin green-striped onesies didn't keep him alive, and once Simone was in the NICU I smacked up against the uselessness of my worry on what felt like a daily basis. What I feared never materialized; what did I never saw coming. Again and again and again my attempts to worry my way into control were thwarted, until it finally sunk in that I could lose Simone at any time at all, in a million different ways, and all the worrying in the world wouldn't change that one whit. Fear should have tightened my grip on her; instead it loosened it. To be honest, it probably should have driven me crazy, but instead it made me saner than I've been in some time. Maybe it's the realization that I'm stronger than I thought I was, or maybe it's just that I've figured out it doesn't matter whether I am or not.

At the end of our first summer we returned to the hospital for another checkup. I was in perilous danger of falling asleep at my post, so we stopped at the coffee shop in the basement where I used to get my tea. The cashier was the same familiar face, and we exchanged smiles and hellos before she motioned to the next customer and I moved down the counter to wait for my cup. I noticed that the woman ordering had one of the flimsy plastic badges they give to parents of long-term patients, and I waited for her to turn so that I could get a look at the department, though I already knew what it would say. She looked just like I must have, all the mornings I hurried here before doctors made rounds: her shoulders hunched, her eyes straying to the middle distance, someplace behind the case of croissants. Perhaps she was seeing numbers scrolling before her: probable days until discharge, percent oxygen saturation, weight in grams.

Simone was babbling in her stroller, smiling approvingly at her recently discovered left foot. She waved it aloft in its sock, and spoke nonsense to it confidentially, like a friend.

"Excuse me," I said, stepping back down the counter, "Do you have a baby in the NICU?"

The woman startled, then nodded. I pointed at Simone, who took no notice of us.

"Twenty-five weeks," I said. "I never thought we'd make it, but we did. We're doing just fine."

Epilogue

I disapprove of endings, on principle. A story has to end sometime, but the choice of when is maddeningly arbitrary, and yet an ending will go back over the story without your permission and change perfectly ordinary bad news to foreshadowing, and add all sorts of undertones and overtones that weren't there before. They're pushy, endings. They're fine for fiction—where weather has meaning, and there really is a fore to shadow—but in nonfiction, disingenuous. I've always loved that Joan Didion line, *We tell ourselves stories in order to live,* and I agree with the statement, but I think it would also be true without that "v" in the last word.

I'm not calling you, personally, a *liar,* understand. Like I said, a story has to end sometime. And it's not really the ending that's the problem, it's us, and our compulsion for narrative integrity. It is not so different from what we do with people and personality, the determined shaping of things into familiar forms, the low tolerance for non-sequiturs or outlying data points. We doggedly pursue causation where there is none; we wrest anecdotes into parables. A friend and I chatted about this at length after her divorce, the way the divorce rewrote people's perception of all the days of the marriage that came before it, undermining the validity of their previous happiness. Had a bus killed the two of them before the topic of divorce came up, the happiness would have been left intact, though with a new, tragic patina.

I like the ending I chose; it's a nice one, pleasantly illustrative of distance traveled. It's a little pat, maybe, to more or less reduce the poor woman at the coffee counter to a symbol of an earlier me, but it adds a satisfying circular quality to the thing. However I could just as easily have ended things a few months later, maybe on the day I took Simone in for an appointment at the NICU follow-up clinic. I could have written about the scene that ensued when Simone failed to turn in the direction of a ringing bell, or in fact to respond to any sound, at all. I could have written about the way she didn't even flinch as we clapped next to her ears and called her name and crumpled paper noisily. I could have ended the story *that* way, and without much additional work, as much of the episode could be cribbed from *The Miracle Worker*. I could have shown you the sad face on the doctor that day, one of Simone's old neonatologists, when he told us that Simone likely had a hearing loss, and might well be profoundly deaf. Maybe I'd keep going for a day or two afterward, and show myself in the kitchen shaking a bottle and bursting into tearful but genuine laughter as I remembered the etymology of "Simone," and realized that I had given my probably-deaf daughter a name meaning "She Who Hears."

I thought a lot about endings in the weeks after that appointment. I was writing a magazine article at the time, and had ended it with the scene in the hospital's basement coffee shop because it seemed—and obviously still does—such a fitting cap to the story of my NICU experience.

Did I have to change the end of the article? The encounter and the emotions around it had been real, but now it felt dishonest, as if I were claiming an illusory triumph. Sure, I'd *felt* triumphant, and intensely aware of how changed I was since Simone's birth, but wasn't omitting her hearing loss the equivalent of writing a memoir of a Miss America win and omitting the fact that my crown had been revoked six-weeks later after it was discovered that—though I hadn't recognized him during the competition—I'd dated one of the judges, back when we were high-school lab partners?

Just that August I'd thought a lot about the way new events recast older ones, as I'd found myself unexpectedly grieving the loss of Ames, and to my annoyance some people acted as if my lack of grief while Simone was in the hospital had thus been proven a lie. People took satisfaction in this development because it brought mine and Ames' story back in line with expectations: the loss of a baby is supposed to be a simple narrative of sorrow, and either my surviving baby had mucked it up or I'd just plain reacted wrongly when I neglected to properly mourn him. Some found my sadness six months after the fact as inappropriate as others did gratifying, diverging as it did from the schedule. *Choose,* both camps seemed to say, *pick a reaction and stick with it.* For a while I avoided writing about Ames on my website, because it seemed like an entry about missing him would imply that I was missing him *right then,* or consistently, when in truth it only cropped up during my more contemplative moments for a few minutes at a time, quickly replaced with laughter at Simone or preoccupation over work, and casting no lingering pall over either. I wondered if *anything* I wrote would be a lie, because wasn't that what storytelling was, in its inclusion and emphasis of certain details and omission of others?

Every word I select, writing this book, is a rejection of other ones, based upon my perception of how closely the chosen word reflects or recreates reality, or at least the reality I remember. I make decisions about what to include and not to include, what was important and what, ultimately, wasn't. Of course it's hard to know what's important before all the facts are in—and they never are.

A month after our Miracle Worker moment, testing revealed that Simone, in fact, had *perfect* hearing—masked by a cat-like ability to ignore that in which she lacked interest. *Ring that stupid bell all you want,* she'd apparently been thinking, *I'm going to keep playing with these diverting plastic cups.* When the therapist stood to the side and clapped briskly, Simone had continued staring at my face not because she couldn't hear the clapping but because it didn't seem pressing—while I, on the other hand, might have been concealing milk about my person. It was a relief to have the question of the truth of my article's ending rendered moot (doubly moot a few months later, when the magazine folded), but while we'd been waiting for Simone's hearing testing I'd felt like all of my thoughts about our time in the NICU had been thrown into disarray, and I've been thinking about that feeling ever since.

I believe there should be a permanent embargo on the phrase "miracle baby." Finding a news story about a preemie that doesn't use this phrase is about as easy as finding a usage of the phrase "men's empowerment" that doesn't make my eyes roll like possessed marbles (in my defense, type it into the search box and even Google asks, pointedly "Did you mean *women's* empowerment?") Miracle babies are described as "fighters," and "brave," and there is the suggestion of a specialness not present among the babies who were not miraculous enough to make it. My other issue with "miracle baby" it is that it devalues the work done by researchers, doctors, and nurses, giving the impression that sorcery is the chief ingredient of a NICU Success Story.

Which, incidentally, is the one phrase I hate even more than "miracle baby," because what *is* a NICU Success Story? A baby who makes it out of the NICU alive, or a baby who makes it out of the NICU unscathed? Is there such a thing? Is it meeting the much-vaunted goal of "caught up by age two," or does it mean *staying* caught up? What does "caught up" even mean?

There is a tool, now, on the website of the National Institutes for Health, that lets you enter a few pieces of data about a premature infant— gestational weeks completed, birthweight in grams, gender, a few others—and upon pressing a button it will generate the statistical probability that your baby will live. It doesn't take into account any of the post-birth catastrophes that might change the picture, brain bleeds or the lack of them, or the statistically encouraging sign of continuing survival over time, or whether your particular NICU uses developmental care or your particular doctor has any particularly specialized experience.

It wasn't around when Simone was born, but if I feed it her information now, it tells me that she had a 72% chance of survival, a 44% chance of Death or Profound Neurodevelopmental Impairment. She had a 38% chance of Survival Without Moderate to Severe Neurodevelopmental Impairment. A preemie with delayed motor skills at 18 months might be classified as "moderately impaired," but a year later therapy might have caught him up. A preemie might test normal at 22 months and develop sensory issues a year later.

And then there are the full-term children who walk "late" or don't say a word until they are three. The list of conditions that may be linked to prematurity is long, and I have several of them myself, despite having been born punctually. ADD, terrible eyesight, problems with anxiety and sensitivity to stimulation. Had I been born prematurely, would these traits disqualify me from being a success story? Many are genetic, and if Simone inherits my ADD, do we pin it on prematurity, or her crazy mother?

Simone's lungs are not the same as a fullterm baby, and she has only one really effective kidney. She seems like any other two-year-old, but I see no point in arguing against the fact that she is different than she might have been had she arrived less hastily. A brain that develops in a womb is different from a brain that develops elsewhere—that's just science. What bothers me is the notion that this is something worth moping over, that there is some inherent SIMONE that was *supposed* to be and was thwarted by her early arrival on the scene, some perfect genetic expression of potential that will never be realized. Genes, it is my understanding, may be turned on or off by experience. Having a gene that makes you prone to migraines isn't like having the genes that give you blue eyes. Some genes sit around unused for ages, some are turned on by a fluke of chemistry. It seems to be built into the coding, that our experiences shape who we are and leave other possibilities behind. Prematurity is an extreme example, but there are so many factors that go into making a person, I don't see the point in coming over all wistful about The Simone That Never Was. It's like whining about all the ways in which you might have been different if your childhood had contained less factory work and more bracing fresh air. By all means, be angry, and organize other factory working children to rise up upon their bandy, ricketed legs and throw off the shackles of oppression. But let's not get carried away and blame all that loom time for everything that ever went wrong with your life. As far as I am concerned, Simone's exactly right as she is.

There seem to be two warring schools of thought among preemie parents. There is a group that steadfastly maintains that once a preemie begins meeting appropriate milestones, she is just like any other child. For these parents it is truly a matter of "catching up"—the process is linear, and preemies are babies born a few steps behind, who need only a few developmental cram sessions to bring then equal with their peers. The other faction is as resolutely pessimistic as the other is optimistic: preemies are damaged, will always be damaged, and a fair amount of bitterness is attached to this fact, along with strong opinions about the inadvisability of resuscitating very premature infants. These are the people for whom their child's status as "preemie" will always color every shortcoming and success.

To no one's surprise, I am sure, members of the former group tend to be those with better outcomes, the latter with worse. The optimists seem irritated by any discussion of the real, lingering problems of premature birth; the latter unwilling to allow for the possibility that statistics vary widely according to hospital practices, and that there are, against all odds, English-cucumber-sized babies who grow up free from all but the ordinary troubles.

The tension between triumph and tragedy in the land of premature parenthood borders upon the absurd. I don't see why one has to rule out the other, myself. I have no desire to frame Simone's early birth as anything other than a tragedy, but I don't see why that should reduce her to one. The saddest stories are the babies who come home from the NICU in the triumph camp, and then die a year or two later from a respiratory disease. They get shunted into "tragedy," then, and it irks me. Why should the good be denied because something terrible happened later? Can't they be NICU success stories, too? Why do they have to be "stories" at all? What if Simone dies of bee-stings one summer, like the unfortunate boy from *A Taste of Blackberries?*—the book that instilled in my six-year-old self a healthy suspicion of bees? What if she gets the swine flu, or pneumonia?

Will they take away our NICU Survivor badge?

The ending shouldn't determine the meaning of anything, a story *or* a life. Logically, I don't think it can—didn't Heidegger say something to that effect? That the meaning of all our moments cannot be contingent upon an end-point over which we have no control? That if we are happy right now, that means something, even if we die tomorrow? Narrative integrity is overrated. I don't need to know that the story of my life has a happy ending to enjoy it. A good thing, too, because I hear all the characters die in the end.

While narrative integrity may be overrated, what is underrated is denial. "Live like there's no tomorrow!" you hear, and if that isn't the stupidest idea since the pain scale I don't know what is. It's important to appreciate what you have, but if you really want to enjoy it, you can't be constantly anticipating its loss. I say live as though there IS a tomorrow. Anyone who has ever lived otherwise knows what a brutal and untenable way it is to exist. The NICU is a tomorrow-less place, at least it was for me in the beginning, and I'm glad to be rid of it. I come over all gooey with gratitude at least once a day, scooping up my toddler and smelling her hair and tickling her hysterical, but I have also been known to wonder, during a particularly emphatic tantrum of hers, how young is too young for military school. And this, I feel, is exactly as it should be.

Take George Bailey, a year after the action of *It's a Wonderful Life*. One would hope that he saved ZuZu's petals and still looks at them fondly from time to time, but that he is also occasionally driven slightly mad by a child boisterously playing the piano, and has long since dispensed with the "Merry Christmas, you wonderful old Building and Loan!" effusiveness, because if he hasn't I suspect he's beginning to try the patience of poor Donna Reed.

"Oh for god's sake, George!" I imagine her saying as they drive through town and he leans out the car window to ardently greet the movie house for the eight-hundredth time, "Will you give it a rest, already?"

There is a fine line between gratitude and paralysis. Here is where I was going to put my very favorite quote, except that I find the Internet insisting that said quote does not exist. Instead it is my own plagiarism of one of Hume's dialogues, which I have been going around attributing to G.E. Moore, probably because I find him so adorable. The quote, as I misremember it, said *while it is all very well to stay up until three in the morning discussing the theories of Bishop Berkeley, when we leave we do so through the door and not the second-story window.* The point being that while it may be technically *possible* that this table doesn't exist, I might as well behave as though it does because I need somewhere to put my coffee. I could die in a tragic sailing accident tomorrow (if I put myself out on a boat it might even be pretty likely, since I haven't the faintest idea of how to sail), but I'm planning to turn in my rent check, just in case. I'm letting Simone go to a petting zoo, despite the troubling fact that donkeys kill more people each year than do airplane crashes. I try to remember that the idea that pianos are more likely to fall on the obliviously happy is only a narrative convention, and that happiness is not actually a risk factor for falling pianos OR anvils or even upsetting telegrams. I am an advocate of preparing for the worst, but expecting whatever is most statistically likely.

When I am feeling beset by misery, I remind myself that the statistical likelihood is that I will eventually feel better, which is what propelled my feet each morning back when I was marching myself to the cathedral. It's also likely that I'll feel worse again at some point, but from day to day, chances are greater that nothing terrible will happen than they are that it will. I relied upon this when I began writing letters to the Science Babies, and later when I walked through the birth center to get to the NICU each day. It's inevitable that I will sometimes fall on the unpleasant, slenderer end of statistics, but impossible to anticipate when and how. I disapprove of endings on principle, I said, and I meant it. Simone's early birth wasn't any less regrettable because I ended up happier afterwards than I was before. She's no less glorious now if she turns out to be a Republican or one of those insufferable people who responds to a freeway lane closure by speeding ahead instead of merging like the rest of us. I don't know that I'm any less afraid of death, or loss, or aging than I ever was—I still have attacks of dread and ennui brought on by television shows featuring the elderly, and a healthy aversion to stories of sick children or unexpected cancer diagnoses. I try not to think about tumors or accidents or the slow slide to decreptitude, which is made easier knowing that thinking about them won't do a goddamn thing to change them. I mentioned before that the unexpected boon of being smacked around so thoroughly and with such unpredictable variety by the universe was that it decisively disabused me of the notion that my worry affected anything at all except the stock of benzodiazepines at my local pharmacy. You can call it resignation or hope or denial—or maybe it's mindfulness, and we've come all the way around again to Zen.

Another of my favorite quotes is one I heard for the first time only recently: *It is only possible to live happily ever after on a day-to-day basis.*

At this particular moment, Simone is sprawled in a chair sucking on a Duplo, and looking at her I see neither a miracle nor a time bomb, just my baby, the one who refused to eat the perfectly adequate dinner I prepared, and who is responsible for breaking most of my wine glasses, and whom I will sing to sleep tonight while she kisses my hair extravagantly. Simone was a late walker, not because of any physical delay, but because of a refusal to relinquish her hold on the furniture. She cruised around our apartment, obviously steady on her feet, for months, keeping one small hand on the couch or a table or a chair, using a push-walker to cover distances that exceeded her arm-span. Her pediatrician told me not to worry, and that some babies go for ambulation all at once, teetering and lurching and losing their balance, while others preferred to wait until they were better prepared. Physiologically, he told me, walking is only controlled falling. At first it's bound to terrify, but eventually everyone learns to take for granted the leap of faith it takes to step forward. And he was right—one day Simone just took off, and she hasn't stopped since. You should see her go.

ACKNOWLEDGMENTS

The longest overdue thanks belong to my first and second grade teachers, Mrs. Joyce and Mrs. Wisen, and my elementary school librarian, Mrs. Fruehling. I would also like to thank my beloved books and their writers, for keeping me such good company for so many years.

My own book, the one you are holding now, owes its existence chiefly to my readers at Flotsam, my virtual home. They encouraged and inspired and bolstered me, and have my eternal puppy-like devotion as a result. I would especially like to thank Amanda Milloway and Tara Austen Weaver, the latter of whom introduced me to my patient and marvelous agent, Danielle Svetcov, who set in motion a happy avalanche of circumstances that led to Jennifer Kasius at Running Press. Jennifer's belief in this book helped sustain my own, and she never stopped returning my increasingly neurotic email messages even as the DAY OF RECKONING (er, manuscript delivery) drew near. Everyone at Running Press deserves a thank you, particularly Craig Herman and Nicole DeJackmo in publicity for their kind enthusiasm and Josh McDonnell for creating a cover by which I would happily have my book judged.

Jennifer Gilbert was a wise and sharp reader of an early draft who responded to a two-page stretch of exposition on intraventricular hemorrhage with the gentle editorial comment that I could likely count on readers to know that blood in the brain = BAD even *without* my explanation of intracranial pressure. Elizabeth McCracken not only believed in me but made that belief public, to my everlasting awe and delight, and A.J.

Jacobs agreed to read my manuscript based upon nothing but the word of a friend, even though said manuscript had yet to be finished and was certain to contain multiple instances of the word "cervix."

I thank my brother Max, who was my biggest fan long before I'd ever finished writing anything. Ember, Tammy, and the NICU staff at Children's Hospital already know what I thank them for, and I can never thank them enough.

The only reason I am not typing this from a padded cell is Fernanda Moore, Nimble-Witted Tamer of Swivets, Champion of the Unlikely and Possibly Unwashed, and the best friend I could ever ask for. She edited much of this book, and kept me, on multiple occasions, from flinging it off a bridge in a fit of pique.

Lastly I thank Scott, for holding my bucket—both literally and not so much—and not-leastly I thank Simone, just for being there at the end of every day: my own shrieking, food-smeared *raison* d'everything.